A First Language
Taught and Learned

This book is printed on recycled paper. ♻

A First Language Taught and Learned

by

Ernst L. Moerk, Ph.D.

Professor of Psychology
School of Natural Sciences
California State University–Fresno
Fresno, California

·P·A·U·L·H·
BROOKES
PUBLISHING C⁰

Baltimore • London • Toronto • Sydney

Paul H. Brookes Publishing Co.
P.O. Box 10624
Baltimore, Maryland 21285-0624

Typeset by Brushwood Graphics, Inc., Baltimore, Maryland.
Manufactured in the United States of America by
The Maple Press Company, York, Pennsylvania.

Library of Congress Cataloging-in-Publication Data
Moerk, Ernst L.
    A first language taught and learned / by Ernst L. Moerk.
        p.   cm.
    Includes bibliographical references and index.
    ISBN 1-55766-081-6
    1. Language acquisition.   2. Mother and child.   I. Title.
P118.M63   1992
401'.93—dc20   91-17036
                                                                CIP

Contents

Foreword *Grover J. Whitehurst* vii
Preface xi

Chapter 1   Conceptual Models and Methodological
            Implications 1
Chapter 2   The Now: Interactional and Cognitive
            Processes in Acquisition of the Present
            Progressive 19
Chapter 3   The Here, There, and Then: Training and
            Acquisition of the Prepositional Phrase 47
Chapter 4   Speaking of Time: Processes in the
            Transmission and Acquisition of Temporal
            Morphemes 75
Chapter 5   The Transmission and Acquisition of
            Future-Tense Morphemes 111
Chapter 6   The Training and Learning of Syntax 147
Chapter 7   The Transmission and Acquisition of
            Language-Learning Strategies 185
Chapter 8   Theoretical and Methodological Approaches
            in Research on Language Transmission and
            Acquisition 211
References 235

Index 247

Foreword
All About Eve

Shakespeare's Owen Glendower says, "I can summon creatures from the vastly deep," to which Hotspur answers, "So can I. So can any man. But will they come?" (Henry IV, Part 1). Ernst Moerk summons those who are interested in a theoretical understanding of the development of language to consider evidence and argument that a first language is taught and learned.

This is a unique book that is well worth the careful attention it requires. Methodologically, it falls into the category of case study, in that all data come from transcripts of verbal interactions involving one child, Eve. This is the same Eve and the same transcripts that first appeared in Roger Brown's seminal work, *A First Language: The Early Stages*. But this is a case study with a very important twist: an extremely detailed microanalysis of the linguistic interactions of Eve and her mother over time. Diaries, or biographies, of children's language development have a rich history that reaches back at least to the 18th century. Case studies of language development have been published by the hundreds since the 1970s. They differ from their historical predecessors primarily in the advances in detail and systematicity that are afforded by the use of audio or video recording. Most diary studies have focused exclusively on the child, and those few that have looked for relations between maternal and child speech have ignored time altogether, or have framed their search in macro units. Gerald R. Patterson, one of the most influential and prolific students of human social interaction, says of his own work, "The entire set of assumptions underlying the analysis of structure and process rests upon the idea that behavior is governed by immediately impinging events" (Patterson, 1982, p. 170). If Patterson is right, then Moerk is right: We cannot hope to understand the sociogenetic basis of language development unless we analyze interactions in real time. Moerk's case study is a fine grained sequential analysis of mother–child linguistic interactions. There has never been a case study like it.

Theoretically, Moerk's position is more easily defined by what it is pitted against than by what it is. Moerk is opposed to nativism, and antagonistic to the nativists who have set the agenda for developmental psycholinguistics during much of its recent history. In Chapter 8, he characterizes their work as "a considerable setback to the field" (p. 231). Moerk pins his sociogenetic approach to language acquisition on a potpourri of theories and approaches, including behaviorism, systems theory, Piaget's theory, computer models of parallel distributed processing, Gibsonian perceptual learning, cognitive models of the development of skills, and Vygotsky's sociohistorical position. Some of these approaches are usually seen as incommensurate (e.g., behaviorism and cognitive psychology), and in lesser hands such eclecticism could result in confusion. However, Moerk does not so much endorse each theory as draw from it elements that provide a scaffold for his position that language is taught and learned. The theories on which Moerk calls all are committed to organism–environment interaction as one critical component of development, as is Moerk.

Though Moerk's methodological advance is admirable, I believe it has limitations that he does not fully appreciate. Sequential analyses, either of the narrative sort that Moerk has conducted here or the mathematical sort that he proposes for future research, generate interpretative ambiguities. The first arises from the necessity to code behavior before it can be analyzed. A second source of interpretative ambiguity is that sequential methods are forms of correlational analysis. One of the first lessons in research methodology is that correlation is not causation. This is not to disparage time series analyses of linguistic interactions. I have conducted such analyses and consider the method to be an extremely useful way to screen for regularities in interaction. It is the drawing of causal conclusions from such regularities that requires caution.

Substantively, Moerk's book is an interesting melange of detailed data and scholarly discussions of the meaning and place of those data. For example, Chapter 6 begins with a fascinating discussion of the psychological differences between copula and copula-like sentences (e.g., "That is a kitty." "See the kitty.") versus full verb sentences (e.g., "Eve chase kitty."), which then provides a basis for analyzing the syntax of Eve's sentences. Many of Moerk's observations should prove useful to those with an applied interest in language development. Particularly relevant here are Moerk's descriptions in Chapter 7 of Eve's learning-to-learn strategies, such as build-up sequences and frame variation.

But, as Hotspur says, "Will they come?" In 1980, I would not have been optimistic about the market for this book. The nativists and structuralists were in full cry. Perhaps they still are in some environs. However, I think there are two growing audiences that will be sympathetic to Moerk's position, and interested in his data. First are language and speech professionals who must grapple with delays and disorders of speech and language development. Teachers are always pragmatic empiricists. Positions such as Steven Pinker's that language development is so robust that "there is virtually no way to prevent it from happening short of raising a child in a barrel" (Pinker, 1984, p. 29) have always rung hollow to professionals who spend their time with children for whom it hasn't happened. The second group of interested readers should be developmental psycholinguists who have tired of the nature–nurture issue and the rhetoric associated with it, and who wish to embed their work in the mainstream of psychology and developmental neuroscience. Since Moerk grounds this book in the nature–nurture controversy, it may seem strange to say that it should be of interest to those who have tired of that controversy. However, it is not necessary to adopt Moerk's sociogenetic position to find great value in this book. Moerk's root metaphor for language acquisition is skill learning. Any complex human skill, piano playing for example, involves a complex interplay of various biologic, cultural, and cognitive components that can be analyzed at many levels. The centrality of any of these components and levels of analysis will fluctuate depending on the question being asked. For instance, we may look primarily to sociogenetic (cultural) variables to explain why some children take piano lessons and some do not, biologic variables to explain why the stroke victim has lost certain musical abilities he or she once had, or instructional–interactional variables to explain why one teacher's students regularly learn more than another's. Moerk has chosen to focus on sociogenetic variables in language acquisition, and while he has tied his data rhetorically to the nativism–empiricism issue, an extremely important characteristic of this book is that it is not about rhetoric, it is about data. Thus whether you see sociogenetic variables as a piece of the pie or the whole pastry, this meticulous work of scholarship can inform.

Grover J. Whitehurst, Ph.D.
Professor of Psychology and Pediatrics
State University of New York
Stony Brook, New York

REFERENCES

Brown, R. (1973). *A first language.* Cambridge, MA: Harvard University Press.
Patterson, G.R. (1982). *Coercive family process.* Eugene, OR: Castalia Publishing.
Pinker, S. (1984). *Language learnability and language development.* Cambridge, MA: Harvard University Press.

Preface

*It is a capital mistake to theorize
before one has data.
Insensibly one begins to twist facts
to suit theories,
instead of theories to suit facts.*
Sir Arthur Conan Doyle: A Scandal in Bohemia

A First Language Taught and Learned is a fully empirical book. It shows how the major grammatical facets of a first language are taught and learned in verbal interactions, largely between a mother and her child, Eve. A demonstration of how language is taught and learned logically implies *that* it can be taught and learned. This book is consequently also very practical, with "practical" meaning that it is applicable to the practice of remedial language teaching. By showing the detailed processes of how specific linguistic constructions are taught and learned efficiently, models are provided that indicate how these constructions could be taught when learning does not happen spontaneously.

Because the process analyses show that these teaching and learning procedures were sufficient for the acquisition of language, the book is also implicitly theoretical. Vague causal speculations of various forms of "innate linguistic knowledge" become superfluous. While this theoretical conclusion follows necessarily from the factual evidence, the emphasis in this work is only minimally on the predominant theoretical controversies of the past.

Throughout the book, the bidirectionality of cause–effect relationships is emphasized. The child's interests and mastery affect the mother's linguistic input, and that, in turn, affects the child's learning of new items. A developmental spiral results from these dynamics, where, ultimately, the child is always the critical partner because the mother's teaching depends upon the child's readiness. Concepts such as "schema," "discrepancy," and "equilibration," borrowed from Piaget and, more broadly, from cognitive psychology, are therefore integrated into the conceptual apparatus of a more strictly learning–theoretical provenance.

In order to make the demonstration of the teaching and learning of a first language as cogent as possible, the focus of the analyses in this book is on morphological and syntactic learning. Innate knowledge has been deemed a requirement, particularly for syntax acquisition. The data presented in this work can provide strong evidence for the learning of the structural aspects of language. Vocabulary acquisition is generally acknowledged to be due to input and learning, because, obviously, languages have idiosyncratic vocabularies

that need to be rote learned. Therefore, vocabulary learning is not a focus of
the following analyses, although many teaching and learning principles that
are demonstrated also apply to the acquisition of vocabulary items.

Chapters 2–6 cover the transmission and acquisition of the present progressive, the prepositional phrase, past-tense and future-tense morphemes,
and the basic S-V-O frame. The chapters focus on the mechanisms of developmental change and therefore on interactional processes. Chapter 7 adds a new
perspective to these process analyses by discussing how the child "learns to
learn," that is, how she acquires learning strategies that are modeled after the
mother's teaching strategies. This aspect stresses specifically the activity and,
partly, the "creativity" of the child. It is, however, a creativity that is learned as
"procedural knowledge."

While Chapters 2–7 represent the empirical core of the book, Chapters 1
and 8 serve to introduce the reader to the model underlying the analyses. It is
by now an epistemological cliché that all data are conceived from specific perspectives. Those perspectives and the methodological implications are therefore spelled out in Chapter 1, and their appropriateness to verbal interactions
and learning is reevaluated in Chapter 8. The perspective that underlies the
presented analyses is that of skill learning. The learning of language skills is
seen as a subset of the broader domain of culture learning, because language is
a subset of the cultural skills that all children must acquire.

This general model has a very practical aspect. No mysterious innate capacities, which some children could be presumed to lack, prohibit intensive
efforts to teach specific language skills and the overall assembly of skills to children whose spontaneous acquisition of these skills is delayed.

There is another perspective underlying the empirical analyses in this
work. From the child's and largely the parents' perspective, specific verbal interactions are hardly judged by their function as training and learning opportunities. For both parent and child, language is a communicative tool and a
means to express their mutual enjoyment of each other's company and of the
mastery of the "toy," that is, language. As is well known from research on baby
talk, musical and poetic devices are quite common in maternal speech. Rhythmic and other prosodic devices also serve to make underlying patterns more
obvious and memorable, which is demonstrated in this work. Parallel methods
for memorizing Greek and Latin poetry, especially the epical devices that support the storage and recall of oral poetry, are indicated. Awareness of these
mnemonic devices might prove helpful in the analysis of the storage and mastery of linguistic skills.

This last emphasis may also prove useful for the practitioner. The verbatim
data and longitudinal sequences presented might also show the remedial practitioner what not to do. Input and parental teaching are stressed as necessary,
but not exclusive, factors in the acquisition process. Motivational factors, such
as functional communication and enjoyment of mastery of this tool are also
very important. Whatever the fashionable terms might be, whether the child is
seen as "creative" or as "generating language," the practitioner must focus on
the child as an active and, increasingly, as the leading participant in dyadic
processes. The practitioner must let the child lead the therapist by indicating

his or her interest and readiness for specific acquisitions. Awareness of the bidirectionality of effects, including motivation and intellectual readiness, may resolve theoretical questions, for example, concerning the effectiveness of corrections. Such awareness might serve as an important reminder for the therapist who is too prone to employ the experimental paradigm and who always assumes the lead in interaction.

Language teaching and learning is obviously an extended process and the structure of inquiry must be compatible with the structure of the subject. Single observations of cross sections of input and acquisition are not able to provide information about the teaching and learning processes that begin in the immediate exchange of utterances and continue over weeks and months. Methodological innovations, such as Markov chain models that capture interactional phenomena, are employed for microprocesses, and methods approximating bivariate time series analyses provide information about long-term developments. For intermediate time periods, approaches are employed that resemble Skinner's "cumulative record" and also memory research, which uses varying intervals between learning and testing.

It is possible and hoped that these methodological innovations represent a major contribution to the field. The methodology might prove especially valuable for the practitioner who wants to follow improvements over varying intervals in order to provide a bivariate evaluation of the effectiveness of remedial intervention in improvement.

The ambitious goals of this study could not have been approached without important contributors. First, Professor Roger Brown was very generous to lend his data in 1977–1978 to a relatively unknown investigator, long before these data became generally accessible through the CHILDES system. This rich data set made it possible for this investigator to become familiar with the family's general interaction style and with the child's changing language level, almost as if he were a member of the family.

The extensive analyses would not have been possible without a second source of help in the form of two research grants from the Spencer Foundation. These grants not only provided time away from a heavy teaching load and the chance to devote much time and energy to the project, but they also made it possible to hire very able research assistants. Rosa Vilaseca from the University of Barcelona, Spain, was the assistant centrally involved in the analyses leading to this book. She spent a full academic year steeped in data analyses and completed some of the tables in the following chapters. She was a very valuable contributor to the effective achievement of the tasks that we set out to accomplish.

Finally, my sincere appreciation goes to Dr. K.P. Wong, Dean of the School of Natural Sciences, California State University–Fresno. Dr. Wong brought about many innovative changes that made research possible within this institution's financial and administrative constraints, and he supported creative activities with his interest and encouragement. This interest in research extended to chairmen of the Department of Psychology where Professors William Coe and Alex Gonzalez provided flexibility and support when the conflicts between a heavy teaching load and research goals required special consideration. Their moral and tangible support was an important factor in this research. Finally, after years of relatively isolated work, it was a great pleasure to encounter in the publishing house of Paul H. Brookes Publishing Co. an enthusiastic and efficient team who expedited the publication processes and fully shared my goal to create the best possible work.

Benjamin B. Burton
1923–1987
and
Donald D. Kritley
1938–1989
in fond memory

Chapter 1

Conceptual Models and Methodological Implications

An art which cannot be specified in detail
cannot be transmitted by description,
since no prescription for it exists.
It can be passed on only by example
from master to apprentice. M. Polanyi: "Personal Knowledge"

A number of theoretical discussions of language development have emerged in recent decades. This extensive theoretical network was, however, built on an exceedingly small and incomplete database, which in many theoretical arguments was almost absent. Even more damaging, some of the best known factual studies were based upon weak methodologies and came to premature, and probably incorrect, conclusions. Researchers are again focusing on establishing sound databases and on methodological clarifications. The cross-language data collection of Slobin (1985) is such an example. The extensive work of Wells (1985), in his Bristol Language Development Study, and of Bates and her research team (e.g., Bates, Bretherton, & Snyder, 1988), included larger numbers of subjects in their samples. Moerk (1983a) focused on microanalyses of a considerable variety of training and learning processes. The CHILDES database at Carnegie Mellon University encompasses data from many subjects and continues to expand. Bohannon and associates (e.g., Bohannon & Hirsh-Pasek, 1984), and Moerk (1983a, 1986), have explored some major methodological issues that need to be resolved before data and theory can be optimally integrated. Many methodological challenges, however, still exist.

Developmental psycholinguistics is thus returning to the basic modus operandi of scientific research: Extensive factual studies, with methodological refinement, precede the construction of theoretical systems. Intuitive armchair speculations, even if the armchair sits in front of a computer console, remain at best heuristic tools and at

1

worst, worthless if not tested against reality. This work adheres to this epistemological emphasis on facts, although aware that the selection and collection of data are already based upon implicit models. Chapters 2–7 are devoted to careful presentations and micro- and macro-analytic explorations of data for evidence of underlying processes. Chapter 1 specifies the preliminary models that guided these studies.

To avoid entanglement in speculative controversies, for example, the predominant and unproductive nature–nurture debate of the 1960s–1980s, the topic of this investigation is carefully delimited and focused on the acquisition of items that are specific to the English language. Even the most ardent nativist would not deny that specific morphemes of the English language that express the present progressive, the past, and the future are learned through interaction with the environment. Similarly, vocabulary items that specify diverse locative and temporal relationships by way of prepositional phrases must be acquired from input because they are different in every language. A strong innate component could be postulated only for the overall syntactic structure of sentences, and it has been presumed to influence the ease and speed of syntax acquisition. Yet in this domain also, language-specific aspects certainly have to be learned. A careful evaluation of the learning and training processes in this domain, compared with those that depend exclusively upon learning, permits preliminary evaluation of possible differences in the processes. Such differences were postulated by Newport, Gleitman, and Gleitman (1977), who considered "universal aspects of language and structure . . . insensitive to individual differences in maternal speech style" (p. 133).

THEORETICAL PERSPECTIVES

Philosophers of science emphasize that all databased studies are guided by theoretical models that determine the selection, definition, and analysis of facts. If the theoretical models of a study are clearly identified, the investigation and results can be better evaluated. A brief survey of the major models that guide this investigation precedes the presentation of data. Two models are briefly surveyed, culture learning, and skill training and learning, which are considered to be in a set to subset relationship. Following this, the model of language training and learning that guided the investigation is briefly outlined in relation to the two preceding, broader models.

The Model of Culture Learning

Culture learning is the model that guided conceptualization of this study and the search for optimal data definitions. Culture learning is almost as broad an area as the combined fields of psychology and anthropology, and the term "cultural psychology" (deVos & Hippler, 1969) expresses the integration of these two fields. In a more restricted sense, other terms for a similar concept are acculturation and enculturation. Extensive anthropological and psychological work in the field of culture and personality (Kluckhohn, Murray, & Schneider, 1953) primarily addresses the effects of culture learning, but also considers the processes. Roots of the conceptualizations employed in these fields are found in Dewey (1922), Mead (1934), and Pierce (1934). The volume edited by Bain (1983) contains valuable surveys and discussions of principles. Bronfenbrenner (1979), focusing on "the ecology of human development," carefully analyzed the many changing influences affecting the child in the course of development. Rogoff (Rogoff & Gardner, 1984; Rogoff, Gauvain, & Ellis, 1984) employed conceptualizations of cultural learning similar to those considered optimal for language acquisition. Rogoff and Gardner (1984) refer to "instruction . . . as joint problem-solving . . . [by an] expert (the mother) and a novice (the child) [who] structure their interaction so as to transmit information" (p. 95). The expert structures the training and monitors the novice's progress. The training and learning is sequential, additive, and repetitive, since earlier acquired tasks are repeated and thereby rehearsed. In this conceptualization of culture learning, major features stand out that need to be evaluated for applicability to language training and learning.

The Ubiquity of Information   Culture continuously surrounds learners since it is consistently displayed in the artifacts and the behavior of members, with or without their awareness of the display. Members cannot help but behave in a culture-appropriate manner, and thus they display information for the learner in every act. Cultural skills are also taught intentionally in a master–apprentice relationship. The parents normally represent the masters of cultural precepts for the young child. Combining unintentional and intentional teaching of culture, the vivid image of a "bain du langage" (Delacroix, 1934, p. 18), indicating that language stimuli completely surround the young child as the bathwater surrounds the baby, can be adapted as "la mer du culture." Culture surrounds each of its members like the water of the ocean surrounds its inhabitants. Neither can avoid absorbing and integrating the contents of the surrounding medium.

J.J. Gibson's (1979, 1982) concept of "affordances," derived from research on visual perception of the inanimate environment, carries similar implications. Mace (1977, p. 43), describing these affordances, exhorted the investigator, "Ask not what is in the head but what your head's inside of." He poignantly expressed this sufficiency principle:

Since we are surrounded by information and have sensory organs to process input, we cannot avoid taking in the surrounding information, whether exhibited in inanimate, nonhuman behavioral, or cultural realms. Such a wealth of information results both in "incidental language teaching" summarized by Warren and Kaiser (1986), and in "incidental learning," researched by Greenfield and Lave (1982) and Kaye (1982). This argument can be put into a broader perspective. More basic than cultural "information display" is the ethological concept of "behavioral display," such as the courting behavior of many animal species. In this case too, information is displayed by co-species members, independent of the conscious intention of the displayer.

Interactional Routines   In many aspects, culture learning is simpler than the incidental learning of the inanimate environment. Culture is learned largely through interactional routines in feedback processes. Through these interactions, models can be adapted to the receiver, simplifying the comprehension of information. In addition, behavioral routines are often repeated with only minor variations, and exhibit the breakdown of larger routines into small components. For example, "Say 'Good bye,' " or "Shake hands," may be emphasized as elements of the greeting routine. Systematic positive and negative feedback may be provided by parents and later by the school system. Simple interactional routines are demonstrated in Greenfield and Lave's (1982) report about the teaching and learning of weaving. Ochs (1986, p. 2) offered the integrative characterization: "Socialization [is] an interactional display (covert or overt) to a novice of expected ways of thinking, feeling, and acting." This is reflected in Vygotsky's theories and in Bruner's (1983) emphasis upon "scaffolding": "Where before there was a spectator, let there now be a participant" (p. 60). A participant always receives covert or overt feedback and may eventually act as an independent performer (Vygotsky, 1978).

Iterative and Incremental Acquisition   Culture is not and cannot be learned as a single undifferentiated unit. Many steps are needed to acquire diverse aspects, and these steps are often arranged in developmental sequences, such as in toilet training, the learning of eating skills, and the acceptance of social responsibilities. In brief, culture learning proceeds iteratively and incrementally by stage-like sequences.

Distinct domains require distinct input and learning processes for their acquisition. Toilet training may be based on reward and punishment, with a component of modeling. University education, however, is based on complex logical understanding and rule learning. A relationship between contents mastered and the processes used to master them, whether sphincter muscles or logical systems, is plausible. Thus, the concept of culture learning represents a broad abstraction that hides a multiplicity of psychological tasks, processes, and steps in mastery. Refined analyses of a particular domain and its required learning processes are needed to understand the acquisition process.

The principle of incremental and iterative acquisition involves several aspects: 1) The aspect of "readiness," or "the zone of proximal development" (Vygotsky, 1978), is important. Adults usually adapt the level of culture instruction to the child's developmental level, because mismatch leads to failure. 2) Dependent upon this readiness is the progression from simple to complex training and learning. This applies both to the learning process and the contents. 3) Since culture learning is enormous and the developmental course has to follow incremental steps, the acquisition process is lengthy and continually changing. Early teaching and learning processes cannot fully account for results occurring later. The early training in control of sphincter muscles cannot fully explain the later and more sophisticated control of adult emotional expression, although both require control of bodily functions, and the acquisition of the former might, in some way, affect the acquisition of the latter. Such early training is even less likely to account for later achievement motivation or acquisition of other phenomenologically different cultural skills. Phenotypic and genotypic discontinuities and changing influences are to be expected in culture learning and require careful examination. Though distant causation might be a factor, proximal causes are more pertinent to later and higher achievements.

Flexibility of Cultural Skills   Obviously, cultural skills do not comprise fixed sequences of behavior. They represent schemas, scripts, or general formats applied flexibly to changing situations and demands. An abstraction process is superimposed on originally specific behavior patterns, such as "Wave 'bye-bye,' " in the course of learning. This leads to the result of flexible greeting behavior. Although the early "Bye-bye" may be based on a conditioned response principle, later selection of different greeting behaviors, adapted according to partners and situations, may be described as rule-based performance.

From Controlled to Automatic Processing   Though not all important features of culture learning are considered here, a last point is of great importance in the conceptualization of skill learning generally and language learning specifically. Controlled processing with focal awareness undergoes a transition to become automatic processing with only subsidiary awareness. Sub-routines become automatized and are integrated into larger routines, which will run semi-automatically once started. Frequency of performance is an important variable in automatization. The mastery of cultural skills, such as greeting routines, involves many semi-automatic or automatized sub-routines. Since the child lives submerged in his or her culture and has many opportunities to employ specific routines, such automatization is a necessary consequence of frequent exposure and exercise. When frequency and automatization are less automatically guaranteed, cultures and their representatives cultivate such skills assiduously: "What do you say?" urged consistently leads to the automatic "Thank you."

The Model of Skill Learning

In the above analyses of culture learning, the learning of specific skills was mentioned repeatedly. Whether language skills, obviously one aspect of cultural skills, or specific social, technical, or sports skills, great similarities appear to exist in their acquisition. The headings used to discuss culture learning are retained in the following discussion of skill learning to show clearly the similarities between these types of learning.

The following remarks are brief and cannot cover the broad range of the field of skill learning and its application to the acquisition of cognitive skills, so the reader is referred to several excellent sources. Kaye's (1982) discussion of motor skill acquisition in young infants through interactions with their mothers focuses upon the very immature learner and is closely applicable to the infant's and young child's acquisition of language. Another publication closely applicable to later discussion of language acquisition is Anderson's (1981) edited book and his analysis (Anderson, 1982) of cognitive skill acquisition. Extensive literature exists on skill acquisition generally, such as Holding (1981), Kelso (1982), and Sage (1984). All specifics of skill learning discussed here are elaborated in these sources. Moerk (1986) presented a detailed exploration of the application of these conceptualizations to first language transmission and acquisition.

The Ubiquity of Information   Although information is less obviously ubiquitous in the domain of skill learning than in culture learning, its availability is nevertheless equally important. Only those who are surrounded by information about a skill will become highly competent at it. In famous musical families, such as the Bach family, the Mozarts, or the Strauss family, it is apparent that children grew up surrounded by music.

A similar phenomenon is reflected in Austria's outstanding success in worldwide skiing competitions. In much of Austria, which consists largely of mountains, skiing is a daily activity for a considerable part of the year. Good skiers are a natural consequence of these conditions.

Where such intense models are not immediately available, learners are exposed to extensive modeling and instruction to establish equivalent intensity.

Interactional Routines   Interactional routines between trainer and trainee are elaborately established in intentional skill training. Generally, a model is provided and then imitated by the trainee, and this trial receives immediate, and often extensive, feedback. "Augmented feedback" may be provided through video replays of the performance. This augmented feedback largely concerns knowledge of performance (KP) and not knowledge of result (KR), though both types are often combined. The difference between these two types of feedback can be illustrated with an example. Basic performance, that a discus thrower can throw a disk, is assumed. The distance thrown, the major aspect of the result (KR), is related to the particulars of the throw. Knowledge of performance (KP) is provided to explore how performance could be improved. Bandura (1986) provides extensive evidence supporting the effectiveness of such "corrective feedback." Contiguity between provision of the model, attempted performance, and feedback is important (Newell, 1981).

Iterative and Incremental Acquisition   Acquisition of any complex skill takes a long time and requires many levels of accomplishment. The beginning skier would think it absolutely impossible to perform on the level of the Olympic competitor. Burton, Brown, and Fischer (1984) provide a discussion of "skiing as a model of instruction" with the ICM paradigm. "Increasingly Complex Microworlds" (ICM) are constructed between the initial and final state, based on training of sub-skills and error correction. Similarly, the first steps in spelling and writing do not directly presage the achievement of a Nobel prize in literature. The learning process can be very lengthy and almost infinite, as demonstrated by Grossman's (1959) report that learning increments can be detected even after millions of trials.

All specific features of such incremental learning discussed in connection with culture learning are implicit in the discussion of the incremental nature of acquisition: 1) Higher skill levels can be taught effectively only after lower levels have been mastered. Readiness and "fine tuning" of teaching to fit successive levels of attainment are very important. 2) Skill acquisition proceeds from the simple to the complex. The process is cumulative, and simple skills are integrated into complex routines or form the stepping stones to them.

An interesting paradox, relevant to language acquisition, is that the rudiments of a skill are often learned quite rapidly, but refinements can be added, seemingly ad infinitum. The reasons for this phenomenon are relatively clear. A skill would never develop in a given culture if it were not learnable. In order to be learnable, a skill must be able to be broken down into small steps that can be readily mastered. This mastery constitutes success in training and learning. Without this success, a learner would give up, and the skill would not develop.

Analyzed into elements, even the most complex skill can be acquired through relatively easy steps if the right training approach is employed. What would appear impossible if only the beginning and the end stages were compared is experienced as a natural and manageable progression of many simple steps over long periods of training. 3) Based on this aspect of the skill training and learning model, a controversy in developmental psycholinguistics can be resolved. Gleitman and Wanner (1984) correctly argued that input from the earliest stages of language acquisition cannot account for adult language competence, nor does it need to. New contents have to be taught, and new methods of learning may be needed to progress from simple to complex forms of a skill. The learning of how to snowplow cannot directly explain the later skill of parallel skiing, nor can addition and subtraction explain the advanced mathematician's explorations of number theory. Without carefully following the intervening training and learning steps, the end products appear miraculous and unexplainable.

Flexibility of Skills   Skill learning is not the learning of specific sequences of acts, but the learning of abstract patterns that are flexible to changing situational demands. Schmidt's (1975) "schema theory" details this distinction: "A key prediction of schema theory is that the abstract representation of a class of actions becomes stronger the more variable the precise instances of it from previous actions" (Newell, 1981, p. 223). Formulated as a structuralist conception: "Practice that is variable will develop a schema which is more impervious to decay and more flexible or generative in production" (Newell, 1981, p. 223).

Kaye (1982) reports a pertinent observation: "Variations were introduced subtly over a series of repetitions, as though the mothers were holding down the variability so that their infants could tune in to the regularity" (p. 26). The regularity results in schemas, and the variability assures that learning is not merely routine sequences of actions. Since flexibility is a goal of training, the acquisition of such schemas is a precondition of skill learning. On a simple level, specific walking movements may change with age, with the type of load carried, and with the terrain, yet the general pattern or schema remains the same. This also applies to the skier mastering different slopes and to the speaker uttering an infinite variety of sentences based upon two schemas, the S-V-(O) and the copula sentence. It is central to skillfulness that one can adapt skills flexibly. Schmidt (1975) labeled this phenomenon the "novelty problem" and related this to Chomsky's (1965) description of "the generativity" of the language producer.

From Controlled to Automatic Processing Automatization of routines and sub-routines is central to skill training and learning. Smooth and flexible execution of skills requires the execution of minor routines without focal awareness and with minimal processing. Polanyi (1958) analyzed in detail the contribution of "tacit knowledge" to skilled performance, and Schneider and Shiffrin (1977) discussed how the information is processed. Bandura (1986) tied tacit knowledge directly to language acquisition and performance. The overall principle is that frequently exercised routines become automaticized and subject to only subsidiary awareness, conserving resources of information processing. Primary attention to or focal awareness of changing situations allows the flexibility needed in goal-directed performances. The goal can be conveying a message, achieving a victory in sports, or succeeding in any nonsymbolic motor activity. Focus on gradual automatization of single routines or of accreted sub-routines of a performance contributes to a full understanding of any type of skill training and learning.

Language Teaching and Learning

Some parallels between the acquisition of cultural skills, motor skills, and language learning are self-evident. Correspondences between speech and skilled behavior concerning temporal structure were drawn by Lashley (1951). Fitts (1964) elaborated on the close relationship between verbal and motor processes. Fischer and Corrigan (1981), as well as Schmidt and Paris (1984), applied skill conceptualizations to both structural and pragmatic aspects of language development. Moerk (1986) substantiated these analogies with detailed parallels in training and learning processes. These points are briefly summarized here to introduce specific methodological consequences that the skill learning model has for the factual studies of language acquisition presented in following chapters.

The Ubiquity of Information Human beings are loquacious animals, and the fact that mothers converse with their babies from the moment of birth on is established in decades of studies. The language input that an infant receives varies with the cultural group, social class, and individual family. Language proficiency that children later exhibit is known to vary with early input. It ranges from Genie (Curtiss, 1977) with minimal or no language skills, to children entering school with low levels of verbal skills, to children fluent in reading and writing before they enter school. Cause–effect relationships between intensity of stimulation and degree of language acquisition have been demonstrated in decades of applied developmental research (cf. Warren & Kaiser, 1986, for discussion). Accepting differences in input and acquisition, it nevertheless remains that in the "average expectable environment," (Sullivan, 1947) abundant language input is provided by adults or older children.

The intrinsic interest that infants exhibit in co-species members and in their activities is a basic tendency of human beings and a major factor contributing to this abundance of verbal stimulation. This attention to co-species members leads almost automatically to observational learning of their behavior patterns. On the highest levels, interest in co-species members results in culture learning and in language mastery.

The instructional value of the language input has been questioned, since it has been asserted that syntactic structures are not observable in input (Bever, Fodor, & Weksel, 1965). This is based on inaccurate conceptualizations of "stimuli." When an organism behaves, whether it is Konrad Lorenz's famous stickleback or a mother speaking to her child, the behavior is structured, and thereby potentially informative. When an interacting partner observes and "comprehends" the meaning of the behavior, he or she has automatically analyzed and interpreted its structure also. No particular instruction is necessary to turn structured behavior into information display. Structured behavior *is* information display.

Gibson (1979, 1982), explaining his concept of affordances, elaborates carefully this concept of the direct perception of information and structure contained in environmental "invariances over transformations." The principle is illustrated by the following example. Children may observe trees, four-legged animals, or human beings and draw them spontaneously as abstract stick figures. Neither the trees, nor the animals, nor human beings intentionally taught these abstract patterns. Invariances over transformations, experienced often, are sufficient to produce schemas or patterns. This explains the phenomenon that practically all normal children will acquire the basic structural features of their language if they are able to observe structured linguistic information.

Interactional Routines   In many ways, language learning is easier than visual absorption and recognition of patterns in the environment. The child receives considerable help in language learning through interactional routines. The dyadic nature of early language interaction has been explored since the 1960s, beginning with the studies of R. Brown and his associates. Turn-taking routines are established during the first months of life (Beebe, Alson, Jaffe, Feldstein, & Crown, 1988). As soon as the infant approximates a level of preliminary comprehension at the age of 7–8 months, the mother simplifies her input (Snow, 1977a) in order to be comprehensible to her child. Fine tuning between mother and child continues for several years (e.g., Bohannon,

Stine, & Ritzenberg, 1982; Moerk, 1975). Extensive evidence for such fine tuning is presented in following data analyses.

The dyadic interactions in language learning follow the pattern of model, imitative attempt, and feedback. Both the imitation and the feedback follow the model closely, at least in early stages of a learning episode. The feedback often combines acknowledgment and confirmation with changes and corrections. In this manner, the maternal imitation and expansion is equivalent to an improved audio replay: It combines description and prescription, similar to multifunctional feedback in sports training. This feedback demonstrates discrepancies between the model and the attempt since it is often adapted to the specific mistakes of the preceding performance.

In language training, too, the feedback generally concerns performance, or knowledge of performance (KP), and not results (KR). Results, or successful communication, are assured before the baby produces a single word. As will be seen in the following chapters, knowledge of performance is provided consistently, often in the form of Brown's "expansions." These demonstrate where the performance of the child was not up to expectations. The expansions combine corrections, by including missing elements, with confirmation. During the extended course of first language acquisition, variations in informative feedback and other interaction patterns, that is, changes in immediate causal aspects, have profound effects on learning processes and outcomes. Adjustments in modeling and feedback processes are the focus of the studies presented in this book. Microanalytic evaluations of actual adjacency pairs demonstrate the versatility and complexity of immediate feedback. Macroanalytic explorations of extended feedback demonstrate longitudinal changes, especially those discussed in the following section.

Iterative and Incremental Acquisition   Not all forms of input or all types of feedback, however, represent real affordances. Several conditions must be met before objective information becomes an affordance for the child and before the affordance results in learning and mastery of a linguistic construction. To clarify this point, two meanings of the term "acquisition" need to be differentiated. First, the meaning that underlies data selection and analysis in previous studies referred to "the temporal course of increasing productions" with little or no focus upon cognitive processes and cause–effect relationships. Second, the meaning that may be found in the discussion sections of the same studies views acquisition as the "psychological and cognitive processes that result in linguistic productions." In spite of this expressed interest in cognitive processes, training or learning processes generally have not been explored in these studies. The concept of "rule learning" is an example of this second interpretation and derives from linguistic studies that focused exclusively on linguistic products.

The subsequent analyses are focused on the second aspect of acquisition, that is, the teaching, learning, and cognitive processes involved in the incremental mastery of the linguistic constructions.

Principle of Readiness   Input and feedback have to be matched to the child's level and momentary processing abilities. For input to be effective, the child has to be ready for it. Vygotsky's zone of proximal development, the concept of fine tuning, and the master–apprentice model refer to this match. Fine tuning can be best achieved in feedback because the filial utterance is readily remembered. Yet, as studies by Snow (1972) and others show, a second form of tuning seems to exist as an overall adjustment to the age and appearance of the communication partner. This is a first rough tuning. Rondal (1979) studied and confirmed the maternal awareness of the child's overall level.

Progress from Simple to Complex Skills   The early establishment of turn-taking skills at approximately 4 months (Beebe et al., 1988) reflects a learning of more macrotemporal patterns found in other interaction routines, such as feeding. The phonetic and phonological learning of sounds of the language and of suprasegmental intonation contours (e.g., Peters, 1983) relates largely to the sensorimotor level. The semantic level, with one- and two-word utterances referring to objects and actions, follows. The grammatical level, involving abstract patterns and comprehension of rules, appears later.

In contrast to previous theories that stressed miraculously fast language acquisition, the model of skill learning suggests that learning processes occur gradually and may never end. If a skill does not have strong innate components, it requires up to 1 year to progress to even a simple level of performance, such as one-word utterances. As with most skill learning, it takes additional years to attain a reasonable level of mastery, and refinements continue into adulthood (Menyuk, 1977). This is, of course, exactly what is observed in language acquisition.

Not only do the contents of learning proceed from simple to complex, but the processes of learning do also. Pattern abstraction is reflected in the early abstraction of suprasegmental intonation patterns and also in the abstraction of patterns of individual sounds and syllables. Considered from the perspective of memory, simple imitation of brief utterance elements progresses to the utilization of cues only, and finally to spontaneous recall from long-term memory. Whitehurst and Vasta (1975) summarized this progression in the comprehension, imitation, and production elements of the CIP hypothesis. Stimulus dependency is replaced by goal dependency, as in all skill learning. Reliance on short-term sensory register gradually shifts to reliance on long-term memory recall, with adjustments so that the recalled items fit immediate contingencies. Related conceptualizations proposed by MacWhinney (1978) include a progression from rote learning, to pattern abstraction, to rule learning.

Piaget's (e.g., 1977) conceptualization of a progress from "empirical" to "reflective abstraction," or from "figurative to operative knowledge," seems homologous with the change from pattern abstraction to rule learning. Gagne's (1968) emphasis on a variety of learning processes is similar, though more differentiated. This resolves the controversy whether language acquisition is based on imitation and rote learning or rule learning. It is both, more, and neither. Rumelhart and McClelland (1987) and an earlier study by Bybee and Slobin (1982) indicate that to a large extent it is based on neither process. Pattern abstraction in the Gibsonian sense, or Piaget's empirical abstraction, comes closest to the phenomena observed in the earliest stages of mastery. Yet language acquisition presents a long developmental sequence, and it cannot be presumed that the same approach to information processing would be applied at all times or to both familiar and new items. In Heinz Werner's (1948) microgenetic sense, early patterns may be based upon vague overall outlines, as Peters (1983) described the earliest intonation contours. More detailed representation of patterns might follow, and rules might be abstracted later or not at all. Careful factual analyses by Bybee and Slobin (1982), and Rumelhart, McClelland et al. (1986), and in this work attempt to provide more answers.

Incremental Progress   The training and learning process necessarily advances incrementally, by integrating the progression from simple to complex developmental levels and accommodating the considerable parental adaptation to the child. Feedback increases gradually in complexity since it is provided in response to actual filial constructions. Single words, more-word constructions, and bound morphemes are trained and learned at different levels as are diverse grammatical constructions. To understand filial advances, both cumulative/distant and proximal causation have to be integrated. A central weakness of the typical psychological pre–post measurement is that such measurements of behavior at the start and finish, or at similarly long intervals, hold little promise for elucidating the intervening processes. Yet the psychological processes leading to acquisition are of greatest interest, and only minute, detailed exploration of these can enlighten the sufficiency controversy.

The arguments and analyses put forth may lead to a conclusion that appears somewhat revolutionary, not because it is difficult to establish logically, but because it goes against the dominant convictions of the last decades. This conclusion is that language acquisition is really quite simple, if analyzed microanalytically in its continuous time course. The acquisition proceeds in minute steps, supported by an abundance of environmental information structured and attuned to the child's mastery level. The old conception of the immensity of the task was a misconception, derived from overly global cross sectioning, that compared a near-zero point in the developmental level with full competence. This was Gleitman and Wanner's (1982) jump from the "earliest utterances" to the final product, "grammar covering the full range of adult competence" (pp. 39–40).

Partial support for this new conceptualization is found in the following factual analyses. They are based on continuous-time analyses. Full support for this conceptualization can be expected only after the research program derived from this conceptualization and resulting methodological innovations provide further evidence.

Flexibility of Skills   Little theoretical discussion needs to be added in this area. It has been extensively propagandized under the label of generativity. Schmidt's (1975) elucidation of the novelty problem discussed above showed that every mastered skill can be applied flexibly. The following chapters indicate how the child progresses from rigid routines to increasing flexibility by substituting new elements into existing frames. These developments have been noticed in even casual observation, and they have been extensively documented in second-language acquisition (Fillmore, 1976). In brief, careful developmental research demonstrates increases in flexibility as a result of learning processes and makes recourse to concepts such as generativity superfluous.

From Controlled to Automatic Processing   Automatization is as important in language performance as in the performance of any other complex skill, and the principle is widely acknowledged. The result of automatization is identified as the "transparency" of language, that one can "see through the code" directly to the meaning a message conveys. The code is deciphered with little or no conscious awareness. The same phenomenon appears in discussions of the "stratification of language," or in Hockett's (1960, pp. 4–6) famous "duality of patterning." The sub-routines of the lower strata are performed automatically so that full attention is given to the meaning of the message. The gradual change from performance requiring much attention and information processing to increasingly automatic performance has been insufficiently explored. Such transitions are known to every second-language learner. Transitions depend upon consistent practice, which is readily provided by the ubiquity of linguistic information in the child's environment, as discussed earlier. It is well known that children engage in active practice, that is, frequent talking.

Substantiation for gradual automatization is found in the literature. Scollon's (1976) "vertical constructions" preceding "horizontal"
ones suggest an early struggle with the code that demands much information processing capacity. Dysfluencies, partial imitations, and imitations of unknown elements (R. Clark, 1977) indicate heightened attention to aspects of the code. The process of accretion of sub-routines,
such as the progress from one-word to more-word utterances, or the
gradual inclusion of functors into utterances originally constructed
only of contentives, provides indirect evidence of automatization.

METHODOLOGICAL IMPLICATIONS

The theoretical conceptualization has been progressively narrowed
from general culture learning, to skill learning, to learning of language
skills, and the methodological implications of these models can be
summarized. Methodological considerations are encountered in the
data and analyses throughout this work.

Measurement Aspects and Relational Data

The data are considered largely as relational. This contrasts to the
reliance in many previous studies upon "punctuate" data, such as
frequency counts of single constructions. This relational conceptualization applies in three domains.

Microanalytic Domain   In the microanalytic domain, this conceptualization pertains to relationships between adjacent utterances. For
example, the relation between the model of a specific linguistic construction and the child's subsequent attempted production, and the relation between the child's production and its feedback are considered
more informative than counting the number of models or the number
of filial trials. Discrepancies between model, production, and feedback
are seen as exhibiting critical features that are readily noticed and that
lead, over many repetitions, to improvement.

Intermediate Domain   On an intermediate level, relations are also
more important than individual data points. Special emphasis is placed
on temporal intervals, resulting in massing versus spacing of training
episodes. The temporal interval between the model and production is
of interest because it reflects storage and retrieval processes. The increase in intervals can show how the child proceeds from stimulus dependency, to reliance on cues, and to internal guidance for his or her
linguistic constructions. These temporal relations are interdependent
with similarity relations. Immediate stimulus dependency leads to
rather identical imitation. Delay can be expected to result in the loss of
some specific features and reflects schema abstraction, which results in
substitutions in the child's utterances. The similarity relationship is

important in the input, as conceptualized in invariances over transformations, and realized in Stokes and Baer's (1977) emphasis on the advantage of "multiple exemplars" in training. If relationships between such exemplars exist, "positive transfer" or "abstraction of similarities" can be expected. Attention to multiple exemplars is important in language learning since few structures exist to be trained in early stages (see Brown, 1973). On the level of global syntax, these structures are the copula sentence and the full-verb sentence. Looking at one sentence constituent, the prepositional phrase, two frames exist, with one predominant. These frames are prepositional phrases with and without a determiner. Substitutions in elements of the phrase are common during training, which results in the transformations over invariances discussed. It follows that research needs to focus not on one specific construction, but on many related patterns and the temporal and similarity relation between the presentation and the training.

Macroanalytic Domain   Relational principles are most important in the macroanalytic domain. Chapters in this volume present data, conceptualized as bivariate or multivariate time series, and compare curves of input over many months with acquisition curves to explore cause–effect relationships. Cause–effect relationships are presumed to be bidirectional, with the child affecting the mother's input and feedback, and the mother affecting the child both immediately and cumulatively. Furthermore, comparisons between learning curves are made to demonstrate iterative aspects and changes in proximal causes. The forms of individual curves, whether typical sigmoid growth curves or other forms, are important indicators of the acquisition processes.

Continuous-time analyses, or "serial methods" (Smith, 1984), or "continuous series" (Dray, 1957), ranging from seconds, to months, to years are employed. This methodology can be compared to a sort of developmental calculus: The differential component focuses on microchanges and on determining slopes of progress, or the edge of learning. The integral component specifies areas of mastered content and integrates previous accomplishments. The intervals between comparisons (dt) can be defined as microintervals, or immediate responses to input, or as longer intervals in order to effectively explore dynamic transmission and acquisition processes.

Data Reduction and Synthesis

No quantitative inferences to circumscribed populations are possible when focusing on a single dyad. The goal is, nevertheless, to explore general laws, comparable to Eppinghaus's famous learning and forgetting curves. Thurstone's (1919) "learning functions" and Hull's (1943, 1952) "acquisition functions" reflect similar endeavors to explore general laws. Thurstone attempted to specify parameters, which is not yet possible from the present data.

Curvilinear presentations of general relationships and tabular summaries of transformations over invariances have been chosen to demonstrate major principles. A century of research on learning and memory and the practical results on skill learning are presupposed in these presentations. The phenomena reflected in these data are in close accord with the laws past research established in these fields. This concordance suggests that the same general law also underlies the learning process represented.

Generalized parameters and parameters that change with the multivariate complexity of language acquisition will have to be explored with the mathematical tools of time and event series analysis. Conceptualizations based on transitional probabilities (cf. Moerk, 1983a), periodicity (including rhythmic phenomena), and on developmental functions or curves (e.g., growth curves) provide foundations for the following data presentations and interpretations.

Chapter 2

The Now

Interactional and Cognitive Processes in Acquisition of the Present Progressive

Where now?
Who now?
When now?   *S. Beckett: The Unnameable*

Samuel Beckett's famous questions represent not only the topics of hu-mankind's most basic research, but they also point to the earliest topics of verbal interactions. Since the data for the following analyses do not begin with the very first steps in language learning, the topic "Who now?", referring to people as subjects and objects of sentences, has been mastered to some extent. The other questions, "When now?" and "Where now?", are just entering the conversations in the tran-scripts. The early steps in the training and learning of these topics are explored.

Infants and young children live exclusively in the "here and now." Because of this cognitive limitation, parents and other·interlocutors must adapt to this capacity and restrict their focus to the same range of experiences. The here and now is of great emotional importance since this is the arena of need fulfillment, whether of joy or distress. The here and now, so central cognitively and behaviorally, is also the cen-tral focus of early language interactions. This and the following chap-ter concentrate on the acquisition of two sets of linguistic items, the present progressive (PPr) that communicates about the now, and the prepositional phrase (PPh) that communicates about the here, there, and then.

As stated in the preceding chapter, co-species members and their movements are of special interest to children. "What doing, Mommy?"

is one of Eve's most common questions. Children watch movements intensively and talk about them often. The maternal acts and the child's own activities constitute major topics of discussion. The child has much opportunity and a considerable need to master the linguistic means to refer to these activities. In accordance with this, Brown (1973) reported that the present progressive -*ing* appears early in the three children he studied, and it was the first bound morpheme to be mastered by Adam and Eve. (Mastery was defined by Brown as at least 90% use in obligatory contexts in the children's speech.)

An exploration of acquisition of the present progressive morpheme provides insights into very early learning processes. Additionally, Brown's (1973, pp. 326–327) own analyses provide indications of possible processes underlying this acquisition. Brown's analyses and this extensive study complement each other with their findings and interpretations.

Brown reports that the verbs often employed by Eve in the progressive were: "do, eat, make, go." A larger number (19) of process verbs were, however, not used by Eve in the progressive form. This first report indicates a possible frequency effect because the four verbs are common in all households. Brown provides another indication of the effectiveness of input frequency. He reported about samples 4–6: "For the five process verbs which Eve most often used in the PPr . . . they were [used by the mother] in the progressive precisely as often as they were in the generic form" (Brown, 1973, p. 326). Since these verbs are frequently used, Eve had plenty of opportunity to hear them in the progressive form. In contrast, "The 19 process verbs which in Eve's samples looked like state verbs since they never were in the progressive . . . were [used by the mother] in generic form about 7 times as often as in the progressive form." Brown concludes that Eve might have employed these present progressive forms "based upon her mother's practice" (p. 327), and not based upon any cognitive principle. The analyses in this chapter provide evidence to confirm these preliminary suggestions by Brown.

Brown adds another central consideration for the evaluation of the acquisition processes employed by Eve. He stresses that "the involuntary state verbs were never in the progressive," and ponders that the causes for "the absence of error with the progressive" (Brown, 1973, p. 327) may be due to innate knowledge. He concludes that "there are fatal difficulties" (Brown, 1973, p. 328) for the nativist argument and chooses instead the argument for acquisition processes. This theoretical conclusion is in agreement with the following evidence, with a minor qualification.

Contrary to Brown's statement, the use of the present progressive was not error-free. Eve's mother herself once reported frequent pertinent errors. After her father had trained Eve in the PPr during the mother's hospitalization, Eve's mother commented, "Almost with every verb [Eve] has -*ing* on it whether it should be or shouldn't." (The mother was remarking here upon strong training effects.) Examples of this incorrect use were found in the recordings and are presented below. These also indicate training, specifically frequency, effects, and they support Brown's hypothesis of the dominant effect of frequency upon learning.

These examples also suggest another phenomenon: Not one of the incorrect uses of the PPr in these examples occurs with a state verb, and Eve avoids a major category error. In contrast, all incorrect uses of the PPr occur with process verbs, and in situations where the generic form should have been employed. This suggests that input might serve a delimiting role, and words that are not heard in the PPr form are not used in this form. If the PPr form is familiar, then the child may employ it incorrectly. This suggests cognitive confusion about the underlying semantic principle, or lack of principle, as well as effective input storage and lack of productivity. More evidence needs to be considered to evaluate these preliminary causal interpretations.

This study first carefully describes the role of input in acquisition. Second, the major cognitive processes employed by Eve in acquisition are explored.

METHOD

The subject of the analysis is Eve, the girl observed by Roger Brown and associates, whose language acquisition was reported in several studies, especially by Brown (1973). Eve was observed in her home, interacting predominantly with her mother, and, to a lesser extent, with her father, and the observers who soon became well-known visitors. Eve was 18 months of age at the start and was observed for 10 months. For these analyses, the first nine samples were studied (to Eve's 22nd month). In sample 9, Eve employed the present progressive in 90% of obligatory instances (Brown, 1973). This report suggests that she was close to mastery. Since the goal was to explore the acquisition processes of a grammatical form, it seemed best to focus on this early period. Processes employed during acquisition are probably different from those employed in skilled performance, as reported in skill learning (Kleinman, 1983). For the application of already acquired skills, gradual fine tuning based on feedback clarifies the exact conditions of when to apply them.

Longitudinal approaches that follow the acquisition process in all nine samples are used with microanalytic approaches, which specify immediate cause–effect relationships in Eve's interactions with her mother. Quantitative indices of the learning processes and qualitative examples are provided.

RESULTS

The results are reported in light of five major considerations. First, overall longitudinal trends are presented, and the development of specific verbs employed in the present progressive form is explained. These analyses indicate when intensive acquisition processes occurred in the course of development. Second, microanalytic explorations of these events contribute to specification of the dynamics shaping developmental trends. Third, longitudinal perspectives and fine grained process analyses are combined to describe the maternal influences and filial processing that contribute to acquisition of specific verbs in the present progressive and to the overall construction of the present progressive. Fourth, it will be shown that production of a form does not automatically imply knowledge of correct usage. Incorrect productions challenge the mother to provide corrective feedback. Fifth, Eve's dependence upon priming is demonstrated by the close timing of Eve's productions to a maternal cue.

Overall Longitudinal Trends

Table 1 presents overall longitudinal information of sample length and gradual introduction of the present progressive by adults and by Eve. Eve's mean ages for each sample are given in Row 1 as a basis for comparisons and for computations of correlations between age and dependent variables. The cause of the trend of increasing use of the present progressive could have been due simply to an overall increase in the amount of verbal interactions. Rows 2 and 3 show that, with the exception of sample 8, the amount of interaction is relatively stable and declines slightly in hours of observation and pages of transcripts. The increased use of the present progressive can, therefore, not simply be due to the amount of interaction.

Row 4, "Total types," reports the number of different words employed in the present progressive form. With the exception of sample 9, an increasing trend is observed in the range of verbs to which the new grammatical form is applied. Rows 5 and 6 distinguish this trend for the mother and for the child. (The term "mother" is used to refer to adult performance, but the more encompassing term "adult" is employed also, especially when input of an observer or the father is obviously included in a specific discussion. Labeling performance as sim-

Table 1. Descriptive data and longitudinal trends in use of the present progressive: Frequency data

Row	Item	Samples S1–S9								
1.	Age	18.0[a]	18.15	18.29	19.13	19.27	20.18	21.0	21.14	21.26
2.	Hours/sample	4	3	4	2	3	2	2	5	2
3.	Transcript pp./sample	30	26	27	24	25	20	23	37	19
4.	Total types	14	17	20	23	26	24	31	33	15
5.	Types M	14	17	20	21	26	22	24	30	12
6.	Types E	3	3	2	7	11	12	21	20	11
7.	Proportions of types $\frac{E}{M}$	$\frac{3}{14}$	$\frac{3}{17}$	$\frac{2}{20}$	$\frac{5}{21}$	$\frac{11}{26}$	$\frac{10}{22}$	$\frac{14}{24}$	$\frac{17}{30}$	$\frac{8}{12}$
8.	Maternal types employed by Eve (%)	21	17	10	23	42	45	58	56	66
9.	Types employed only by Eve	0	0	0	2	0	2	7	3	3
10.	Tokens M	44	50	41	44	74	49	61	64	42
11.	Tokens E	4	4	3	10	29	33	51	48	38

[a]Age is given in months and days. Days represent a rounded average across hours per sample.
M = mother, E = Eve.

ply adult input or feedback would be misleading since most of the linguistic information came from the mother, and it is shown that the other adults were not as responsive to Eve's informational needs as the mother.)

Rows 4, 5, and 6, as well as row 9, show that for samples 1, 2, and 3, Eve used the present progressive only with the verbs that the mother used in the sample. From sample 4 on, the number of maternal types is smaller than total types, indicating that Eve employed types not employed by the mother. Eve's increased independence from her mother's immediate model is evidence of either long-term storage of the specific present progressive verb construction or of the application of a morphological rule. In either case, linguistic progress is indicated. The following analyses attempt to specify the processes that Eve was employing.

Before these more complex questions are faced, a simpler aspect of filial information acquisition is indicated in rows 7 and 8. These indicate what fraction (row 7) or percentage (row 8) of maternal present progressive types Eve employed. This percentage increases steadily, as is particularly evident in row 8. The correlation between age and this increase is .93. Eve is, obviously, utilizing maternal input more effectively. Rows 10 and 11 demonstrate that this increase in diversity is accompanied by an increase in total frequency, particularly for the child.

The correlations are: Eve's age and tokens M, $r = .31$; Eve's age and tokens E, $r = .91$. In the early samples, the mother led in frequency and diversity of tokens, but Eve had caught up by samples 7 and 9 in the types she employed, as seen from a comparison of rows 5 and 6.

A preliminary indication of interactional dynamics is found in the relationship between samples 4 and 5 and between tokens M and E (rows 10 and 11). Maternal tokens are stable in sample 4, while Eve's tokens increase almost threefold in sample 4. In sample 5, the mother almost doubles her tokens, and Eve triples hers. This lead by the child, indicating readiness for a specific learning task, was also reported in other linguistic domains. Sachs (1979) found that the child led in semantic contents, but the mother led in supplying the linguistic forms for their correct expression. The effects of Eve on her mother are analyzed in more detail in a later section.

Table 1 suggests that Eve's acquisition process might have occurred in three stages: In samples 1–3, Eve used very few types of the present progressive and similarly few tokens. Sample 4 represents a transition period that prepared for the dynamics of samples 5 and 6, where types and tokens of the present progressive increased considerably. Samples 7 and 8 represented a doubling of types and a plateau in token attainment. Sample 9 appears exceptional because it is the shortest of the samples in number of pages and, consequently, fewer phenomena are analyzed.

To explore the topic of memory span, an additional row in Table 1 was planned that would reflect the average delay between maternal model and filial production. This came to naught, since already by sample 1, Eve produced one or more tokens spontaneously, that is, in random intervals from the maternal model. Whereas most filial productions followed a maternal model with an interval of one utterance at most, a single extended interval of 22–100 utterances, appearing in each sample and based only on pragmatic factors, obliterated any mean differences in increases in the delay of imitations. A more complete presentation demonstrates some dynamics of Eve's morphological learning.

Extended Acquisition Process of Frequent PPr Forms

The global factors affecting use of verbs in the present progressive are summarized in Table 2. A small set of verbs became "productive" for Eve, meaning that they were employed in several later samples in the present progressive form. These verbs were used by Eve's mother in many samples with considerable frequency.

The first three verbs in Table 2, "doing," "sitting," and "making," were employed by the mother in all nine samples. "Doing" is encoun-

Table 2.   Longitudinal trends of verbs employed in the PPr form: Frequency data

Verb	\begin Samples S1–S9																		Total	
	M	E	M	E	M	E	M	E	M	E	M	E	M	E	M	E	M	E	M	E
Doing	12	0	17	0	12	0	10	0	23	11	11	2	16	2	22	4	13	2	136	21
Sitting	3	0	2	1	2	0	1	0	4	0	6	0	3	1	2	8	3	7	26	17
Making	1	0	1	0	1	0	2	1	4	1	1	1	2	3	1	0	1	0	14	6
Eating	0	0	9	2	2	0	1	0	6	5	1	1	5	9	1	1	7	6	32	24
Having	3	0	3	0	2	0	1	0	0	0	2	0	2	0	1	0	8	6	22	6
Writing	4	1	0	0	4	0	2	0	0	0	4	12	1	4	3	3	4	6	22	26
Going	11	0	6	0	1	0	1	0	5	3	0	0	2	0	0	0	1	0	27	3

M = mother, E = Eve.

tered in maternal "What are you doing" questions. Eve uses it most commonly in the form "What doing, Mommy?" This form appeared in a massed training session (i.e., used 23 times by the mother and 11 times by the child in sample 5) and is subsequently used in every sample, although infrequently, by Eve. The term "massing" is employed here with a slightly different meaning from that usual in learning psychology. It refers to frequent repetitions within a brief period but does not imply forced training with no interval between repetitions. The intervals between rehearsals also are not uniform. In this case, the child is largely in control, and the repetitions are integrated into normal conversation.

"Sitting" is employed by Eve's mother less frequently. It is used by Eve in sample 7, and becomes productive in samples 8 and 9. Although "making" is employed by Eve's mother in all nine samples, its frequency is low, and it did not appear productive in Eve's use.

The two verbs, "eating" and "having," generally used with the meaning of "having something for lunch," are only employed in eight samples, although they refer to an activity of considerable importance for Eve. Eve first produces the present progressive "eating" in sample 2, when the mother employs it often (again evidence for the effects of massed training). Eve did not use it in samples 3 or 4, when the mother employs it infrequently, and seems to acquire it permanently in sample 5, again in connection with frequent maternal use. "Having" is employed by the mother less frequently and enters Eve's regular use in sample 9, in a massed training situation.

For the last two verbs, "writing" and "going," the same impact of maternal frequency can be seen. "Going" is counted in the present progressive meaning, referring to locomotion, but not when employed to indicate intent for future action, as "going to/gonna." Both items are employed by the mother in seven of nine samples, but "writing" is used more frequently in most samples. Eve uses "writing" in sample 6 and maintains its use thereafter. Eve begins to employ the less consistently modeled "going" in sample 5 with the mother's frequent models. With subsequent infrequent maternal use, however, Eve does not continue to employ it.

The columns of Table 2 that present overall frequency data for mother and child provide the evidence in compact form: Whether a form is incorporated by Eve and when it is incorporated depend upon the frequency of maternal modeling and consistency of maternal use. The overall correlation between frequency of maternal input and filial use is .34. Yet if the items are categorized according to their spacing, or use by the mother in nine samples, or eight, or seven, and are totaled within these categories, the correlation with the frequencies of Eve's use jumps to .99. This suggests that regular spacing has a considerable impact in addition to overall input frequency. Although these covariations are suggestive at best due to the small number of items on which they are based, they do indicate two factors that influence acquisition: frequency and overall spacing of input. Additional effects of local massing were indicated repeatedly, and pragmatic variables are certainly important also, as they affect frequency and learning.

These considerations of causes, consisting of overall frequency, overall spacing, but with massing during the initial acquisition episode, were too global to provide detailed insights into the processes underlying acquisition and early use. More fine grained analyses should provide additional insight.

Fine Grained Analyses of the Acquisition Process

The most plausible cause for learning a new construction is to be found in models provided by the adult environment. Exact models of the PPr are an obvious source. Analyses of the interactions revealed that an equally frequent antecedent of a filial production of the present progressive was a maternal "What are you doing" question. When referring to activities of other people or animals, the form of the question was adjusted. The entire set of these questions is included as "What doing" questions. Additionally, any closely antecedent adult model of the ending -ing, independent of the verb stem, could have served as a cue for the child to employ the same morpheme in her utterance. In Tables 3, 4, and 5, the intervals are given between such potential elicitors and the child's production of a PPr.

When Eve produced a present progressive that did not follow within a brief interval one of these three categories of models, the construction is termed "spontaneous." An interval for differentiation of "imitative" versus spontaneous utterances was set at approximately 30 utterances, which was ½–1 page of transcripts. This conservative criterion was chosen to counteract the possibility of underestimating Eve's productivity. (Because the imitative character of Eve's speech is emphasized in this work, it seemed prudent, when in doubt, to go against the major hypothesis.) To substantiate this differentiation of imitative and spontaneous utterances would require computation of probabilities. A preliminary indication is that most verbs occurred in the PPr within a brief interval after a cue, and the probability of their occurring uncued was close to zero. Spontaneous productions were, however, found in Eve's speech beginning with sample 3. Spontaneous productions were recorded with the distances from models, if models could be found within the same recording hour or in the hour immediately preceding. (Often in Brown's recordings, 2 hours were recorded without interruption. Other recordings were actually separated by a few days but still considered by Brown [1973] as one sample.)

Early Uses of the Present Progressive

Table 3, summarizing Eve's early use of the present progressive and its antecedents, presents a diversified picture. Before sample 3, Eve employs few verbs in the PPr, and those she did use were repeatedly not dependent on imitation of a preceding model. "Writing" in sample 1 is employed independently of an exact model or a "What doing" question. This also applies to one instance of "eating" in sample 2, the second instance of "banging" in sample 3, and for "swimming" and one occurrence of "running" in sample 4. Certainly, instances suggesting the influence of an immediately preceding model or cue predominate ($N = 13$).

The interpretation of cuing by model of -ing must be considered as preliminary. Because the mother commented upon events in the present and plans for the immediate future ("going to/gonna"), frequent -ing morphemes occurred in maternal speech. Some close co-occurrences of maternal and filial PPr morphemes are expected merely due to chance. Only if close co-occurrences predominate can cause–effect interpretation become plausible. For most of the PPrs in the columns "Model of -ing," an assumption of random co-occurrences seems advisable. Conservatively interpreted, the data in Table 3 provide indications of both spontaneous productivity and immediate input effects.

The vocabulary items underlying these spontaneous constructions refer invariably to the domain of Eve's activities. (The exception is "swimming" in sample 4, which was produced to describe the activity of fish in the aquarium in Eve's home.) It can be plausibly assumed,

Table 3. Interactional antecedents and intervals before Eve's production of the PPr

Verb	Sample 1			Sample 2			Sample 3			Sample 4		
	Exact model	"What doing" question	Model of -ing	Exact model	"What doing" question	Model of -ing	Exact model	"What doing" question	Model of -ing	Exact model	"What doing" question	Model of -ing
Coming			2[a]									
Writing			26									
Swimming		0/1[b]										58
Sitting						2						
Eating				0		22						
Dancing						11						
Drinking							0		0			
Banging								0/57			1/0	
Making										0		
Running											0	32
Cracking										9/0		
Lying down												6
Wearing												6

[a]Interval between antecedent and production measured in number of utterances.
[b]The slash separates data from filial productions.

and partly substantiated by the examples below, that mother and child often talked about Eve's activities before the actual recording session. The data in Table 2 have shown that this applies for all recorded samples.

The term spontaneous suggests that an item was produced by relying upon stored information. Yet neither in the term spontaneous nor in the specification of the intervals between models and Eve's production is there any implication of the psychological processes that Eve employed. Spontaneous productions could be based on rote memory of the entire construction or on construction from morphological and semantic rules. This also applies to constructions occurring shortly after a model. Only distributional analyses, whether Eve produced constructions only after a model or independently of it, or whether -*ing* was used with types not modeled by the mother or only with modeled verb types, can provide answers to the complex questions regarding the psychological processes employed in linguistic performance. The clearest evidence of processes might come from detailed study of the developmental course of specific acquisitions.

There are several items in Table 3 that provide insight into various stations of the learning process. "Coming" in sample 1 is immediately preceded by two maternal questions: "Where is your car going?" and "Is it going?" Additionally, near the end of the preceding hour of observation, the mother employed the construction "Oh, the choo-choo is coming?" In this case, an exact model and two closely related cues are found as antecedents. Eve's more spontaneous construction "writing" had been modeled also by the mother in the preceding hour, and her "swimming" came in response to a maternal question "What are the fish doing?" Two aspects of priming are observed: priming through the immediate cue, "doing," and priming through an identical model, "coming" or "writing." Nevertheless, the exact form "swimming" must have been constructed or retrieved from long-term memory because no immediate, exact model was observed.

In sample 2, Eve's "sitting chair" follows the maternal description "Eve's having lunch," and Eve's first "eating" (describing her own action) shortly follows a maternal description "You're drinking your milk." (Note the structural and semantic parallels between the model and Eve's production.) Eve's next "eating" is in immediate response to a maternal question "What are you eating?" In contrast, Eve's "dancing," describing her activity, seems to rely on a cue, but not depend on a preceding model. Table 2 suggests that this item was not frequently employed. Pragmatic importance might be an influential factor and outweigh both frequency and immediacy of modeling.

When the mother asks Eve in sample 4, "What are you doing?" Eve responds, "Dance," and the mother improves, "Oh, you're dancing." An item produced as PPr in sample 2 is produced incorrectly in sample 4, in spite of the immediately preceding maternal cue as to the present progressive form. This argues against rule-based performance in cases when Eve does produce the correct PPr ending. It seems more likely that Eve has learned to associate formulas: "sitting chair" with "having lunch," and "eating" with "drinking your milk," which she heard often in her daily routines. Low frequencies of "dancing" in both maternal and filial use might account for the loss of this previously mastered form.

"Drinking" in sample 3 describes an important activity and appears consistently in discussions across samples. The mother modeled "drinking" twice at the beginning of sample 3, and Eve produced it approximately 140 items later in response to the cue of -*ing*, "What are you going to do now?" The second appearance was an exact and immediate imitation:

M: *Papa's drinking water.*
E: *Drinking water.*

Eve not only likes to dance, but also to bang. She announces, proudly and spontaneously (0 and 57 utterances after "What doing" questions), "Banging," and her mother responds, perhaps somewhat mournfully, "I know you're banging." In sample 4, Eve responds to "What doing" questions, "I banging pencil," and "I banging." She obviously has mastered the activity and the means to describe it. The syntactic construction itself, however, especially when it is complex, and includes the subject of the activity, still benefits from the support provided by priming, "What are you doing," questions.

Eve's "running," again describing her own activity, is produced first spontaneously, and then after a cue (intervals 32 and 0). Therefore, it is mastered by Eve but may also be cue dependent. Partial mastery and effectiveness of cuing are not mutually exclusive phenomena.

Learning processes become very evident with two items appearing for the first time in sample 4. Eve produces her first recorded "making" after two successive examples by her mother, "Making pennies." The first maternal model was uttered as a correction of Eve's "Make penny," which in turn followed two constructions that could have functioned as cues: a maternal "What's he doing?" and a model of -*ing*. The central interactional sequence is:

M: *Yes, Pap's at Emerson.*
E: *(Make) penny.*
M: *Making pennies. Yes.*
E: *Papa penny.*

M: *Pennies. Yes. Making pennies.*
E: *Making penny.*

This brief sequence provides several insights. Though Eve has been using the present progressive -*ing* for several weeks, and though she knows the verb "make" and even the phrase "to make pennies" (i.e., to earn money), she does not produce the PPr form after the two cues specified above. Maternal improving feedback and the second maternal model are needed before Eve repeats, "Making penny." This sequence shows that Eve does not always include the PPr even in rote-learned phrases, nor does a single maternal cue seem sufficient to prompt the ending. (The parentheses indicate reduced intelligibility of the item on the tape.)

An impressive example of teaching and learning is found in the acquisition of the phrase "cracking nuts" in sample 4. The mother introduced "to crack" and "nuts," and, as the evidence suggests, Eve had to learn the words and the present progressive form "cracking." The overall processes involved have been detailed in Moerk (1985b). The present emphasis concerns acquisition of the present progressive form of a new vocabulary item. After the mother used the present progressive "cracking" four times, but Eve continued to employ only the stem "crack," the following interactions were observed:

M: *Are you cracking the nut?*
E: *Yep.*
M: *Okay. You keep trying. You keep trying.*
E: *Mom crack nut.*
M: *Yes, I'll crack the nut.*
E: *(A) crack nut.*
M: *Mommy will crack the nut.*
E: *Eve cracking the nut.*
M: *Are you cracking the nut?*

Five exact maternal models, four preceding the one quoted above, and two cues, in the form of "trying," were required before Eve produced her first construction of "cracking." Note also the close syntactic match:

M: *Are you cracking the nut?*
E: *Eve cracking the nut.*

In this case, Eve retains the article, which is usually omitted. Almost two pages of transcript later, we find the following:

M: *Mommy's cracking the nut.*
E: *(Mommy) cracking nut.*
M: *And Eve's cracking the nut, too.*

In this instance, an immediate model (but only one, not five) was needed for Eve to use the PPr for the new word. In the text between these conversations, Eve repeatedly referred to cracking nuts, but in all instances she employed only the stem "crack" without the PPr morpheme.

The use of "lying down," describing a frequent activity of Eve's, appears based on long-term memory, aided by a cue, -*ing*. This also applies to "wearing." The above analyses suggest that the PPr morpheme -*ing* is not yet productive for Eve. She employs the PPr with well-known word stems or influenced by immediate models, but by herself she does not yet combine the word stem and ending. This suggestion requires careful evaluation on the basis of additional evidence.

Expansion of the Variety of Verbs

The trend toward employing new verbs in the PPr was observed in sample 4 in the imitation of new models and responsiveness to -*ing* cues. This trend is enhanced in sample 5 of Table 4. In sample 4 Eve had increased the number of types to 7 (from 2 or 3 in the first three samples), and she then increased this number in sample 5, employing 11 types.

In sample 5 Eve immediately imitates 5 of 11 PPr verbs newly used by the mother. In addition, two immediate imitations follow verbs infrequently used before by the mother, and frequently employed PPrs are imitated also. These facts suggest that Eve had conceptualized the PPr as a phenomenon deserving her attention and as an item to be imitated and mastered.

This impression is reinforced when verbs employed by the mother in previous samples (Table 2) are considered. The mother used "doing" often beginning with sample 1, but Eve had not employed it until sample 5, where she employs it 11 times. Eve had not tried "going," referring to locomotion, once in spite of consistent and frequent maternal models. In sample 5, five maternal uses are matched by three filial uses. "Eating," which had been employed twice by Eve in sample 2 but not subsequently, despite consistent maternal use, is now employed by Eve five times in imitation of six maternal uses (Table 2). This attention to the present progressive strongly suggests that the construction has now entered Eve's zone of proximal or active development.

The fine grained analysis of the acquisition of "doing" in a massed training situation is most informative. Eve began the hour repeating the question "What doing, Mommy?" twice, exhibiting a newly acquired formula. Despite several maternal questions of "What are you doing?" Eve does not incorporate the copula in her four subsequent questions. The formula appears fixed but not completely static. Eve

Table 4. Antecedents and intervals before Eve's production of the PPr

	Sample 5				Sample 6			
Verb	Exact model	"What doing" question	Model of -ing	Other[a]	Exact model	"What doing" question	Model of -ing	Other[a]
Doing				11×[b]		0		1×
Making		5[c]			22			
Writing								12×
Swimming								6×
Going	0/[d]0		25					
Holding	0						4	
Running	0	45				0		
Building	0							
Hiding	0							
Skating	0/0							
Digging	0							
Splashing	0							
Crying					2			
Eating	0/0/0/0/0					0		
Sleeping						0/2	3	1×
Lying down							33/0	
Riding						0		
Squashing					0			

[a]Indicates only the frequency of occurrence of specific PPrs.
[b]× = times.
[c]Interval between antecedent and production measured in number of utterances.
[d]The slash separates data from filial productions.

produces spontaneously, "Tinker-toy doing here?", and the source in maternal questions is obvious. The PPr "doing" is consistently used in immediate imitations along with various subjects, but other elements are often omitted. (*O* is the observer):

M: *He's doing what?*
E: *(He) doing what?*
O: *What's the horsie doing?*
E: *Horsie doing?*
O: *What are these people doing?*
E: *People doing?*
O: *What's this man doing?*
E: *This man doing?*

Several cognitive processes can be inferred from these examples. First, processing restrictions appear to be at work when Eve systematically omits "What" in her imitations of unfamiliar constructions, though she employs "What" spontaneously in her own question "What doing, Mommy?" Second, the effect of immediate models upon the range of Eve's constructions is obvious. With the exception of "Tinker-toy doing here?" Eve spontaneously employed only her formula, but she inserted four different subjects in her imitations. All these imitated constructions follow the model immediately, without an intervening utterance from either partner. Eve does not show evidence of retention of newly modeled constructions when other utterances intervene. These observations accord with several reports (Bloom, 1977, 1979; Watson & Ramey, 1972) that 1-second intervals maximize learning for infants, and longer intervals interfere with it. Since Eve is beyond infancy, optimal intervals may be longer than 1 second, but are still relatively brief.

Similar phenomena are encountered in Eve's use of "going," employed three times. The mother's "Where are they going in this picture?" is immediately imitated by Eve as "Going picture." The mother, when her question did not result in any meaningful response, tries again, "Going where?" Eve's unintelligible utterance prompts her mother to provide the answer "They're going shopping," which is imitated by Eve as "Going shopping." Only Eve's "Truck going," in the next recorded hour, appears not immediately modeled. But this appearance may hide important cognitive processing phenomena. In reading a picture book with Eve, the observer prompts her, "and we saw a boy with a . . ." which Eve completes as "Truck going," which was reaffirmed by the observer as "A truck going." (This last construction is linguistically peculiar, but may be contained in the text of the book, which was not provided. The observer's prompting and confirmation suggests a rote formula that is used with minimal linguistic analysis.)

Focus on Eve's intensive training of "eating" during sample 5 confirms these findings. The maternal "They are eating lunch" is immediately imitated by "Eating lunch." A maternal testing question "He's eating what?" leads first to conversational failure, with Eve responding, "Eating what?" The immediately following maternal model "He's eating banana" leads to the correct imitation of "Eating banana." Immediately after this less than optimal interaction, the mother asks, "And he's eating what there?" and Eve answers correctly, it seems, "Eating parsley." The mother reiterates this effective format, "And he's eating what there?" which is answered by Eve, "(Eating) bacon." The mother continues, "Yes, bacon. What's he hiding behind?" Did the mother study psychological research on warm-up and massed training? Probably not, but she certainly applies the principles in her interactions with Eve.

Sample 6 shows both continuity and change. Continuity is found in Eve's attention to constructions in the PPr, and she focuses on "writing" and "swimming" and incorporates them into her repertoire. Both appear in several massed clusters, and much imitation and self-repetition is involved, but they are better mastered than "eating" and "going" because Eve produces the first occurrences spontaneously. She also produces the form "sleeping" 55 utterances after the start of the recording and without any cue. Yet she trains it thereafter following maternal cues. The first use, however, is semantically inappropriate: Eve's "Baby S. sleeping" is responded to by her mother with "Baby S. is waking up." The additional three uses are also repetitions of "Baby S. sleeping" (S. is the newborn baby sister), suggesting the source of the construction. These PPr items are not newly acquired in the session, but are as intensively trained as are very recent acquisitions. As seen in Table 2, Eve employed "writing" only once (sample 1) in the preceding samples, "eating" twice (sample 2), and "sleeping," never.

In contrast to sample 5, Eve uses only two new words in the PPr form in sample 6, "squashing" and "riding," of the eight new PPr phrases that the mother employs. "Riding" is produced by Eve in response to a "What doing" question and is imitated by the mother. The transcript provides additional indications of cognitive processing:

M: *What are you doing?*
E: *(   ) riding.*
M: *You're riding?*
E: *Eve . . . Eve ride tink-toy. Eve ride tink.*

Here Eve produces a correct PPr in a very simple sentence, which was probably "I riding" ("I" is barely audible on the tape). Yet as soon as she tries to expand her construction by adding her name and an object, the information processing load becomes overwhelming, and she drops the PPr ending. Similar restrictions in information processing capacity were discussed in the context of the acquisition of Eve's "What doing" questions. "What" was dropped with an increased processing load.

This last example and much of sample 6 can serve as a reminder that the adult question "What are you doing?" is an effective cue for Eve to produce a present progressive, prompting production of the PPr six times in a brief time. Several words never appear uncued in the PPr, while two, "sleeping" and "doing," are also used spontaneously as rote phrases: "Baby S. sleeping" and "What doing, Mommy?" Nevertheless, they are still trained after cuing and then are employed in more complex and flexible syntactic constructions. Without a cue, the PPr morpheme is often missing in obligatory contexts. These findings suggest extensive reliance upon immediate conversational cues, partial reliance upon rote formulas, and they argue against rule-based performance.

Increase in the Range of Effective Cues

Table 5 presents PPrs from samples 7, 8, and 9, with emphasis on samples 7 and 8. Sample 9 is an exception, and the processes in the sample are described and analyzed separately.

Sample 7 reflects a continuation of the trend in samples 5 and 6. Features of this trend are an increasing productivity and independence from exact models, and enhanced responsiveness to "What doing" questions and to the ending -ing independent of the verb stem the mother uses. This last is theoretically most interesting, suggesting that Eve vaguely grasped that the verb stem and ending are two separate elements that can be combined spontaneously. As seen in Table 5, Eve's productions follow maternal priming by at most several utterances. A major causative factor for Eve to form the PPr is still the adult model or cue, but this time it is a model that has been analyzed into verb stem and ending. While the effects of exact modeling, of "What doing" questions, and of the ending -ing are quite obvious, no clear evidence is found that a semantic or linguistic rule governs Eve's use of the present progressive.

Eve's mother noticed this herself. As mentioned previously, Eve's father had trained Eve in the use of the PPr. As a result, Eve used -ing "almost with every verb . . . whether [she] should or shouldn't" (mother's report). Two processes could underlie this phenomenon: 1) Eve could have formed her own category of verbs and a conceptualization that it is desirable to add -ing to items of this category, or 2) she could have devoted special attention to forms ending in -ing without analyzing or synthesizing the word. Of the 20 words employed by Eve in the PPr form, 7 had never been used without the -ing ending, which supports the second hypothesis. Analysis of the samples supports the suggested interpretation that Eve does not seem to have grasped the difference in semantic conditions that require adding -ing. Several examples that support this hypothesis are presented below in the microanalyses.

This interpretation depicts a course of acquisition quite different from that presumed in most linguistic discussions of "competence." Instead of rule awareness, much trial and error, based upon the vagaries of idiosyncratic input, would have to be accepted, and "incompetence" emphasized instead of competence. In sample 8, an intensity of learning and training processes can be observed that surpasses that in sample 5. "Coming" and "sitting," frequent in maternal input in previous samples, are incorporated into Eve's productive repertoire and used five and eight times, respectively. Several previously trained items have progressed into more or less spontaneous use. These might still be primed by maternal use of -*ing*, but the interval between the model and the child's constructions is generally 10 or more utterances, and these co-occurrences could be random phenomena. The influence of the model cannot be due to short-term memory storage, as was predominant in sample 7.

On the other hand, the effects of priming follow quite special dynamics (cf. Jacoby & Witherspoon, 1982). Hearing a person's name less than a minute earlier would facilitate retrieval for an adult. Similar effects can be assumed for children. Since most of Eve's PPrs are produced briefly after maternal modeling of -*ing* and not spontaneously, cues still seemed to facilitate the use of PPrs, although the effects of the cues lasted longer, and Eve showed more initiative.

These influences are seen most clearly in the column "Exact model." Eve's use of a word usually follows the maternal model immediately or after one utterance for previously used words and especially for new ones. Of the nine new words in the PPr form that the mother employs in sample 8, Eve immediately imitates three, which indicates that she is still alert to new PPr constructions. This alertness appears to result in rapid learning and productive independence, as seen in the item "giving." "Giving" was first found in sample 7 and trained by mother and child with the help of a picture book, "Giving hay 'raff." In sample 8, Eve employs "giving" six times without even a single maternal model. All these occurrences pertain to "Mommy giving baby S. milk/cereal," a content that makes clear the origin and the pragmatic roots of this construction. Then, in sample 9, Eve says after a "What doing" question, "Giving baby S. (some) cereal," and much later she indicates increasing mastery by uttering, "(Not) giving Papa this one." That is, she replaces two constituents in the previously rigid formula.

Finally, sample 9 suggests, as did sample 5, a break in the intensive training process, or a change in emphasis. Few exact imitations of new items are found in Eve's productions, and the range of verbs employed in the PPr is small, whatever the interactional antecedents. This may be due in part to the shorter sample length. Some more established types of the PPr are trained quite extensively, however. The processes taking place in this intensive training need to be elucidated. The PPr forms of "writing," "sitting," "having," and "eating" are employed three, seven, six, and six times, respectively, by Eve. The interactions per-

Table 5. Antecedents and intervals before Eve's production of the PPr

Verb	Sample 7				Sample 8				Sample 9			
	Exact model	"What doing" question	Model of -ing	Other[a]	Exact model	"What doing" question	Model of -ing	Other	Exact model	"What doing" question	Model of -ing	Other
Doing	0[c/d]			1×[b]				4×	0/0			
Making			8/9/10									3×
Writing	0/1	0/1				0		2×				7×
Sitting			24					8×				
Swimming			1				32				6	
Dancing		0				0						
Banging			2									
Reading	0/1		1		0		19					
Wearing	0											
Jumping			15									
Brushing		0	4									
Cooking		10	4									
Mixing			141									
Remembering			0									
Rocking			4		0/24							
Carrying		0										
Ringing	0	37										
Coming						26/27	11/12/13					
Crying							4					

38

Eating		9×[b]		18	6×
Drinking	8/0	5×			28/29
Trying			36	14/17	
Putting				30	
Running		0		13	
Lying down		0			
Climbing			18		
Walking			31		
Blasting		1			
Picking		1			
Shaking		0	0		
Playing				1/2/3	
Turning				1/2	
Bringing				3	
Giving	0/1	0	6×	3	
Having					6×

[a]Indicates only the frequency of occurrence of specific PPrs.

[b]× = times.

[c]Interval between antecedent and production measured in number of utterances.

[d]The slash separates data from filial productions.

taining to "sitting" are not studied in detail because Eve uses her two phrases "Sitting chair" and "Sitting down" correctly, and her mother provides only reaffirming feedback.

Production without Mastery and with Maternal Corrective Feedback

One construction repeatedly employed is "writing." Eve acquired it in sample 6 and used it in each subsequent sample, and she employs it spontaneously in sample 9. The developmental course of this construction provides indications as to the type of competence underlying Eve's performance. In sample 6, all 12 items of "writing" are either in response to "What doing" questions or as exact imitations of a model. They are used appropriately. This applies to the four occurrences in sample 7 and the first occurrence in sample 8. The following two occurrences of "I writing Fraser pencil" are interpreted by the observer as inappropriate, since Eve's message appears to be"I want to write . . . ." Similarly, the first spontaneous instance in sample 9 is "Let me writing" (just before she starts to write). This provides two indications that the construction is employed incorrectly: 1) "Let me . . ." is directed toward a future activity and cannot be combined with a PPr, and 2) the remark of the observer, in parentheses, also shows that the PPr was inappropriate.

This mistake is interesting since a few lines later Eve says, "Let me turn back," as she turns pages, and then she shifts to "I turning back," "I turning . . ." correctly describing her turning pages. ("Back" should probably read "page," but "back" is in the transcript.) Immediately afterward, responding to the model "Now we'll write on this page," Eve repeats, "Write this page. Write there," as she writes. In the latter case, use of the present progressive form would appear to be more appropriate. A few pages later, Eve says again, "Let me writing," immediately after her utterance "Let me get it."

Within one-half page of the transcript, Eve first employs the present progressive incorrectly, then differentiates, more or less correctly, the construction "Let me turn" from "I [am] turning" and immediately afterward does not employ the present progressive where it would be expected. Across pages and transcripts, Eve employs the PPr where she expresses a request and produces interchangeably "Let me + PPr" and "Let me + verb stem." This counterindicates a semantically based use of the PPr.

Eve interacts in the previous sequence with the observer and her father, who do not provide corrective or guiding feedback to this demonstrated confusion. The feedback the mother provides is more finely attuned to the informational needs of her child. For example, after Eve's request, "Let me writing," she receives the answer from her mother, "You don't need to write," which structurally reflects a correct request form ("I want to write"). During lunch preparations and within the same hour, Eve employs one of her rote "having" constructions, "Fraser, I having (fruit)." The word "fruit" was not enunciated clearly, and Fraser misunderstands her, "Yes, you're having food, aren't you? Are you having good food?" Eve responds by answering "No." Fraser is surprised, "No? I think you're having very nice food, aren't you?" Eve seems to give up for the moment and turns to her father:

E: (   ) *Papa.*
F: *What, dear?*
E: *I having (fruit).*
F: *You have good food?*
M: *Fruit, she is having.*
F: *Are you eating fruit?*

The mother corrects the misunderstanding to ensure correct communication. Shortly afterward, Eve switches to "I having lunch" and after a few turns, following the mother's "Yes, I'm gonna eat my sandwich," Eve employs this immediate cue to formulate "Mom, Eve eating lunch," both PPrs employed correctly. The utterances might suggest that Eve has mastered the PPr in spontaneous and rule-governed use. Yet, after conversation with Eve and her mother both employing "eating" and "having" appropriately, Eve makes a mistake and is corrected by her mother:

E: *Mom, I'm eating chocolate ice cream.*
M: *Eating chocolate ice cream? We're not eating chocolate ice cream now.*

The mother emphasizes the relationship between the PPr form and "now," the progressive aspect that is a condition for the use of the PPr. Eve again incorporates the maternal feedback in "Mom not eating chocolate ice cream." It is not clear if she comprehends the demonstrated rule. After a very brief digression, Eve repeats her fixed phrase "I having fruit" and her mother responds, "Okay." When Eve continues "Mom too," the maternal correction comes swiftly, "No, I'm not having fruit. I'm going to have an apple." Eve's simple "Me too" gets the response, "Would you like to have a part of an apple?" Eve replies, "Yup," and her mother confirms, "Okay."

Eve learns from the model to differentiate intention from use of the PPr and says correctly "I'm going have chocolate." The mother's "(   ) going to have chocolate?" echoes this formulation and thereby accepts it. The maternal responses of "Okay" versus "No" to Eve's correct and incorrect assertions, respectively, as well as the effectiveness of these maternal interventions, are of great theoretical interest since they demonstrate positive and negative feedback, respectively, which have been broadly denied since the 1970s.

These detailed qualitative analyses demonstrate theoretically important phenomena. First, appearances can deceive. A calculation of Eve's use of the PPr in obligatory cases might suggest that Eve has mastered it, but further analysis shows that she also employs it inappropriately and has not mastered the rules governing applications of the PPr. The level of appropriate use may be a coincidental result of the focus of young children and their parents on the here and now. In this perspective, the PPr is correct in many cases, independent of understanding of any rules. Furthermore, Eve's use of the PPr is often contingent on models or "What doing" questions. Therefore, mere quantitative analyses could obviously overinterpret the child's competence.

Second, once Eve has mastered a form and proceeds to overgeneralize it, diacritical feedback for appropriate versus inappropriate use becomes important. In these situations, the immediacy and systematic nature of maternal corrections is impressive. Corrections are swift and informative, whether about the "truth value" of an utterance (Brown & Hanlon, 1970) or the grammatical misapplication of the PPr. Eve responds to the corrections by at least repeating them. It appears doubtful that a few corrections helped her understand the rules of applications of the PPr. It seems more probable that many instances of corrective feedback and correct models will be required for selection criteria to be clearly understood.

With this discussion of corrections, a preliminary stage has been reached in the developmental trajectory. Eve produces the PPr in 90% of obligatory contexts, has analyzed and probably synthesized the PPr form as two separate morphemes, and now she provides a new challenge and a task for her mother. Her mother now needs to demonstrate diacritically the conditions in which to produce these forms and when to avoid them. With this challenge, the training and learning process continues iteratively on a higher level, moving from cue-dependent performance to rule-dependent competence.

Cue Dependency of Eve's Productions

The data strongly suggest that during early stages of acquisition of the PPr, Eve was predominantly dependent on immediately preceding stimuli that functioned as cues.

Figure 1 demonstrates the overwhelming predominance of productions that follow a cue with zero interval. In the form of a typical inverted J-curve, frequencies decline steeply at intervals of 1 and 2.

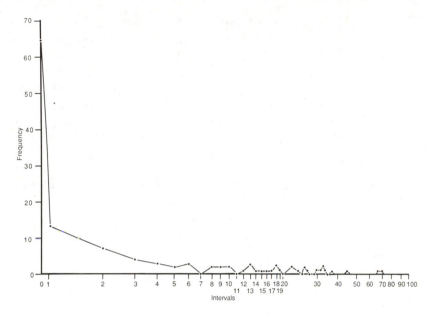

Figure 1. Intervals between priming and Eve's production.

When intervals approach five or more utterances, the frequency is one or two items per specific interval. The point of inflection of this inverted *J*-curve is at an interval of one utterance, and causative influence trails off rapidly after an interval of two or three utterances. The total productions after intervals of five or more utterances are less than the total after an interval of zero utterances. This includes the few rote-learned phrases. This shows Eve's overwhelming dependence upon priming in her production of the present progressive during these early stages.

Figure 1 also suggests (far right of the inverted *J*-curve) that the contribution of long-term memory, exceeding intervals of 20–30 utterances, is minimal. This is somewhat misleading, as has been previously discussed. Since the mother consistently produced PPr forms, these items are reflected as models of -*ing* even if Eve would not have needed the model or employed it as a cue in her constructions. The rather random fluctuations after an interval of seven or eight utterances suggest that co-occurrences with preceding cues are random. The potential underestimation of Eve's productivity has been discussed previously, and Eve's probable independent use of rote formulas was emphasized.

Awareness of this does not imply that Eve's productions were not primed even if retrieved from long-term memory. As research has emphasized, priming and long-term recall are mutually supporting, not mutually exclusive, factors. Future experimental approaches may positively ascertain the influence of each factor.

To this evidence about the effects of immediate stimuli, add the demonstrated fact that during the early stages of acquisition, items appeared only after such priming and then became less dependent on immediate support. In these early stages, the probability of occurrence without priming appeared to be zero for many items. To compute meaningful probabilities for each cross section of the developmental course would require large samples. Since these do not exist, the non-quantitative evidence presented must suffice. This evidence is overwhelming, even without statistical computations.

DISCUSSION

This longitudinal and microanalytic study of one child's increasing use of the present progressive led to differentiation of sub-periods that were characterized by distinct psychological principles. In the earliest period, Eve employed a small range of vocabulary items in the PPr form, all referring to her own daily activities. Although they were learned before the recorded period, it can be assumed that labels of these activities were often modeled for Eve while she performed them. For these acquisitions too, a frequency principle is plausible. The frequency principle was demonstrated to affect later learning also, in combination with regular spacing across samples and intensive massing. There was no indication in this period that Eve had conceptually separated the ending -ing from the word stems. The forms seemed to have been acquired as unitary vocabulary items.

In the next phase, Eve seemed especially alert to the PPr form in the input, and she repeated a large number of the PPr items modeled for her. Repetitions were performed most often immediately after the model, and they were generally not incorporated into the child's spontaneous use. An item had to be exercised in a massed form within a brief time in order to be stored in long-term memory. In this phase, the production of acquired forms was largely elicited by adult "What doing" questions. No spontaneous or "creative" application of the -ing to new word stems was observed. This again indicates that Eve learned the PPr forms as unitary vocabulary items.

Such learning also explains an impressive fact reported by Brown (1973, pp. 326–327), who found that Eve did not apply the PPr ending to any state verbs that grammatically could not accept the PPr ending. Although Brown suggested input frequency as an explanation, he concluded that evidence was not strong enough for any definite decision

(Brown, 1973, p. 328). These microanalytic analyses confirm Brown's descriptive report, but they also provide evidence for an interpretation. Eve seemed to have acquired all the pertinent forms in her use through rote learning of these items as vocabulary items, that is, based on input frequency. As has been shown, such rote learning and imitation would exclude generalization to new verb stems, whether linguistically permissible or not.

In the final period of early development of the PPr, a new principle is suggested. Eve still imitates new forms of the PPr immediately. "What doing" questions are still important to production of PPr forms. Yet she is also stimulated by adult models of the PPr to produce immediate PPr forms with different verb stems. This indicates the first differentiation between verb stem and ending, as well as a first understanding of the constructive nature of the PPr. Mastered verbs are still produced spontaneously without adult cues or models.

The probability of incorrect applications increases with increased frequency of filial PPr forms, and another principle becomes strongly evident. Eve seems to have little insight into the semantic rules underlying the application of the PPr. Items that have been heard in the present progressive form are used freely along with generic forms, whether appropriate or not. The discriminative stimulus is largely the preceding adult utterance containing a "What doing" question or a verb ending with -ing.

The data and analyses suggest that preliminary semantic understanding follows considerably after the acquisition of a linguistic construction. During the early stages of acquisition, employment of a linguistic construction depends on immediately preceding discriminative stimuli—and nothing else. Whether the same principles apply to all linguistic constructions and to all children remains a question of empirical investigation. The reports of R. Clark (1974, 1977) and Fillmore (1976) provide evidence of such imitative learning of grammatically unanalyzed formulas. A careful comparison of this work with the theoretical analyses of Derwing and Baker (1986) would also show similarities in findings and conclusions.

Chapter 3

The Here, There, and Then
Training and Acquisition of the Prepositional Phrase

> *Everything positively contradicts the credulous references*
> *to the absence of any need for teaching of language, as it*
> *contradicts the underestimation of the role*
> *of parents. . . . R. Jakobson: "Main Trends in the Science of Language"*

Jakobson's assertion pertains to one of the two major aspects of the present study: the demonstration of the parental role in providing rich linguistic information that results in acquisition of sentence constituents. As discussed in Chapter 1, the transmission process is conceived of as informal. The term "teaching," as used by Jakobson and in this work, does not presume that the parental behavior is intentionally instructional. Ethnomethodological concepts of the teaching situation (cf. Garfinkel, 1967; Heritage, 1984) and skill learning approaches (e.g., Bilodeau, 1966) more accurately describe the situation. Both approaches focus on the total instructional sequence of initiation, reply, and feedback in goal-directed activities, with the goal-directed activity as the emphasis, and teaching and learning as incidental.

The acquisition of prepositional phrases (PPh) can serve as an example to explore multifaceted learning processes because the same processes underlie the structuring of full sentences. Prepositional phrases, which are composed of a preposition, a determiner, and a nominal, express compound meanings. Prepositional phrases share an important characteristic, which is that surface strings of elements fill slots of an underlying pattern. The underlying pattern, in the same manner as the "deep structures" of the transformationalists, might never be directly observable (cf. discussion in chap. 1, this volume). Teaching and learning of linguistic patterns can, therefore, be studied through the transmission and acquisition of prepositional phrases in mother–child interactions. They can thereby be observed in a domain, where it would be agreed that learning is the exclusive factor. The variety of ways to express the locative (or other modalities) across languages is too great to even suspect universal underlying principles.

It can be argued that a close correspondence exists between the prepositional phrase and the complete sentence, especially the copula sentence. Both consist of three major elements, and the middle element is usually of minor importance, or semantically quite empty, in both. Consequently, the copula is omitted in some languages. Similarly, young children first learning the prepositional phrase often omit the article, which has only a grammatical function.

Principles encountered in the teaching and learning of prepositional phrases might therefore be relevant to the learning of syntax in general. They are pertinent to the controversy between Braine (1963, 1965) and Bever, Fodor, and Weksel (1965) about how young children learn syntactic structures although these cannot be perceived directly as input stimuli. The results of the analyses in this work might be able to provide a solution to the central question of the learnability of language.

Although prepositional phrases seem especially suited for study of teaching and learning processes, an extensive search of the literature suggests that little attention has been focused on the processes involved in their acquisition. Brown (1973) discussed transformational theories of prepositional phrases and reported on the order of acquisition and the age of acquisition of specific prepositions. Wells (1985) gave data on the ages at which classes of prepositional phrases were acquired.

H. Clark (1973) provided a fascinating discussion of the cognitive bases of space and time concepts. Wales (1986) summarized the results of studies focused on cognitive bases of prepositional development. E. Clark (1973) explored the established mastery of prepositional phrases but not acquisition processes. Parisi and Antinucci (1970) also neglected input phenomena. Johnston and Slobin (1979) considered diverse linguistic systems the child encounters, but presumed "standard communicative settings" (p. 530) across a variety of cultures. Yet settings certainly cannot be uniform with respect to specific prepositions and prepositional phrases, and standard learning situations cannot easily be presumed. The work of Carey (1978) indicated that children can acquire new vocabulary items after few exposures, often within one learning episode. If learning situations are not standard, and if some learning can be acquired after little exposure, it is highly improbable that the course of learning is uniform.

Generally, it is a fascinating comment on scientific attitudes and procedures that pertinent input has not been studied during the last century. Research in this period was largely based on a "learning psychology" orientation that emphasized learning from environmental input.

An exception to this general criticism is the work of Brown (1973), who explored a possible relationship between input and acquisition. He related the input frequency provided by the parents of his subjects to the age at acquisition of the 14 earliest morphemes, which included "in" and "on." He concluded that no relationship existed between input frequency and age at acquisition. Most astonishingly, he found that Eve used some prepositional phrases, such as "in the wastebasket," correctly without any input recorded in his transcripts. Cognitive principles of generalization, or of rule learning, seemed to be suggested by this finding.

Moerk (1980a), however, analyzing the same data and transcripts as Brown (1973, pp. 366–377), arrived at very different results. He found impressively high correlations between input frequency and age at acquisition, ranging from .50 to .80 when cause and effect data from adjacent time periods were related. He also demonstrated that the construction "in the/a wastebasket," for which Brown had found no model, was in fact modeled intensively shortly before Eve produced it.

Repeated models contributed to improvements in Eve's attempts at employing this construction. Strong effects of massed immediate input and cumulative input were thereby demonstrated. Moerk's (1980a) conclusion as to processes involved relied more on rote learning and pattern abstraction than on rule abstraction based on complex cognitive principles.

Moerk (1980a), employing Brown's transcripts, but independent of his quantitative analyses, demonstrated that prepositional phrases with "in" and "on" were trained intensively and consistently in Eve's home. Modeling, corrective feedback, massing, and spacing all were demonstrated at different times. Observing this wealth of teaching, it appears logical and almost necessary that these constructions would appear as two of the earliest minor morphemes in Eve's active use.

Moerk (1977b) explored evidence for the effects of imitation on a variety of linguistic elements, including the prepositional phrase, with a different sample of children. He reported that prepositional phrases appeared more frequently in imitative than in spontaneous speech during the early stages of acquisition, and he also found a clear developmental progression: 1) Prepositions plus nouns were produced in imitative speech, with the article missing. 2) Then preposition plus article plus noun appeared in imitative speech. 3) Dependent on input frequency, some prepositions plus noun, but without any determiner, appeared in spontaneous speech. 4) This appearance was often followed by the insertion of a possessive pronoun between preposition and noun. 5) The preposition plus article plus noun were produced spontaneously. Steps 2 and 3 might appear in reverse order. This sequence indicates the strong effect of immediately preceding input and cumulative cause–effect relationships in an extended learning process.

METHODS

Samples 7–9 are the focus of this analysis, spanning a mean length of utterance (MLU) range from 2.5 to 2.7 morphemes and an age range of 21–22 months. In these samples, Eve attained a 90% level of correctness in obligatory use of the prepositions "in" and "on" (Brown, 1973). The samples seem to represent a period of special attention to the PPh, demonstrated by Eve's extensive imitations and her somewhat spontaneous use of a considerable variety of prepositions and prepositional constructions.

The analytic approach relies mainly on microanalyses of immediate feedback processes. To a lesser extent, macrolongitudinal analyses of the unfolding of skills over minutes, hours, and weeks of interactions are employed.

The conceptual basis for these microanalyses lies in probability theory and, more specifically, in methods employing transitional probabilities. General discussion of these approaches can be found in Gottman and Notarius (1978). Application to verbal mother–child interactions is described in Moerk (1983a). No computations of probabilities are presented here, and statistical considerations are not a focus of this study.

Methods of inferential statistics are not employed because a sample of one dyad does not allow generalizations. Inferential statistics are not needed because emphasis is on psychological processes and not specific quantitative parameters. The psychological processes are assumed to be widely employed or even universal, reflecting well-established principles of learning psychology and cognitive research. Specific parameters of interactional features pertain only to the dyad studied, but the psychological processes, such as learning due to frequency of exposure, reflect general psychological laws. Data show how these laws apply to language acquisition, and that they transcend this one particular dyad.

The data presentation focuses on interactional phenomena, cross-utterance relationships, and psychological processes and thus describes the dynamics of the acquisition process. Data exhibit microanalytically the information display by the adult, information utilization by the child, and the variables affecting each. The presentation fully integrates the descriptive and explanatory aspects. Therefore, a distinction between "description" and "explanation" is not appropriate. These microanalyses are a subset of the broad range of methods generally labeled "discourse analysis," but they are a narrowly defined subset because of their emphasis on psychological and mathemagenic (knowledge producing) processes and their relative neglect of message content.

RESULTS

In the period under consideration, Eve is approaching 90% accuracy with the prepositions "in" and "on." The microanalytic study investigates two complementary aspects: refinements in the use of already familiar PPhs, and early steps in the acquisition of less common prepositions. Table 1 focuses on Eve's productions of relatively rare prepositions and antecedents.

Uptake of New and Rare Prepositions

Table 1 is largely self-explanatory: The vertical arrangement of examples corresponds to their time sequence in the transcripts. The sequences are identified by sample number, hour of recording, and utterance number. Utterance numbers are consecutive within each analyzed episode and, generally, within hour of recording.

Table 1 shows Eve's productions of rarer or newer prepositional phrases, which are generally based on closely preceding maternal models. The uniformity in sequential pattern might obscure the diversity of imitative processes, however. There are cases of immediate imitations, such as in sample 7, hour 1, utterance numbers 2516–2517, and sample 8, hour 2, utterance number 551. In sample 8, two successive maternal models contain the two rare constructions "at you" and "one day." Eve imitates those two and not the more familiar words, and she does not use those phrases spontaneously. This suggests that she may not have comprehended their meaning. In addition to Eve's attention to novelty, primacy and recency effects seem to affect this imitation as evident from the word order in the mother's models. The same immediacy of model use is found in sample 8, hour 2, utterance number 571, "After supper," and sample 8, hour 4, utterance numbers 2083–2085, "Breakfast. For breakfast." Maternal repetitions confirm and reward the learning attempts.

With more frequent but new constructions such as "After S." (the baby sister born recently), which are linked with daily meal routines, Eve is less dependent upon a maternal model. In sample 7, hour 1, utterance number 2699, Eve produces "Turn after S." after an interval of

Table 1. Eve's utilization of closely antecedent maternal models

Sample number	Hour	Utterance number	Mother				Utterance number	Eve			
7	1	2516	That's part	of	the	top	2517	That part	(of	the)	top
7	1	2690	You may have a turn	after		S.	2699	Turn	after		S.
8	2	541	She'll be able to smile	at		you					
		550	One day soon S. can smile	at		you	551	one day	At		you
		552	One day soon smile	at		you					
		561	( )she'll smile	at		Eve					
8	2	570		After		supper	571		After		supper
8	4	2082	No, that's	for		breakfast	2083		For		Breakfast
		2086	yes	for		breakfast	2085		For		breakfast
9	1	3477	All you do is go and look	at		it	3500	Look	at		Eve.
9	1	3817		for		dessert	3889		(for)		Papa
		3818		for		dessert	3890		(for)		Mommy
							3891		(for)		Eve
9	2	4155	What d'you want that I do	with		it	4156	Blow	with		spoon
		4157	Oh' blow	with	the	spoon					

( ) indicate reduced intelligibility.

eight utterances from the maternal model. She produces "After S." once spontaneously in sample 7 (not shown in the table). Since this spontaneous use occurs before the cued use in sample 8, hour 2, utterance numbers 570–571, a consideration of causality is in order. It appears that maternal models can cue productions for Eve, even if they are not necessary for a production. Psychological research on cuing, priming, and everyday experience (Jacoby & Witherspoon, 1982) indicates that recent hearing of an item facilitates its reproduction, which confirms this principle. Repeated cuing and subsequent production result in easy retrievability of an item and, gradually, in its mastery. A cue is not necessarily cause for a filial production, although it might facilitate it and, through the rehearsal it provides, contribute to learning.

In addition to Eve's input dependency, Table 1 also indicates a form of filial independence from maternal models. In the three examples from sample 9, Eve substitutes nouns for the pronouns or uses a different noun than the mother employed in her model. These substitutions might suggest that Eve has abstracted an underlying structure of at least two elements, the preposition and the nominal, and that she conceptualized a set of nominals that can fill the slots in these prepositional phrases.

Although this interpretation would be acceptable to linguists, scientific precaution requires that a less sophisticated principle be considered. The specific prepositions in the maternal models "at," "for," and "with" might have functioned as partial cues for Eve in eliciting a rote formula. The content of Eve's utterances suggests that she had heard these phrases repeatedly, and she could have learned them by heart. This juxtaposition of maternal models and filial formulas might serve as the basis for pattern abstraction and for the learning of linguistic structures. The data in Table 1 do not permit a determination of the interpretation that reflects Eve's cognitive functions. The following tables, however, do contribute to such differentiations.

Table 1 might provide the impression that instances of information provision about the prepositional phrase are dispersed in conversations between Eve and her mother, and that Eve is alert to this information. Table 2 shows that the interactional patterns are often more conducive to learning and easier for the child.

Intensive Teaching Episodes

Table 2 demonstrates the massed density of the mother's input. Since the close repetitions of the PPh involve varied surface strings, the maternal input also displays the contrast between the stable underlying schema that contains three slots and the flexibility of supplying fillers for these slots.

Table 2. Intensive teaching episodes

Sample number	Hour	Utterance number	Mother				Utterance number	Eve		
7	1	2296	There's one	in	the	kitchen				
		2297	There's one	on	the	counter				
		2306	You have animal crackers	in	the	kitchen				
				on	the	table				
7	1	2576	She doesn't know how to drink	out of	a	glass				
		2632	Oh, you want some	out of	the	bottle!				
		2692	Fraser's going to drink his coffee	out of	a	cup	2741	Baby S. drink	out	bottle
7	1						2868	Baby S. drink	out	milk
										bottle
		2871	Babies drink	from		bottles				
		2872	Big people drink	from		cups				
		2873	I drink my milk	from	a	cup	2875	I drink	out	cup
		2874	I drink my beer too.	from	a	cup	2876	Grape juice	out (from)	
							2877	( ) Fraser		
		2880	And Mommy drinks coffee too	out of	a	cup	2878	He drink coffee	out	cup
		2881	When you're big you drink	out of	a	cup				
		2882	Look at that big girl drink	out of	a	cup				
8	1	154	She can't drink	out of	a	cup	155	She drink	out o'	cup
							156	Baby S. drink	out a	cup
		157	Baby S. can't drink	out of	a	cup	158	Baby S. drink	out o'	bottle
		159	She drinks sometimes	out of	a	bottle				

8	4						2261	(One)	by	Papa	stool
		2262	Is there one	by	Papa's	stool					
		2264	There's a round one there	by	that	chair					
							2266	Get (one) chair			
		2267	There's a bead	under	the	fireplace					
				Under	the	fireplace					
			there's a bead				2270	Bead			
							2271	Put ( )	in		
								too			
		2272	Well not	in	the	tinker-toy can.					
		2273	That goes	in	the	toy box					
							2274	Put	in		
								too			
		2276	It doesn't go	in	the	tinker-toy can					
		2277	It goes	in	the	wagon					
		2278	That one goes	on	the	wagon					
							2279	Go			wagon
		2281	(You) put it	over on	the	wagon					
							2282	Put	over		wagon
9	1						3552	(Lemme) play	(with)		bouillon cube
		3553	No, (you) can't play either	with	the	bouillon cubes					
		3560	You're writing	with	your	pencil					
							3561	Writing	with	Fraser	pencil
		3562	You're not writing	with	Fraser's	pencil					
		3573	You're playing games	with		Fraser					
							3577	I playing game	( )		Fraser
							3581	I playing game	( )		Fraser
							3583	I playing game(s)	with		Fraser

(   ) indicate reduced intelligibility.

The first example in sample 7, Table 2 is a relatively transparent pattern display: Two instances of "in the kitchen" are separated by "on the counter," and the sequence concludes with "on the table." One element, the determiner, is constant. The preposition is retained in a similar form with "in" and "on." The nouns involve some alliteration ("kitchen" and "counter") and some consonance ("t"s in all nouns). With these prosodic means, the mother seems to make the pattern acoustically clear. Additionally, all four prepositional phrases utilize a strict rhythmic pattern, consisting of two feet that each contain one stressed and one unstressed syllable. This isochronic rhythmic pattern, predominant in English nursery rhymes (Burling, 1966), provides important prosodic support for the abstraction of the demonstrated linguistic pattern.

Such disambiguated pattern teaching episodes are not at all rare. On the first page of transcripts, in sample 1, hour 1, the following interaction is found:

E: *More . . . cookie.*
M: *You want a cookie?*
     There's a cookie on the table
                    in the room
                    on the table
                    with the rest
                    of your crackers.

Without doubt, the theme word "cookie" will hold the child's attention. "On the table" is repeated, "room" and "rest" are alliterative, the child encounters consonance with the "t"s in "table" and "rest," and "crackers" at the end refers with alliteration to the initial "cookie," forming a cyclical, rondo-like structure of motivation and content. Weir (1962) described similar phenomena in the bedtime monologues of her son. No wonder that du Preez (1974, p. 375) concluded, "Mothers . . . virtually sing their speech to their children." Papousek and Papousek (1981) similarly reported that "syllabic sequences are sung in short structured melodies with distinct patterns of rhythm and accent" (p. 210) when mothers talk to young children. On the basis of these rhythms, the child masters the pattern on a sensory level (cf. Peters, 1983). This level can then provide the framework for easier discrimination of semantic and syntactic maternal input.

The next major theme begins in sample 7, Table 2 and is taken up again in sample 8 and concerns instruction in methods of drinking. The preposition "out of" in the context of "drinking out of" has been trained previously and is employed by the mother three times over intervals of approximately 60 utterances. Eve's production "baby S. drink out bottle" (utterance number 2741), approximately 50 utterances after her mother's "out of a cup" (utterance number 2692), and almost 110 utterances after a model of "out of the bottle" (utterance number 2632), indicates a certain degree of mastery.

Eve produced quite spontaneously (utterance number 2868) "Baby S. drink out milk bottle," with the most recent related utterance her own in utterance number 2741. This utterance suggests that Eve might have conceptualized "drink out" as a verb that has either "bottle" or "milk bottle" as its argument. It is fascinating to observe her mother responding to this ambiguity. Normally she speaks of drinking "out of" bottles or cups, but she models the phrase "drink from" four times (utterance numbers 2871–2874), and twice she specifies that the object of the verb comes before the PPh: "I drink my milk" and "I drink my beer."

Eve seems to struggle with this new information, but she struggles successfully. After one attempt, she produces the correct word order, with the object before the PPh, in utterance number 2876. She also tries to incorporate the maternal "from" in her utterance. Finally, in utterance number 2878, she has managed to produce a full S-V-O-PPh sentence and to arrange all constituents in the correct sequence. Three instances of confirming maternal feedback (utterance numbers 2880–2882) reward and strengthen this new acquisition. Interspersed in this specific instruction were (not in Table 2) two PPhs with "on," one rehearsal of "from," and one case of corrective feedback employing "at." These constructions are closely positioned and provide models for replacements of the preposition in the PPh.

In sample 8, hour 1, utterance number 154 and following, Eve and her mother return to this pragmatic instruction. The mother's feedback provides a correction of truth value, and results not only in Eve's correct statement, but also in a linguistic advance. In sample 7, Table 2, Eve employed "out" as a preposition without the element "of" and without any determiner. She now twice attempts "out o' " (utterance numbers 155 and 158) and "out a" once (utterance number 156) and uses the full two-element preposition or preposition plus determiner.

In sample 7, hour 1, 11 different prepositions were taught and rehearsed, often in closely spaced substitution sequences. These sequences involved massing of the underlying pattern and a judicious combination of similarities and differences, or transformations combined with invariances, that demonstrate change as well as stable patterns.

The sequence in Table 2, sample 8, hour 4, beginning with utterance number 2261, demonstrates how the mother employs a practical task to train spatial prepositions. Three occurrences of "by" are followed by two of "under," which in turn are followed by four uses of "in" and two of "on." It is not clear whether to consider "over on" (utterance number 2281) as two prepositions or as an adverb plus preposition. Eve was certainly not troubled by this question, and she repeats the new item as "Put over wagon." It is not necessary to analyze in detail all grammatical and stylistic phenomena involved in the substitution sequences of this episode. The instructional and abstracting value of these sequences can be seen by the reader. It is enough to emphasize that within a few minutes of conversation, 10 prepositional phrases and 11 substitutions of items in these phrases are modeled by the mother.

A similar sequence is encountered in sample 9. Eve initiates the theme "playing with," and her mother responds with variations and corrections. The mother's determiner noun in hour 1, utterance number 3560 is immediately reflected in Eve's determiner noun in utterance number 3561, and the content is corrected by the mother in utterance number 3562. When the mother employs the rare model "playing games with," Eve needs three trials to approximate this in utterance number 3583. Such repeated rehearsals of new items are found often in the protocols, and they are also reported by Weir (1962) in her son's crib speech. In earlier learning, Kaye (1982) observed that infants "work up to" a close imitation after repeated trials.

Table 2, in emphasizing massed maternal modeling and substitution sequences, could easily produce the impression that the mother was the predominant initiator of informative interactions and that the child passively responded to this intensive input. This impression is not accurate. Table 3 provides a complementary perspective by presenting sequences that begin with a filial utterance and by focusing on the maternal feedback to the filial production. The conversational initiative is taken by the child, who makes requests, describes her own activities, or reports on environmental givens. The mother's response, closely related in content and linguistic form to the child's preceding utterance, displays improvements in linguistic form that remain close to the child's expression and, therefore, within range of the child's abilities to process information.

In this volume, an utterance designated as feedback has to be related in content, form, or both to a closely preceding utterance. Feedback can consist of acknowledgment only, such as "yes," or can be a repetition of the content of the preceding utterance. Often this feedback provides correcting and improving information, which may be incorporated by the child.

Maternal Informative Feedback

Mistakes are possible in each unit of the typical three-unit prepositional phrase. The preposition may be missing or incorrect, and the determiner may be missing or incorrectly or incompletely supplied. There may also be a problem with the nominal. Informative and corrective feedback would be expected to each of these elements if Eve made mistakes. Table 3 indicates the mother's responses to Eve's utterances, which are usually less than perfect.

The examples largely speak for themselves and require only summary points and interpretative comments. Table 3 clearly shows that the mother consistently corrects the child's omissions. In the 38 episodes in Table 3, the mother provides a missing or more correct determiner of the prepositional phrase 33 times. She repeatedly adds examples of the PPh that expand or vary Eve's utterances. The mother in her feedback to this element provides more models (41) than Eve produced as original constructions. Since Eve made approximately 30 mistakes in these constructions, the models exceeded the mistakes by approximately 33%. Intensive feedback indeed!

A similar though less intense response pattern is observed for the prepositional element. Because Eve makes fewer mistakes, her mother needs to provide only 20 straightforward corrections, generally supplying the missing preposition. In addition to the 20 corrections, the mother provides additional models by her variations on the theme suggested by Eve. The maternal feedback again approached in number more than two thirds of Eve's original productions.

Eve makes few mistakes in the nominals of her prepositional phrases, giving her mother few opportunities for corrections. In all cases, however, the corrections do follow: In sample 8, hour 1, utterance number 40, "Emma" is corrected to "Emerson," in sample 8, hour 1, utterance number 195, the word stem "write" is replaced by the gerund "writing," and in sample 9, hour 2, utterance number 3914, "counter" is substituted for Eve's "table." Balancing these consistent corrections are affirmations of Eve's utterances. These affirmations may follow correct prepositional phrases, but are often part of the correcting feedback so that affirmative and rewarding interaction is combined with informative and challenging feedback.

Closer study shows several instances of substitutions in prepositions, determiners, or nominals, or of several items in the same episode, as discussed with Table 2. The careful reader will find additional aspects that have not been emphasized. This is the nature of verbal interactions: They are too rich to be analyzed exhaustively.

Table 3. Maternal informative feedback

Sample number	Hour	Utterance number	Eve				Utterance number	Mother		
7	1	7	I put sugar	in		't	8	I had sugar	in	my	coffee
7	1	2463	(Mom) put . . . put	on		floor	2464	Put it	on for	the	floor Eve
7	1	2563	Eve sit		Pop	chair	2565	You're (gonna) sit	in	Papa's	chair?
7	1	2586	Go		(her)	tummy	2587	It's going	in	her	tummy
7	1	2602	Jumping		Papa	chair	2610	You are jumping (then | from)	Papa's	chair
7	1	2724	Cracker	on		table	2725	You want to have a cracker	on	the	table?
7	1	2738	One			Fraser	2739	One	for		Fraser?
7	1	2741	Baby S. drink	out		bottle.	2742		out of the		bottle.
7	1	2751	( )			study	2752		in	his	study.
7	1	2798		in	the	study	2800	He's	in	the	study.
7	1	2832	Fall down			floor.	2834	I see it	by on	the the	table. floor.

Child utterances:

		No.				
7	1	2858	Buy			AP
7	1	2906	Buy more			AP
7	2	2934	(Piece	a)		paper
7	2	3072	Eve	da		radiator
7	2	3078	( )			radiator
7	2	3082	Sugar		in	juice
7	2	3177	(In)	Papa	study	study
7	2	3265	Cheese ( )			table.
8	1	40	make penny			Emma
8	1	44				Chicago

Model utterances:

No.				
2860	We'll buy some more	at	the	A&P
2907	We'll buy some more	at	the	A&P
2939	Look, here's lots	of		paper.
3073	You are laying	on	the	radiator.
3079	You want to sleep	on	the	radiator?
3083	No sugar	in	Eve's	juice
3085	You don't need sugar	in	your	juice
3178	In		Papa's	study,
	yeah.			
3267	No more cheese	at	the	table
3268	We're gonna eat	in	the	highchair
3269	Now, you had some cheese	at	the	table
41	No, he's not making pen-nies	at		Emerson
47	What's Papa doing	in		Chicago?

(continued)

Table 3. (continued)

Sample number	Hour	Utterance number	Eve				Utterance number	Mother			
8	1	109	(Need) tapioca	in	the	bowl	110	There'll be tapioca	in	the	bowl
									in	a	minute.
									for	a	little while,
							127	Stay happy			
								OK?			
8	1	195	Not write				196	No, that's not a book	for		writing
8	1	246	Like			front door	248	Finding someone you like	at	the	front door
8	1	334	Lie down			radiator	335		By	the	radiator.
8	2	405	Write		the	paper	406	Oh!	On	Fraser's	paper
8	2	573	Baby . . . baby S. (do it)	in		bed	574	She's still	in		bed
8	3	763	Eve put	in		cu / cup	764	What did you put	in	the	cup?
8	3	791		In		toy box.	791	Yes, it's / but where	in	the	toy box, / toy box?
8	3	1054	Eat ice cream cone	(in)		high chair	1055-6	Yes,	in	the	high chair

		ID	Utterance				ID	Utterance			
8	4	2261	(One)	by	Papa	stool	2262	Is there one	by	Papa's	stool?
							2264	There's a round one there	by	that	chair.
9	1	6	Go	on	my	hair	7	They go	in	your	hair.
9	1	3519		In	S.	bed	3520	You're	in	S.'s	bed
9	1	3552	(Lemme) play	(with)		bouillon cubes	3553	No, (you) can't play with either		the	bouillon cubes
9	1	3725	Sitting	in							
		3726	Sitting up . . . oh,								
		3727		In		chair					
							3728	Who's sitting	in	(your)	chair?
9	2	3909	Leave	on		table	3914	It's	on	the	counter
							3922	We'll put those back	on	the	counter
9	2	4050	(I) put (the) duck	in		there					
		4052	I put duck	in		there					
		4057		in	the	kitchen	4058	There's not room	in	the	kitchen
9	2	4133	S. sitting	in	the	kitchen	4135	There's not room	in	the	kitchen
							4136	We'll just leave her	in	the	living room

( ) indicate reduced intelligibility.

Having emphasized that the mother almost always corrects filial mistakes, an important question remains: Does the child learn something from these mistakes and the subsequent corrections? Teaching and learning can be asserted only if maternal interventions can be shown to result in at least immediate improvement. This conservative attitude does not, however, necessarily assume a lack of learning if no immediate effects are seen. As Bandura (1973) demonstrated, information can be acquired without resulting in immediate performance. Whether immediate improvements are maintained is probably a function of additional factors.

Effects of Maternal Feedback

Table 4 reports the immediate effects of maternal corrective feedback. It presents the interactional pattern of child-mother-child, with the child producing an imperfect utterance, the mother providing improving feedback, and the child responding with an utterance closely related to the preceding two. As the examples indicate, there is no guarantee of the total effectiveness of maternal interventions.

In the first example "Eat (on) table," the outcome indicates a partial improvement. The transcript suggests that Eve improved her enunciation of "on" after maternal feedback, but the determiner was still omitted. The effects of maternal feedback become more obvious in the following instances: In the next episode, beginning with utterance number 181, Eve not only enunciates more clearly after maternal feedback, but she also uses a possessive determiner, reflecting the maternal model but replacing the pronoun with a noun. Possessive determiners are still relatively rare in Eve's productions of prepositional phrases.

In sample 8, hour 1, utterance number 342, Eve produces a PPh without a determiner, the mother models three uses with a determiner in her feedback, and Eve repeats the last model and includes the determiner. Similar teaching of the definitive article is found in utterance number 781, and the mother's intervention again produces results. In the more complex episode that begins with utterance number 1047, previous teaching seems productive since Eve spontaneously produces the PPh "on the table," which includes the definitive article. "On the table," however, was trained intensively beginning in sample 1 and might be recalled as an unanalyzed formula. This time, however, the use is not correct, and the mother contradicts Eve. Even in this complex situation, Eve understands and changes her message to "in high chair," replacing both preposition and noun. She is rewarded for this feat with two instances of "yes" and imitation of the major improvement in her utterance. Eve omitted the determiner "the" in the con-

Table 4. Maternal feedback and filial progress

Sample number	Hour	Utterance number	Eve		Utterance number	Mother		Utterance number	Eve
7	1	2530 Eat	(on)	table	2531 Eat	on the	table?	2533 Eat	on table
					2535 You don't have your lunch	on the	table		
8	1	181	( )	hand	182 What do you have	on your	hand?	183 Tapioca	on Eve hand
8	1	342	In	washing ma-chine	343	In	washing machine?	350	In the bedroom
					344 No, (we put it)				
					345	in your	bedroom		
					347	up in the	bedroom		
					349	In the	bedroom		
8	3	781 Cathy spill grape juice on	plate		782 Cathy spilled grape juice yesterday	on the	plate	783 Cathy spill grape juice	on the plate

(continued)

65

Table 4. *(continued)*

Sample number	Hour	Utterance number	Eve	Utterance number	Mother	Utterance number	Eve
8	3	1047	Ice cream cone on the table	1048	On the table?	1051	Ice cream cone on the table
				1052	Not on the table?		
				1053	You don't eat ice cream cone on the table	1054	Eat ice cream(in) cone high chair
				1055	Yes,		
				1056	in the high chair,		
				1057	yes.		
8	4	2170	(Hab) in a kak	2172	Oh, pockets in his coat	2175	Pocket in coat
				2178	Pockets in his coat		
9	1	3556	Writing on my...my pencil	3557	You don't write on your pencil		
				3559	You are not writing on your pencil		
				3560	You're writing with your pencil	3561	Writing with . . . Fraser pencil
				3562	You're not writing with Fraser's pencil		
9	1			3575	You're playing games with Fraser		

	No.	Utterance				
9 1	3742			new	table	
	3743	Not		on	the new	table
	3744		On	( ) new	table.	
	3745	We'll have supper		on	the new	table
9 1	3769	I put . . . . cheese sandwich	(on the)	plate.		
	3770	I know you put it		on	the	plate
	3772		On the	plate		
	3577	I playing game		( ) Fraser		
	3581	I playing game		( ) Fraser		
	3583	I playing game(s)		with Fraser		
9 2	4115	( )	sitting in	chair		
	4117			chair		
	4119	( )	sitting ə	chair		
	4121	And Eve's sitting		in	her	highchair
	4126	( ) sitting		highchair		
9 2	4141	Papa got feet	on	stool		
	4142	Got his feet		on	the	stool
	4143	I have my feet		on	the	stool
	4144	Papa hab shoe		on the floor	Papa chair	
	4145	I have my shoes		on	the	floor

( ) indicate reduced intelligibility.

structed (as opposed to rote) phrase "on the table," and it is provided as corrective feedback.

In utterance number 2170, Eve improves her mastery of the noun with the help of maternal feedback. She succeeds, but omits the determiner in her struggle to process this. Note that her mother gives corrective feedback twice but does not insist upon perfection in Eve. One improvement per step is enough, and further success will be attained in iterative training cycles.

The first example in sample 9 is particularly interesting regarding maternal corrections and Eve's response to them. Eve is struggling with her production (note the dysfluency!) and uses an incorrect preposition. The mother leaves no doubt about this mistake and rejects the incorrect formulation twice, contrasting it with the correct form. Eve incorporates this correction immediately, "writing with." This improvement does not meet the mother's standards of content. She rejects Eve's assertion (utterance number 3562) and provides an improved version (utterance number 3575). Eve grasps this model immediately, although she requires three successive trials to repeat it completely and correctly. Eve again works up to correct productions in these examples.

Eve struggles mainly with inclusion of the preposition and the determiner so these are the items the mother and Eve work on. Maternal feedback leads to inclusion of the modeled definite article in most cases. In sample 8, hour 1, utterance number 181, and sample 9, hour 2, utterance number 4121, the mother's model of a possessive determiner induces Eve to produce an equivalent construction with a substitution of the possessive determiner. It is fascinating to observe the apparent processing restrictions. Eve produced the preposition in utterance number 4115, and the mother modeled both the preposition and the possessive determiner (utterance number 4121), but Eve omitted the preposition in her response to the maternal model (utterance number 4126), similar to utterance number 4119. When changes are required in both the referent and the vocabulary item for the possessive determiner, Eve appears able to manage either the preposition or the determiner, but not both. In contrast, Eve manages in utterance number 4144 to produce both the preposition and the determiner following two structural models. The determiner consists of the article only, and the phrase "on the" had been mastered previously. The substitution of the noun is, therefore, well within Eve's capacity.

An evaluation of Eve's mastery levels from these samples again indicates that her performance does not rely on consistent application of a rule or pattern, neither of which is influenced by minor semantic changes. On the contrary, her performance seems to depend on her familiarity with the specific construction, on the complexity of the processing task, and on the immediately preceding adult cue.

Table 4 demonstrates that situational variables and the number of preceding trials of a specific formula seem to determine Eve's productions more than an unchanging rule or stable pattern. Observed dysfluencies and a lack of clear enunciation that reduce elements to the schwa might suggest, however, that Eve is trying to realize a prototypical pattern but is held back by a variety of processing restrictions. A careful reconceptualization of the competence/performance distinction could give rise to challenging research endeavors. Competence appears to relate to memory of the underlying pattern and number of operations, such as substitutions of referent and vocabulary items, that the child performs to produce an utterance. Performance appears to be influenced by the number of immediately preceding rehearsals, which slow the fading of a standard. This suggests that competence is influenced by performance, as in all skill learning.

DISCUSSION

The evidence presented strongly suggests that the mother not only generally fine tuned her speech input, but also that she adapted it specifically to instructional opportunities presented by filial utterances and maximized its didactic functions. This maximization is largely a function of the juxtaposition of imperfect filial and perfect maternal utterances, or of the interactive parameters stressed by Snow (1977a) and Moerk (1972, 1983a), and of the cross-utterance information carried by the sequential relations in discourse (Shatz, 1982). This cross-utterance information involves many corrections, as shown in Tables 3 and 4, and much pattern display through substitution sequences, where the underlying pattern contrasts with varying surface strings (Table 2).

The demonstration of corrections and their frequency does not conflict factually with the previous findings of Brown and his associates, although it does conflict conceptually. Brown and Bellugi (1964) reported that many expansions are found in maternal responses to filial utterances. The corrections presented in Tables 3 and 4 are nothing other than Brown's expansions. Salzinger (1975), Slama-Cazacu (1977), and Soederberg (1974) recognized that these expansions were really corrections. This point has also been argued extensively by Moerk (1983a, 1983b). Hirsh-Pasek, Treiman, and Schneiderman (1984) and Demetras, Post, and Snow (1986) more recently provided additional evidence of the extensiveness of corrective feedback provided to language-learning children.

Brown (1973) preempted the category of corrections by labeling this maternal didactic feedback as expansions and consequently reported (Brown, 1973; Brown & Hanlon, 1970) that no grammatical corrections could be found. Slobin (1968), in contrast, had already shown how effective these corrections are. He reanalyzed transcripts of two of Brown's subjects, Adam and Eve, and found that these two children incorporated maternal corrections in approximately 50% of the instances that they imitated them. Table 4 provides detailed evidence of this.

Substitution sequences have been reported often, whether the child's substitution sequences, recorded by Weir (1962), those of the mother described extensively by Moerk (1985a), or those occurring in educational settings (Rivers, 1964). In summary, the mother displays much linguistic information, thus providing the affordances that the child needs to acquire the information.

The next major focus must be on the child. Conceptualizations of first language acquisition in the past were based on innate language-specific knowledge or inductively abstracted rules. The analyses of the filial productions presented here have emphasized very different principles. Immediate cuing or priming provided in spontaneous or feedback models was the most important factor influencing the child's productions. Conclusions about children's grammatical competence, based on such productions but without consideration of their antecedents, were likely to overestimate that competence.

It was suggested that familiarity with a construction and processing aspects, such as length and complexity of an utterance or number of cognitive operations, are additional factors that probably determined the outcome of specific coding attempts. The evidence for rapidly shifting levels of performance, from complete three-unit prepositional phrases to phrases with one or more units omitted, also suggested an absence of rules or of underlying patterns.

This contrast in conclusions could give rise to the old conflict between the cognitive/constructionist and the behaviorist/learning paradigms. Certainly, there is a difference in emphasis and terms, but the contrast involves terminology more than conceptualizations. It should be acceptable to proponents of either paradigm that patterns or "structures" are displayed by the mother, noticed by the child, and strengthened with frequent repetition. Frequency phenomena and dense substitution sequences can be considered causative antecedents for the results described by cognitively oriented psycholinguists.

Another approach to reconciling these conceptualizations derives from a careful differentiation of the object of analysis. This analysis focused on production of specific utterances, which necessarily leads to a focus on the influence of performance factors. A focus on regularity in performances, such as Eve's effort to include at least one element before the nominal in the prepositional phrase, might lead to emphasis on the increasing strength of an underlying pattern. The processing difficulties that were indicated by the dysfluencies could then be interpreted as resulting from a discrepancy between the influence of the underlying pattern, or the standard, and the value obtained under momentary circumstances, or the performance.

The relationships between the adult standard, represented by the maternal model, and the standard acquired by the child, which incrementally converges on the modeled standard of adult competence, will remain the subject of further investigations when the internal filial standard can be more objectively described. With this customary referral to "the need for further studies," it is readily admitted that an almost unlimited number of questions could be raised concerning such a complex topic as language acquisition. A few pertinent points can be mentioned here.

The emphasis upon maternal information display raises the question "How does the mother know the child's learning needs?" A lengthy survey of research would be required to even suggest an answer. Bohannon and Marquis (1977) and Bohannon, Stine, and Ritzenberg (1982) carefully analyzed the variables that contribute to this knowledge. The early work of Snow (1972) differentiated general adult expectations from the effects of the preceding filial utterances. Cognitive psychology provided the principle of discrepancy (Moerk, 1976b) to explain the maternal responsiveness to filial information needs. The field of discourse analysis could provide further suggestions. Together these indicate that the mother knows because she has just heard an incomplete or incorrect filial utterance.

Discussions about pattern abstractions go back to Plato's ideal forms, and they were revived by Gestalt psychology and are a central concern of all cognitive psychology. Rumelhart and McClelland (1985) suggested neural models to explain pattern abstraction. Similar neural models have been presented in the extensive work of Edelman (e.g., Edelman & Mountcastle, 1978). It can be assumed as common knowledge that most mammals are prone to abstract patterns out of the abundance of information they receive. Nothing more is presumed in this study.

The entire topic of learning, comprising both the information to be learned and the processes involved, needs continued intensive scrutiny. Interactions presented in the tables in this work suggest that mother and child rely largely on the sensory register and Eve's short-term memory in handling new grammatical forms. Immediate models are imitated by Eve, and the mother provides immediate feedback, which leads to Eve's immediate, improved formulations. K. Bloom (1977, 1979) and Watson and Ramey (1972) have demonstrated that intervals of 1 second maximize infants' learning and that over longer intervals, infants are unable to detect the relation between their behavior and adult behavior. Although Eve is beyond infancy, the complex processes of retrieving examples from long-term memory and comparing them linguistically that have been postulated in the past do not seem plausible to explain the data.

In accordance with the developmental level of the child who was in the "iconic stage," in Bruner's (1966) terminology, or the "preoperational stage," Piaget's (1952) term, perceptual processes seem to dominate in interactions that involve new and difficult constructions. A figure–ground relationship explains the dynamics of the maternal corrections and their effects presented in Tables 3 and 4: The ground is Eve's production, and the figure is the maternal improvement. The optimal level of discrepancy is in most cases a minimal level of discrepancy, and the mother adds one improvement per interactional turn. This phenomenon concurs with what is known about the habitual information processing of 2-year-old children.

In a few cases in the tables and more in the transcripts, Eve repeats items that she did not comprehend fully. A principle similar to that in babble dialogues seems at work: Repeat the sound complex that was heard and acquire it without bothering about when and how to apply it. This principle underlies most of the play of young children and allows them to acquire skills before practical application is required. This special readiness of young children to imitate unknown elements of a model has been reported often. A principle of discrepancy or of figure–ground relationships would also explain this phenomenon: The known items represent the ground, and the unknown is the discrepancy that urges imitation.

The emphasis on short-term memory in the immediate processing of linguistic interactions is not meant to denigrate the importance of long-term memory in learning and retention. The transition from the sensory register to short-term and then to long-term memory is effected by frequent rehearsals, often presented in a massed form to introduce new items. Indications of these effects have been found in the tables presented. A fuller demonstration of the effects of input frequency requires additional analyses, which can be found in Moerk (1980a), and in the following chapters. These analyses show that the mother produces and elicits these rehearsals almost exclusively until the child learns this important learning strategy.

In conclusion, the early stages of language learning can be explained by the child's use of well-known and comparatively simple processing strategies that have been documented in cognitive and learning research since the 1950s. If these simple strategies suffice, then it appears advisable to follow the principle of parsimony and to refrain from postulating more complex strategies. This applies particularly if research in other domains of development shows that complex strategies are not accessible to the young child. These conclusions are of obvious and immediate relevance for practical intervention efforts.

Chapter 4

Speaking of Time
Processes in the Transmission and Acquisition of Temporal Morphemes

Time present and time past
are both perhaps present in time future,
and time future contained in time past. T. S. Eliot: "Four Quartets."

Studies beginning with Stern and Stern (1907) or Decroly and Degand (1913), to Leopold (1949) or Werner and Kaplan (1963), focused on children's *productions* of temporal morphemes. This focus also applied to more recent investigations and reevaluations (e.g., Meisel, 1985; Miller & Johnson-Laird, 1976). Productions were described without consideration of verbal or nonverbal context. From these isolated verbal products, conclusions were drawn concerning mastery of temporal concepts and the linguistic tools to convey them. On close examination, however, such conclusions reveal much possibility for error.

Without simultaneously recording and evaluating the speech of the conversation partners, it cannot be determined if filial productions were rote imitations of immediately preceding models. If they were rote imitations, their production demonstrates only some competence in perceptual differentiation and motor skills for reproduction, including short-term memory. Such mastery is far removed from the mastery conceived of as cognitive differentiation of concepts of past and future, or as acquisition of linguistic rules. Orne (1969) alone seems to have realized that "any generalization from such usage to the development of time experience and concepts in general must be uncertain" (p. 48).

Inference of specific cognitive and linguistic competencies from repeated nonimitative instances in filial behavior must also be approached with caution. Fletcher (1985) argued persuasively that the phrase "I falled," commonly encountered in filial speech, could have been formed as a narrow analogy to a form such as "I called." An inference that the child "overgeneralized" a rule would consequently overinterpret the child's level of mastery. Information in this chapter showing that Eve used temporal morphemes incorrectly indicates even more strongly that items taken out of conversational and pragmatic context can lead to misinterpretation.

ACQUISITION PROCESSES IN CONTEXT

The acquisition process is explored by studying the teaching and learning processes as they transpire in mother–child conversations that employ the future and past tense of verbs. "Performance in context" is the main focus of attention, which few studies in the past have shared. Sachs (1983), who related filial performance to adult models and feedback, is an exception. Farrar (1985) related discourse features to the acquisition of grammatical morphemes. Some pertinent findings are discussed in reference to the acquisition of past and future morphemes. Generally, the studies assumed that the learning environment was uniform. Yet it is only too well known that families within and across social classes differ profoundly in the cognitive and linguistic environments they provide for their children. Likewise, microenvironments change with every utterance and with every word produced and repeated in the course of a conversation.

Linguistic context cannot be uniform over utterances and conversations. Some contexts will provide more support, such as an immediately preceding model, for the production of a linguistic form than others. Therefore, uniformity of processes underlying production of the same linguistic form cannot be presumed, if we assume that the child's productions are not completely independent of environmental stimuli. This independence obviously conflicts with the conversational adaptation that is presumed by all linguists. Either the child responds to his or her conversational partner and his or her productions are influenced by the partner's utterances, or the child is not influenced by environmental stimuli and is unresponsive to conversational input.

Taking the cue from all learning, and specifically from second language acquisition, the term acquisition is used in the following analyses with an emphasis on changing processes. As previously argued, acquisition is certainly not an all-or-nothing phenomenon. The adult second-language learner might be able to explain perfectly well the morphemes required to express a specific temporal aspect. Yet the same adult might neglect to supply these morphemes in conversational contexts or at least have difficulty when faced with many processing demands. Only gradually does the production become more automatic and pose fewer processing demands. Incremental phenomena have to be expected in children, too, concerning knowledge acquisition and competent use. Immediate environmental support during the course of acquisition may have different effects on productions at different times.

The focus of this chapter is on the temporal, not the aspectual, dimension of verbs. Adverbs and conjunctions, other forms refering to temporal aspects, are also excluded from the investigation. The acquisition of the past-tense and future-tense morphemes are discussed in separate chapters. Conceptually and interactionally, past and future learning may be closely linked since both domains go beyond the here and now focus of the young child.

TRANSMISSION AND ACQUISITION OF PAST-TENSE MORPHEMES

To summon up remembrance of things past
                                        Shakespeare: "Sonnet 30"

Theoretical Considerations

Since few previous studies have dealt with acquisition processes, compared to reporting of the products, no extensive literature survey will be given here, which would be minimally relevant to the goals in this study. Only studies that pertain directly to the following analyses and their theoretical concerns are considered.

Several studies that pertain to the theoretical conceptualization of acquisition processes are worthy of consideration in this context. With Berko's (1958) study that demonstrated overgeneralization of the regular past, rule learning was presumed to underlie the acquisition of the regular past. This conceptualization has changed gradually during the 1970s and 1980s. The change may have begun with MacWhinney's (1978) differentiation of three learning processes: rote, analogy, and rule. Bybee and Slobin (1982) argued for generalization of a pattern in the acquisition of regular and some irregular past-tense forms, which they labeled a schema. This is close to MacWhinney's "analogy." The influential work of Rumelhart and McClelland (1985) "by dispensing with the assumption that the child learns rules," (Abstract) and by relating input to acquisition, focused attention on learning processes and variable influences such as frequency and regularity of input. Although the present study does not consider neurologic bases or computer modeling, many factual findings pertaining to input and learning processes agree closely with recent conceptualizations of associative and incremental learning processes.

Another group of studies that should be briefly considered are the two factual studies of language development that include environmental influences. Sachs (1983) reported that the earliest appearance of a past tense in her daughter's speech, "I did it," was obviously a routine. One of the next occurrences Sachs quoted was in response to an immediately preceding model. She also showed that the adult set the context by referring to past events with the proform "did," and that the child responded by using the regular past-tense ending -ed. The same phenomena, largely in the same sequence, are described in the analyses in this chapter.

One of Farrar's (1985) findings is of special importance for these analyses. Farrar reported that maternal recasts were related to the child's acquisition of bound grammatical morphemes. Free morphemes were modeled by more general discourse features. In the same vein, adult feedback is important in providing contrasting and corrective information to the language-learning child. This study shows how this feedback led to improvement in Eve's use of temporal morphemes.

Sample

Samples 9–19 are included in this chapter, and consider Eve from age 22 to 27 months with a range of MLU (mean length of utterance in morphemes) of between 2.7 and 4.2. (Sample 20 was not included in the analysis because Eve's mother was absent during the recording. The interactional dynamics and Eve's verbal output were very different and not meaningful to include in a study of mother–child interactions.)

The morphemes for the simple past, whether regular or irregular, are the focus of the analyses in this chapter, but rare instances of the past participle are also included. These participles are often identical in form to the regular past and, for the most part, similar in function. Therefore, it is not presupposed that Eve differentiated these during early stages of learning.

RESULTS

First Steps in the Acquisition Process

Eve's earliest attempts to encode past events are presented (Table 1) to explore longitudinally the gradual mastery of the specific language skills needed to refer to the past.

Phenomena of Immediate Imitation The vocabulary items in Table 1 were rarely employed by Eve in the past tense, and were the

Table 1. Early productions of past-tense morphemes with antecedents

Sample	Hour	Utterance number	Mother	Eve
9	1	1	She cried.	
		3		I cried.
		5	You did.	
		6	Why did you do it?	
9	1	3593	See what the mailman brought.	
		3594		Mailman brought.
9	2	3921	Did you ever.	
		3922		Did you ever.
10	1	97	You lost two of them.	
		98		( ) lost two.
10	2	589	( ) (All morning).	
		590		(She) slep ( ) all morning.
		591–592	She slept all morning, yes.	
		593		S. slep ( ) all morning.
		610		You slep all morning.
		611	Yes, she did.	
10	2	733	There was a green one.	
		734		Was a green one.
		735	There was a green one.	
11	1	65	Until my shoes are tied.	
		66		('til my) tied.
11	1	304		I bite it.
		305	You did bite it.	
		306	You bit a piece right out of it.	
		308	You bit a hole in it.	
		311		Fraser, I bit a hole in it.
		312	Yeah, you did, didn't you?	
		319		I bit a hole in it.
		388		I bit a hole in it.
		389	No, you didn't bite a hole in it.	
		392	That was broken.	
		394		S. I bit a hole in it.
		395	You didn't bite a hole in it.	
		396	Mom did that a long time ago.	
		397		Mom bit a hole in it.
		398	Mom bit the hole in it, Eve.	
		399		Long time ago.
		400	A long time ago, yes.	
		401		I bit a hole in it.
		402	No, you didn't bite a hole in it.	
		404		I bite a hole in it.
		405	No, you didn't.	
11	1	406		I bite a hole in it.
		407	All right, Eve bit a hole in the dish.	
		409		Bit hole.

(   ) indicate reduced intelligibility.

first occurrences in this tense in the transcripts. Eve probably did not understand the meaning of all elements in phrases such as "Did you ever " or "mailman brought." One of her strategies to begin use of the past tense is evident from Table 1: She immediately repeats a model of her mother's. As the immediate imitation and the subsequent loss of these specific past-tense forms suggest, she seems to rely on the resonance of the input in the sensory register or on echoic memory. (Later analyses demonstrate the rapid fading of Eve's performance, even with short intervals between input and repetition.) Immediate imitation that echoes the entire formula obviates the need to recall a formula from long-term storage or to construct the verb phrase from its elements.

Table 1 shows that adults often respond to these imitative productions with feedback. Such adult feedback provides additional rehearsal, so as many as three occurrences may support the transfer of a specific item from the sensory register into short-term and long-term memory.

Processes Underlying This Imitation   Detailed scrutiny of Table 1 shows various psychological processes at work. Exact echoing, with emphasis on the last elements of the model, is found frequently, which suggests a recency effect. A similar principle of echoing, but based on differential stress in the model, is encountered with "lost two." If the modeled phrase is brief enough, such as "Did you ever" (sample 9, hour 2), or its elements well known, "There was a green one" (sample 10, hour 2), all or most elements of the model can be repeated, although the degree of conceptual and linguistic analysis is unknown.

Cognitive work on Eve's part is encountered in other examples. Eve replaced the subject of the utterance in sample 9, hour 1, "I cried." The adult feedback with "did" emphasizes the reference to the past. The episode that includes "slept all morning" demonstrates intensive interaction. After incomplete imitation and feedback, the acoustically indistinct /t/ of the irregular past form was still not produced by Eve so that it could be ascertained on the tape. Nevertheless, the feedback confirming "Yes, she did" reinforced Eve's attempt. Reference to the past is again indicated by "did," which is a general cue for the past tense in this family. Note the massing of six items and the double maternal feedback in utterances numbers 591–592 that confirms (i.e., "yes") but also corrects by modeling the dental suffix.

Multiple Cause–Effect Relationships   An example of training and partial learning of the irregular past form "bit" is found in sample 11. Several cause–effect processes are clearly visible in this interaction: Eve's intended reference to the past without the past form is followed by three adult corrections with "did" serving as a cue for the past tense. The effectiveness of these corrections is seen immediately in utterance numbers 311 and 319, and, after a delay, in utterance numbers 388, 394, and 397. The mother responds with factual corrections (utterance numbers 398–403) and uses the phrase "didn't bite," with the stem of the verb "bite," not the past form. This model supersedes Eve's previous learning and Eve repeats (incorrectly), "I bite a hole in it." An immediate switch by the mother to "Eve bit a hole . . ." results in Eve's return to the correct form "Bit hole."

In this example, immediate models and long-term memory can be differentiated as causal factors influencing productions of the past tense. It is obvious that the effects of immediate models dominate. This interaction also makes clear the effects of the immediate influences of the cue "did" and the model of the verb stem "bite." The simple model is still more effective than the past-tense cue. The lasting effects of such immediate imitation cannot be inferred from one brief interaction. It is, however, of interest that the form "bit" does not reappear in later samples of the recording period and might have been lost.

These examples suggest that the mother and other adults exhibit a tendency to confirm or correct the child's preceding utterance by repeating it with the necessary changes. This repetition may be combined with other indications of acceptance, but it is usually simply "Yes." "I know" plus the child's phrase. Even when adult feedback may be more of a communication check than an acknowledgment, the adult repeats what was understood, specifying with an "occasional question" (Brown, Cazden, & Bellugi-Klima, 1969, p. 57) the element that was not understood. In the early samples in Table 1, instances of this feedback follow almost every utterance. Only rare instances, when Eve engages in a monologue, pass without a response.

Clarification Through Confirmation and Correction

Eve repeatedly employs the irregular past form "broke" in samples 9, 10, and 12, and pertinent interactions are summarized in Table 2.

Confirmation with Minor Corrections Parental responsiveness and frequency of rehearsal are evident in Table 2. Eve mastered the form "broke" but nevertheless receives consistent feedback. Eve's long-term retention of the complex phrase "Pap you have fix . . ." (utterance number 92) is impressive. Since there are no transcripts of the original discussion, it is not known if Eve adapted the model of this common family phrase to fit the occasion or whether the model utterance was produced in full. The maternal use of the utterance referring to a different subject in utterance number 221 rehearses the construction and is immediately imitated by Eve. The adult repetitions offer the opportunity to add elements or provide corrections while provid-

Table 2.   Immediate and consistent maternal feedback to filial productions

Sample	Hour	Utterance number	Eve	Mother
9	1	3589	Ping-pong broke.	
		3590		Yes, the ping-pong broke.
10	1	9	Oh my graham cracker broke.	
		10		It did break.
10	1	140	My sweeper broke.	
		141		It broke?
		142		What happened to it?
		143	What happen to it?	
		144		What happened to it?
		145		It did break.
12	1	32	S. that Fra that one broke.	
		33		Yeah.
12	1	35	My pencil broke.	
		36		Your pencil didn't break.
		37	Only Fraser's.	
		38		Yes.
		39	Other pencil broke.	
12	1	90	S., we have a party.	
		91		We did have a party.
		92	Pap, you have fix other plate because it broke.	
		93		Oh, the cake plate.
		94		The happy birthday plate.
		95	It broke.	
12	1	221		Pap'll have to fix the box cause it broke.
		222	Pap have fix box cause it broke.	
		223		Yes, he'll fix it.
		224	It broke.	
		225		I know it broke.
12	1	241	My pencil broke.	
		242	Fraser, my pencil broke.	
		243		Your pencil broke?

ing positive acceptance. In earlier samples, improvements consisted largely of expansions (Brown & Bellugi, 1964), and in later samples, pronouns and verb forms are adapted to the conversational requirements.

The mother employs the past-tense cue "did" to confirm Eve's statement in "It did break" (utterance number 145). "Did" in this confirming use models the semantic equivalence of the irregular past-tense form "broke" and the verb stem "break" and between the past-tense constructions "broke" and "did break." The same "did" is then employed to correct Eve's mistake in sample 12, utterance number 91.

When Eve does not specify which plate broke, this is corrected with two improved examples. Eve accepts the topic and comments, "It broke." The mother's insertion of the future morpheme "will/'ll" (utterance numbers 221 and 223) in the references to the past, as well as the context, should have helped to clarify for Eve the conceptual and linguistic relationship between the two tenses.

Corrective Feedback in Confirming Responses   Eve's performance in the production of the past tense required more than just positive feedback. In sample 9, hour 1, utterance number 3590, the missing article was supplied. In sample 10, hour 1, utterance numbers 144–145, the requirement for a past-tense form was emphasized twice. In sample 12, hour 1, utterance number 36, the truth value of Eve's utterance was corrected, and in sample 12, hour 1, utterance number 91, the need for a past-tense form was again emphasized.

Consistency of Corrective Feedback   In contrast to assertions that no grammatical corrections are provided by adults (Brown & Hanlon, 1970), evidence of the incidence and importance of corrections (Demetras, Post, & Snow, 1986; Hirsh-Pasek, Treiman, & Schneiderman, 1984; Moerk, 1983b; Moerk, in press) supports the principle exemplified in Table 3. Quantitative data may explain why corrections have been overlooked and denied in past data. Adults provided only a total of 75 corrections to Eve's failed attempts at producing the past-tense morpheme during the 16 sample hours, or approximately 5 corrections per hour. The probability of corrective responses to filial mistakes was, however, very high and approached 100% when the adult attended to the child's utterance. If the informative value of confirming responses to correct trials is also considered, the feedback is highly consistent to Eve's attempts at using the past tense.

The low frequency of corrective feedback is due largely to conversational realities: Eve did not often speak spontaneously of past events and so she could not make many mistakes. She often imitated correctly adult statements referring to the past.

Several principles of interactional phenomena can be differentiated from Table 3.

Exact Post-modeling   When Eve omits the past tense where required, the exact model of the verb form is often provided, such as in utterance numbers 375 and 3841 (sample 9, hour 1), or utterance number 140 (sample 10, hour 1). The mechanism producing these corrections is probably very simple and not intentionally instructional. When the mother repeats the child's utterance in a very similar form, she employs her own correct grammatical system.

Cuing Through "Did"   Need for a past tense was often indicated not by the past-tense form of the main verb but by the auxiliary "did," especially when the adult response was a question or negation. "Did"

Table 3. Examples of corrective feedback

Sample	Hour	Utterance number	Eve	Mother
9	1	374	Baby fall down.	
		375		Your new fish baby fell down?
9	1	3840	Mom Pop eat (all).	
		3841		I know we ate it all.
9	2	4010	Mom, Fraser drink (all) coffee.	
		4011		Did he drink all his coffee?
10	1	139	What happen it?	
		140		What happened to it?
10	2	590	(She) slep ( ) all the morning.	
		591–592		She slept all morning, yes.
11	1	383	It had a hat on.	
		384		It has a hat on?
		385		Well, it certainly doesn't have a hat on.
11	2	163	I spill my pure cream.	
		164		No, you didn't spill your pure cream.
12	2	85	S., we have a party.	
		86		We did have a party.
12	2	466	S., where S. go?	
		467		Where did she go?
12	3	885	And the scarf falled off.	
		886–887		Yes, his hat and scarf fell down.
12	3	954	S., came in with me.*	
		955		I'll come in with you.
13	1	22	You buy it?	
		23		Yes, I bought it.
13	1	4965	I buy it.	
		4966		You didn't buy it.
14	2	592	C. torn the torn the paper.	
		593–594		Yes, she tore the paper.
15	2	7330	I said "hello."	
		7331		Now, you're saying "hello."
16	1	191	Where it goed?	
		192		Where did it go?
16	1	616	He (goed to) make another one.	
		617		Hmm?
		618	He (went to) make another one.	
		619		He was going to make another one.
17	1	2	That fall (ed) down.	
		3		Oh, that fell down.
17	1	7	Fall ( ) down.	
		8		Fell down.
17	1	13	What did you doed?	
		14		What did I do?
19	1	10523	Because he was want to.	
		10524		Oh, he wanted to.

( ) indicate reduced intelligibility.
*She means the imperative "come."

can serve as an effective cue for use of the past tense when the child understood this function as a past-tense marker. Complications arose, as seen in the preceding tables: In constructions with "did," the verb is used in its basic form, which can be misleading to the child. Adult provision of "did" is especially important when Eve herself intended to question about a past event but omitted this auxiliary. In such cases, the adult correction teaches not only morphology but also syntax (see sample 16, utterance numbers 191 and 192).

Unobtrusive Feedback   In Table 3, sample 11, utterance numbers 383–385; sample 12, utterance numbers 954–955; and sample 15, utterance numbers 7330–7331, Eve employs the past tense of the verb, although the present is required. In these cases as well, corrections are forthcoming. Sample 11 contains two corrections of verb tense and one correction regarding the truth value of Eve's utterance. In sample 12, the mother unobtrusively provides the appropriate tense, compared to the more sophisticated response in sample 15. Eve's statement that she had said "hello" was not true, but her mother did not focus on the truth value but rather the grammatical form to reflect the truth: "Now, you're saying 'hello.'" She indicates twice in this response, with "now" and the present progressive form, that Eve's greeting is performed not in the past but in the present. An implicit matching of tense and event within the dimension of time is provided.

Versatility of Feedback   By the end of this observation period, Eve tried to provide the past tense more consistently when obligatory, although she had not yet mastered its morphology. Morphological and syntactic mistakes were common. In sample 14, utterance number 592, Eve employed the past-participle form "torn," which is very similar to the past-tense form. She was rewarded for the attempt with "yes" and immediately corrected also. In sample 16, utterance number 191, an overgeneralization is combined with a syntactic mistake, and the maternal echoing response provides the correct form. A similar phenomenon is encountered in sample 17, utterance numbers 13 and 14, although in this instance Eve marked the past tense twice. In sample 16, utterance numbers 616 and 618, Eve attempted to express the complex message of intention, which is future oriented, but referred to as having happened in the past. Since Eve employs "go" to indicate the future (to be discussed in analysis of future-tense learning), the resulting construction was "He goed to make . . . ." Note the interactional sensitivity established between Eve and her mother! A simple maternal "Hmm?" suffices to give Eve the message that a reformulation is desirable. Therefore Eve reformulates "He went to make. . ." which is not in accordance with the intended message. After the second attempt failed, the mother models the correct form. In sample 19, Eve exhibits confusion about when to employ the auxiliary to form the past tense and is presented immediately with the correct model in an almost identical syntactic form. This similarity simplifies her analysis of the incorrect and the correct modeled form.

Misleading Effects of Feedback   The linguistic informativeness of adult feedback has been emphasized in the examples and discussion to balance past misconceptions. This emphasis, however, does not imply that adult feedback is always optimal. Cazden (1973) noted that sometimes an adult model is not helpful. Wilson and Peters (1988) presented impressive evidence of a child's incorrect productions that were derived from adult models in interactional routines.

"Did" as feedback can have misleading effects. In both questions and negations the tense marker shifts to the auxiliary "did," and the child hears the present-tense form of the main verb, although the question or negation is uttered in the past tense. If the child followed a strategy of direct imitation, as in Table 1, this model might mislead her. The following interactions from Table 1 provide several examples of this:

E: *I bit a hole in it.*
M: *No, you didn't bite a hole in it.*
E: *I bite a hole in it.*
M: *No, you didn't.*
E: *I bite a hole in it.*
M: *Eve bit a hole in the dish.*
E: *Bit hole.*

Eve's correct use of the irregular past changed to an incorrect use of the present after the maternal feedback "No, you didn't bite . . . ." This also shows Eve's strict dependence on maternal models because she immediately shifts to the past after her mother uses the past form. The following interaction is similar:

F: *What did you say, honey?*
E: *I said . . . I say see see . . .*

Eve began her answer with the correct tense marker, but she hesitated and adapted her verb to the model although this change was incorrect.

E: *Because I I caught . . .*
M: *You caught?*
M: *What did you catch?*
E: *I catch my bicycle an' I . . .*

Eve may have interpreted the maternal feedback as a correction, and she immediately "corrected" her utterance. A similar phenomenon was encountered toward the end of the observation period. Eve spontaneously utters, "And and Papa bought us a new house." The mother corrects the truth value, "Well, he didn't buy us a new house." Eve misinterprets the correction and utters afterward, "An' me an' Papa buy some salt." Her mother responds, "You didn't buy some salt." This correction also might have confused Eve.

Corrections of Grammar and Truth Value A general consideration regarding Brown and Hanlon's (1970) argument against grammatical corrections and for corrections of truth value is needed. Once grammatical corrections, whether in the form of expansions or other forms, as analyzed by Moerk (1983a, 1983b), are recognized and their frequency in adult feedback ascertained, it becomes obvious that corrections of the code are more frequent than corrections of truth value. Based on this frequency differential, it is not surprising that Eve interpreted corrective feedback largely as grammatical correction, especially if the main verb form was changed in addition to the content of the message.

Cue Value of "Did" and Overgeneralization Other types of adult input have the potential to mislead. For example, in sample 17, hour 1, the mother asks, "What happened to Hummm?" Eve correctly responds, "He all gone. He went to school." Eve employs the past-tense form to refer to the past, either based on the cue "happened" as a fixed formula, or as a rule-based decision. She also appears to know the correct irregular past of "go." A few pages later in the same sample after the question "Did you go on the subway train, Eve?" she answers, "When I goed Mama goed." The immediate model "go," combined with the cue "did," took precedence over the correct form stored in long-term memory and employed shortly before, without the misleading cues. Similarly, the example "He (goed to) make another one" followed five closely spaced uses of "did." This rare overgeneralization may have been influenced by massed occurrences of this specific past-tense cue and its form with a final dental consonant.

"Did" as a Past-Tense Marker "Did" is employed frequently in English questions and negations that refer to past events and is a reliable indicator, a distinctive cue, for the appropriateness of a past-tense form. Adult responses to Eve's references to past events suggest that emphasis was placed on "did" as a marker for the past tense. For example, in sample 15, hour 1, utterance numbers 6309–6311, the following interaction was recorded:

M: *Well, you tripped over the railroad.*
E: *I tripped over the railroad.*
M: *Yes, you did.*

"Did" in the sentence-final and episode-final position certainly carries emphasis. A similar example is encountered afterward that pertains to the corrective feedback "They did come." In these instances and in many others, adults could easily have used the past tense of the main verb to provide feedback, yet they frequently chose the form "did." If "did" is used as corrective feedback, it can induce the child to produce a past-tense form. For example: In sample 15, hour 2, Eve refers to the recent arrival of observers with the statement "They come." Since they had already arrived, her mother corrects, "They did come." Later Eve specifies more precisely, "Fraser come and Cromer come," and her mother again affirmingly corrects, "They did come to see you." Eve is alert to the improvement and imitates:

E: *They did come.*
M: *They did.*
E: *Fraser comed and Cromer comed.*
C: *What did we do, Eve?*
E: *Comed.*

The models with "did" seemed to serve as cues for Eve that the morpheme *-ed* was required. Her overgeneralized past-tense form was an improvement over the simple present tense, although not entirely correct adult language. The same phenomenon is encountered in this example:

E: *He buy them all by heemself [sic].*
M: *Did he buy them all by himself?*
E: *He weared them.*

Groping for Correct Syntactic Constructions   In two instances Eve seems influenced by her own cue "did." In both she asks "What did you doed?" The observer echoes "So what did you do then?" and Eve continues "We go (ed) to the beach." In the second instance, after the observer's "That's what I did," she reverted to "And what did you do there?" followed by "And what did you do . . . airplane?" Groping attempts indeed! "Almost random performance" might be a more apt description of these productions than the traditional interpretation of rule-based performance. In a later sample, Eve seems ready for the adult forms.

E: *Di di di did you drink all your coffee?*
M: *Yes, I drank all my . . .*
E: *An' you gave it to Mama.*

The maternal feedback employs the irregular past-tense form, and Eve's shifts to an irregular past tense four utterances later. Nevertheless, in a following sample, Eve still asks the question "Did you turned it?"

Theoretical Conclusions Two learning principles are combined in the described phenomena. First, the frequent input models "Did you?" and "What did you" (11–18 instances each in samples 16, 17, and 18) resulted in Eve's learning and using this turn-taking formula. Second, "did" in this formula was a cue to add a dental suffix to the verb stem. This can lead to overgeneralizations of the regular past ending *-ed*. These findings suggest that the immediately preceding cue had a dominant influence on Eve's productions and led to overgeneralizations. The acoustic resemblance between "did" and the regular past-tense ending is worth noting. The cue effect of "did" therefore may be based on a simple sensory similarity and should not be necessarily interpreted as evidence of rule understanding.

The mother's sudden increased use of "did" as a past-tense cue might account for the environmental shift postulated by Rumelhart, McClelland, and PDP research group (1986) to account for the transition of their model from irregular past-tense forms to regular and over-regularized forms. Increased inclusion of past events as conversation topics resulted especially in increased frequency of "did." This sudden increase might have strengthened the links in Rumelhart's and McClelland's model, or acted as an immediate cue without a corresponding increase in link strength, or both. Whatever the process, an environmental shift seems to have occurred parallel to the child's shift in performance. This shift supports not only the theory of Rumelhart and McClelland, but also indicates factual cause–effect relationships (as opposed to rationalist speculations) that account for the changes observed.

It was presumed more than demonstrated in the discussions of modeling and imitation, positive feedback, and corrections that these interactional phenomena had far-reaching consequences for Eve's language acquisition. Actual evidence was found in Table 1 only, and only for immediate effects. The misleading effects of the past auxiliary "did" could be interpreted easily as negative effects. Focused demonstration of the positive effects of maternal input and feedback follows.

Evidence of Positive Effects of Adult Interventions

Overall Progress The global argument can be presented that Eve was progressing rapidly in her language skills, and, therefore, the maternal interventions were demonstrably effective. This argument can be quite convincing if different maternal styles are compared and related to many children's progress, as done by Cross (1977). This argument cannot be employed in this study because no such comparisons have been performed.

Correlational Approaches   A stronger strand of evidence derives from the correlation of specific input items with identical productions. If maternal use of specific past-tense verbs led to correct use of the same verbs by Eve, then cause–effect dynamics are suggested. Data presented by Moerk and Vilaseca (1987) proved the existence of such covariation. Correct filial past-tense use of specific vocabulary items was clearly related to frequency of maternal use, although additional variables were found to be influential. Global frequency data cannot distinguish if models in confirmations or in corrections were most conducive to filial progress. Additional evidence is needed to differentiate the specific relationship.

Continuous-Time Analyses   A stronger strand of evidence can be derived from a continuous-time exploration of potential cause–effect relationships, which would be longitudinal analysis of the covariation of frequencies in each sample. The relation of the two variables can be estimated by the covariation at many time points, as in a bivariate time series. In a first approximation of this, filial uses of the regular past morpheme and of the auxiliary "did" for individual samples are related to the frequency of adult use and presented in Tables 4 and 5.

Inspection reveals clear covariation between the use frequency of Eve and her mother. For uses of the regular past, the correlation between the sets of maternal and filial values is .73. The values in Table 4 indicate that this correlation is not based simply on a monotonic increase of frequency with the child's age. The relationship with age is quadratic, with a peak in samples 15–17, a high in sample 13, and a decline in samples 18 and 19.

A comparable phenomenon is found in the use of "did" (Table 5), although Eve began to employ this construction much later. Peak maternal frequencies are found in samples 15–18, and sample 13 again represents a high. Eve consistently used "did" only toward the end of the recording period so that computation of a correlation coefficient would not be meaningful. It is also clear that the first use of "did" by Eve coincides with the first peak in maternal use (sample 13), and Eve's regular use begins with the maternal maximum use in sample 17. Eve's productions of "did" generally follow adult models after a brief interval. Massing and close temporal adjacency seem to have been important in the acquisition of productive mastery of "did." The cue function, which relies only on comprehension, seems to have occurred earlier.

Several precautions should be observed in interpretations of these covariations. Correlations cannot indicate causation directly, and in this case two causative interpretations are equally plausible. First, the covariation could result from simple conversational necessity. If one partner talks about past events, then the other must almost necessarily

Table 4. Frequency of regular past morphemes in maternal input and filial production

Speaker	Sample 9	Sample 10	Sample 11	Sample 12	Sample 13	Sample 14	Sample 15	Sample 16	Sample 17	Sample 18	Sample 19
Mother	5[a]	5	9	5(3.5)[b]	19(12.5)	7	17	9	16(10.5)[b]	3	5
Eve	5	4	2	3(2)[b]	10(6.5)[b]	5	16	11	10(6.5)[b]	6	5

$r = .73$ between mother and child.

[a] Frequency is given for the entire sample, usually 2 hours of recording.

[b] Numbers in parentheses represent two-thirds of the total. Adjustments were needed because samples, 12, 13, and 17 contained 3 hours of recording.

Table 5. Frequency of "did" in maternal input and filial production

Speaker	Sample 9	Sample 10	Sample 11	Sample 12	Sample 13	Sample 14	Sample 15	Sample 16	Sample 17	Sample 18	Sample 19
Mother	20[a]	14	25	18(12)[b]	32(21.5)[b]	16	41	24	50(33.5)[b]	31	12
Eve					3(2)[b]			1	7(4.5)[b]	7	3

[a] Frequency is given for the entire sample, usually 2 hours of recording.

[b] Numbers in parentheses represent two-thirds of the total. Adjustments were needed because samples 12, 13, and 17 contained 3 hours of recording.

talk about past events to maintain a conversation, not two separate monologues. Support for this argument comes from this family's script for recalling past events that began "Remember when. . . ." This certainly is an optimal signal to focus attention on the past, but it makes interpretation more difficult by accounting in part for the covariation. In other words, conversational, content-based constraints might be causal factors.

A second interpretation was suggested by co-occurrence in maternal and child speech of specific past-tense forms, and by the absence of obligatory past-tense forms in Eve's speech when environmental support was absent. This interpretation was also indicated by the immediate contingencies between specific input and filial production, as in the examples demonstrating the effects of maternal use of "did" on Eve's incorporation of the past-tense morpheme. This interpretation suggests that in addition to the topic, specific models and occurrences of the past-tense morphemes (specific aspects of the input) affected Eve's production of past tenses. Certainly, these two interpretations are not mutually exclusive, nor do they preclude additional causal variables. Multiple causation must be presumed as the rule in interaction as complex as human communication.

Microanalytic Approaches   The strongest strand of evidence for the positive effects of maternal input and feedback is found in the microanalytic approaches as demonstrated in the tables and examples in this chapter, which detail Eve's imitations and the effects of maternal feedback on subsequent productions.

From Reproduction to Productivity

Table 6 provides an overall view of Eve's acquisition of the regular past tense and presents all formations of the regular past tense, with the exception of the overgeneralizations of "comed" (analyzed later) and "goed" discussed above.

Before attempting any interpretation of the data in Table 6, a systematic difficulty of the analyses should be recalled. The recordings were made every 2 weeks for 1 hour, and, therefore, only a small fraction of actual input and use is captured in the transcripts. The majority of teaching and learning phenomena happened outside the recording sessions. Sudden evidence of mastery is sometimes encountered for which antecedents cannot be established. For some of the following interpretations, knowledge of the average expected environment in Eve's family is used to suggest specific sources of development.

The "Model" columns contain Eve's identical imitations of a maternal past-tense construction. The "Cue" columns contain Eve's productions using a different verb stem than the maternal past tense. Numerical

Table 6. Dependence and independence in acquisition of the regular past

Eve's past-tense form	Sample 9 Model	Sample 9 Cue	Sample 10 Model	Sample 10 Cue	Sample 11 Model	Sample 11 Cue	Sample 12 Model	Sample 12 Cue	Sample 13 Model	Sample 13 Cue	Sample 14 Model	Sample 14 Cue	Sample 15 Model	Sample 15 Cue	Sample 16 Model	Sample 16 Cue	Sample 17 Model	Sample 17 Cue	Sample 18 Model	Sample 18 Cue	Sample 19 Model	Sample 19 Cue
Cried	1																					
Sharpened	0,2	2,0																				
Spilled				64 / 12,0		37				37										28		
Falled								[a],1			94 [a]	0	[a],1,1	0		0		0 / 0,0 / 3,55				
Tied					1																	
Said							0			0				9,76 / 0		78		91,57				3,2
Supposed									0						0							
Folded									0	52				71,72	21,0					23		7,10
Happened									18 / 22	44		53		12		137						
Peed										16 / 0		55										
Covered																						
Tried														76								
Saved														0								
Tripped													0									
Fixed														0				58		1		
Stopped														15								
Turned														100								12
Ironed																1,3						
Squashed																5						
Drinked																6						
Weared																1						
Washed																		65,0				
Cooled																				20		
Throwed																				86		

The numbers in the columns express the intervals between maternal model or cue and filial production.

[a] Interval between model or cue and child's utterance is unknown because sample began the taping session.

values indicate intervals between the model or cue and the production and, inversely, the probability of antecedent influence. The larger the interval, the smaller the probability that the model or cue influenced the child's production. The arrangement of the verbs in Table 6 follows their actual appearance in the samples.

Input Dependency   During early samples, the interval between the model or cue and filial production was short, with the exception of "spilled." The intervals became longer beginning with sample 13, and the ratio between long- and short-interval productions becomes larger. In these later samples, verbs used for the first time in the past tense briefly follow models or cues, which suggests input dependency. Longer interval productions do exist, however.

Creativity versus Cue Dependency   Eve seemingly constructs regular past tenses in many cases using the pattern of verb stem plus dental suffix: She appears to be creative but nevertheless depends on cues by her conversation partners. Research on cuing and priming demonstrated that use of stored information is not incompatible with the use of cues to retrieve this information. Cues may facilitate retrieval of information that might otherwise be relatively inaccessible. Three types of input dependency, singly or in combination, are possible. The first type of cue dependency is global dependency. The mother introduced topics referring to the past, and this global maternal guidance was the major cause of the child's use of past tenses. In this interpretation, the mother established "training opportunities" but did not specifically cue the past-tense forms.

Sensory level dependency is the second type of dependency. In addition to setting the stage by conversing about past events, the mother's use of the dental suffix might have resulted in the child's use of the suffix without understanding its meaning or function.

Semantic-conceptual cuing constitutes the third type of dependency. The child might have understood the principle that past tenses are formed with *-ed*, but she might have needed a cue to be reminded of this principle and overcome a production deficiency, as studied by Flavell (1970).

Detailed analyses of mistakes in later sections permit preliminary differentiation of these types of dependency. It is, however, possible that different types of dependency apply to different verbs at different stages of the learning process before a general rule is established. Table 6 shows that Eve employed *-ed* with few verbs during early stages, so it is implausible that she had formed a general rule.

Slow versus Rapid Progress   Dependency on input cues might explain the retention of the incorrect construction "falled" (Table 6), generally used in the utterance "I falled." Until sample 17, this utterance occurred at minimal intervals following cues indicating required use of a dental suffix. The cue was often the maternal standing phrase "What happened?" The feedback Eve received after "I falled" was often "Did you fall?" The maternal use of the verb stem "fall" and the auxiliary "did" might have reinforced Eve's "falled" if immediate acoustic input was the dominant causative factor.

Contrasted with such slow learning, "spilled" in Table 6 was mastered by Eve in samples 10 and 11. The explanation of this acquisition is relatively straightforward. Spilling things is a common occurrence in the life of a small child and also in the activities of a mother who spends much time in the kitchen. References to these events are frequent and of practical importance. Eve produced the highest percentage or 78% of correct constructions of this past-tense form in the period studied. Three examples of interactions illustrate the probable acquisition process, although these examples occurred after Eve had mastered this form of the verb. This procedure is acceptable presuming that the average expected environment in regard to spilling things and commenting on it did not change greatly during the period studied.

M: *You spilled on the floor.*
E: *I spilled on the floor (too).* .

M: *You spilled the coffee.*
E: *S., I . . . I spilled the coffee.*

M: *I spilled some soup and I wiped it off.*
E: *S., (what why) you wipe off?*
E: *S., you spilled it on you.*

In these examples from samples 14 and 15 Eve, although she had mastered the construction "spilled," still tended to imitate it. This observation provides the occasion to comment on an old controversy: Critics may be correct in arguing that children do not imitate *in order* to learn, but this is irrelevant to the inverse, they learn *if* they imitate. When they have acquired a specific construction, they may still use a model to rehearse the form through imitation.

"Happened," which appeared in sample 13, was another exception to the commonly observed learning process. The interval from the model to production is close to 20 utterances in its first use. "What happened?" is often employed by Eve's mother so that the formulaic source of Eve's construction is clear. As with the case of "spilled," a construction that is modeled so frequently almost necessarily has been learned outside the recording sessions. Yet even here, microanalyses enable the discovery of learning processes. Eve's first formulation in sample 13 "What happen (   ) to my paper?" receives the immediate feedback

"What happened to it?" After intervals of 18 and 22 utterances Eve produces "What happened horse?", "What happened your paper?", and "What happened tape recorder?" In brief, even a formula that is close to mastery can be refined and improved by preceding feedback that corrects an imperfect production.

A verb more abstract in semantic content is "supposed to." This was employed as a past participle and was not productively mastered by Eve during the recording period, but the two instances of Eve's use are informative. In sample 13 Eve produces an immediate imitation, employing a well-established learning strategy. The exchange that led to the second production is more interesting:

M: *Remember when you broke my glasses?*
E: *An' I not supposed to.*

The root of this phrase in adult speech was substantiated by the mother's feedback "You're not supposed to." A formula serves again for Eve to acquire a new form, although she probably has only a vague grasp of the semantic complexities in her utterance.

Prolonged Confusion and Partial Learning   The focus is now directed to Eve's use of the past-tense forms "came" and "comed" that show Eve's vacillation between the irregular past-tense form and an overgeneralized version of the regular past tense. Several variables contributed to use of these forms, and the interactions are presented in Table 7.

In sample 9, Eve still omits the past morpheme and receives the corrective feedback "Yes, he did." The first appearance of "came" in sample 10 was uttered, somewhat inappropriately, while Eve was playing with dolls. This construction was employed when discussing the return of the observers. Eve seemed to enjoy the attention she received from them, and she discussed their return on many occasions with her mother, as Table 7 reveals.

In her first production of the irregular past "came" in sample 10, Eve employs a relatively fixed and overlearned formula in a changed behavioral context. Careful microanalysis suggests another source for an element of this formula. Eve produced "Put back," another common phrase, immediately before "All came back." "Put back" might have been reflected in the subsequent "came back," which suggests influences from immediately preceding utterances and from long-term storage.

The utterance "it came apart" in sample 12 is again a fixed formula. The source is suggested by "come apart again," reflecting the parental "Did it come apart again?" "Down came baby, cradle will rock" in sample 12 does not require elucidation of its formulaic nature.

Table 7. Differentiation of "came" and "comed"

Sample	Hour	Utterance number	Eve	Mother
9	2	4129	Papa come see E., too.	
		4130		Yes, he did.
10	2	94	All came back.	
		95		They all came back.
		96	All came back.	
12	1	113	Oh, it came apart.	
		119	Two. . . two piece that came ap	
		126	Come apart again.	
		127		It did?
12	1	607	Down came baby, cradle will rock.	
12	2	954	S. came in with me.*	
		955		I'll come in with you.
15	2	6873	They come.	
		6874		They did come.
		7234	Fraser come and Cromer come.	
		7235		They did come to see you.
		7237	They did come.	
		7238		They did.
		7239	Fraser comed and Cromer comed.	
		7240		What did we do, Eve?
		7241	Comed.	
17	1	26	S., S., lady came with Fraser.	
		27		The lady did come with Fraser.
17	1		Hippity hop came back.	
17	1	45		How did you get down the stairs so fast?
		46	We (came) go too fast.	
17	2	2	Along came a spider	
17	3	6		We went on the bus, didn't we, E.?
		7		Did . . . do you like going on buses?
		8	And the bus comes, when get on.	
		9		It did, did it?

(   ) indicate reduced intelligibility.
*She means the imperative "come."

The interaction in sample 15 refers again to the arrival of the observers and demonstrates that Eve does not yet reliably supply the past tense of "come" and so a rule-based interpretation would be premature. Eve produces the present tense three times in a situation that required the past tense. In addition, the interaction demonstrated that repeated corrective feedback was effective, but served as a cue for production of the acoustically similar regular past morpheme with the dental suffix and not for production of the correct irregular past. Eve obviously did not employ a rule since in all other samples, she did not produce a single form of "comed," as is evident from Table 7. The principle of cue + analogic response seems to have guided Eve, and the cue could mislead as well as guide.

Eve's productions in sample 17 can be summarized briefly. "Lady came . . .", "Hippity hop came back," and "Along came a spider" are derived from formulaic expressions. "We (came) go too fast" combines a formulaic root and an imitation of an item in the recency position in a preceding utterance. The last item in sample 17 shows again that Eve has not mastered the principle of past-tense use, approximately 4 months after her first formulaic production and in spite of her frequent uses of "came." The immediately preceding model "Do you like . . ." seems to have superseded any principle or rule, or was the only factor in the absence of a rule. As Table 7 suggests, the adult feedback that employed "did," and the relative lack of an exact model, might have been the major causes of the lack of progress observed.

Effects of Input Frequency Careful inspection reveals that Eve's overgeneralizations "comed," "goed," and two instances of "doed" in samples 15–18 occurred when adults produced frequent examples of the regular past tense and "did." In most instances, close proximity of cue and filial production supports this interpretation that cue-guided, rather than rule-guided, behavior leads to overgeneralization. Additionally, whenever input frequencies declined, as in samples 18 and 19 (Tables 4 and 5), overregularizations declined also, which should not be the case in rule-guided behavior. A further indication of the effectiveness of input was found in Table 6. When input was highest, Eve produced the regular past tense of 10 verbs and, in addition, she overregularized "throwed," "weared," and "drinked." She also produced "caught," "told," and "made," verb forms close to the regular past tense by ending with a dental phoneme. Bybee and Slobin (1982) elaborated the partial equivalence of the past-tense dental affix and the occurrence of a dental consonant at the end of some irregular past forms. When the input declines in sample 19, Eve's productions of the regular past tense decline even more steeply.

From another perspective, low input frequency results in slow improvement. This is beautifully demonstrated by comparing the three overgeneralizations "comed," "goed," and "falled." "Comed" appears once and is immediately superseded by "came," known from formulaic phrases. "Goed" appears briefly and is replaced by "went," which was common in input and feedback. In contrast, "falled" appears in sample 10 and is still employed by Eve in sample 17 as "I falled down." When searching for causes of this lack of progress, it was found that there was almost no training. In the more than 20 hours of analyzed interactions, the mother employed "fell" only nine times, the father, once, and an observer, three times. Feedback was either "did fall" or "is falling." Eve's only correct production of fell appears in sample 14, "Jack fell down and a pail of water." It was not employed other than in this rhyme during the observation period. Input of once per sample seems to have been insufficient for improvement.

Acquisition of the Irregular Past

Learning of irregular past forms is generally agreed to be more dependent on rote memorization than is learning the regular past, which is attributed to rule learning. Acquisition of the irregular past is summarized in Tables 8 and 9, and the learning principles are surveyed.

Factors in Maternal Input and Filial Learning   Table 8 provides all maternal input (with the exception of "did") of irregular past-tense forms for samples 9–19. Eve's productions of these irregular past forms are indicated by an asterisk.

A brief conceptual factor analysis is performed on Table 8 to indicate some major factors leading to filial production. The most important factor, amount of input, involves overall frequency and the spacing over samples. This is seen in the early acquisition and consistent use of the past forms "had" and "was " and, to a lesser extent, "went."

Frequency and spacing appear to be more important than meaning in these cases. Auxiliaries generally carry less message content than full verbs. Nevertheless, Eve employed "was" as one of her first past-tense forms. The full verb "went" appeared approximately at the same time as "had" appeared as an auxiliary. No other full verb is employed in the irregular past tense by Eve with any consistency in the analyzed samples.

If degree of meaning is the same, as in the occurrences of "was" and "were," the importance of frequency again stands out. "Were" was employed infrequently by the mother and never by Eve. The importance of frequency confirms the analysis of acquisition of the regular past, both here and as reported previously (Moerk & Vilaseca, 1987).

Additional factors are suggested by Table 8 in the same manner as Moerk and Vilaseca (1987) found an interaction between the two factors of frequency and acoustic distinctiveness for regular past-tense forms. It was seen in the discussion of "had" and "was" that Eve employed both equally, although "was" appeared more frequently in the input. "Had" is similar to the present tense of the verb, and it also is very similar to the regular past tense, ending with a dental consonant. This

Table 8. Maternal input of irregular past-tense forms

Verb	Sample 9	Sample 10	Sample 11	Sample 12	Sample 13	Sample 14	Sample 15	Sample 16	Sample 17	Sample 18	Sample 19
Ate	1	1			1						
Broke	1*	1*		3*			2*			1	1
Brought	1*										
Fell	1		1	3	3			2	3		
Forgot	1	1*			5		3	1	4*	1	
Had	1	2*	*	*	4*	3*	4*	1	2	2*	5*
Put	1					2					
Said	1			2			4		3	4	2
Was	1	6*	2		1*	4*	10*	3*	16*	14*	11*
Were	1	4	1		1	5	2	2	8		5
Came		1					4	2	2	1	
Drank					2	1					
Lost		1*									
Slept		1*							1		
Thought		1				1		1			
Went		3	5*	4		2*	1*	1*	11*	6*	2
Bit			1						1		1*
Hit			1								
Shook			1								

Dug	1					
Put	1				1	
Sent	1*					1
Stuck	2					
Threw	1					
Bought	2*			1*		1*
Gave	5			*	*	
Hurt	1			1	1	1
Made	1	2	1*	3*	1*	1
Saw		3	1*		1*	
Tore		1	1*			
Caught			1*		1	
Told			1			
Took			4		4	
Woke				1		
Could					1	
Cut					2	
Drew					2	
Flew					1	
Shut					1	
Grew						1
Heard						1

*Indicates that Eve produced one or more forms of this irregular past tense in the sample.

Table 9. Dependence and independence in acquisition of the irregular past

Eve's past-tense form	Sample 9		Sample 10		Sample 11		Sample 12		Sample 13		Sample 14		Sample 15		Sample 16		Sample 17		Sample 18		Sample 19	
	Model	Cue	Model	Cue	Model	Cue	Model	Cue	Model	Cue	Model	Cue	Model	Cue	Model	Cue	Model	Cue	Model	Cue	Model	Cue
Broke	135			17			0,3	2,0 2,4,1				6										
Brought	0		0																			
Lost			0,0																			
Slept			19																			
Bit					2,2 0	1,1 3,0																
Sent								17														
Forgot				17,17 63													2,12 20	36				
Was			0			1			1			12		4		0		3,9, 98	0,2	29	0,0 2,0 0,2 0,7	0,3 10
Had				0		1	0		1,3	0		1		0,2 6,80						7,60		26,7 30,9
Did									0,4	2						5	3,0	0,2 1,6 0	0,0 2	15,15 24		22,12 14,0
Bought																						
Went										26		5	28	4		2		1,1,0	0,0 18,4	34,0 0,1 1,0,21	20	58
Saw													0					0				
Caught														0								
Made																						
Found															0							
Gave																		3 3 0,0			25,3	
Sat																		1,4				

The numbers in the columns express the intervals between maternal model or cue and filial production.

might have enabled Eve to use "had" regularly in earlier samples and even in samples where no adult form of this past tense is found. A principle of "generalization from regular verb forms" or "analogic formation after cues" is suggested. In contrast, "was" immediately follows a model in early productions, as seen in Table 9. (Note also the early appearances of single instances of "brought," "lost," "slept," "bit," "sent," and "bought," which all end in a dental consonant. The first four are first produced immediately after models, as seen in Table 9.)

In addition to frequency, consistent repetition, and probable similarity to the regular past-tense formation, massing within a short time is a factor suggested by Table 8. "Was" (sample 10), "bit" (sample 11), and "forgot" (sample 17) suggest the effects of massing on first or early use. Other instances of a single production by the mother accompanied by a filial production establish that massing is not necessary for all productions. Massing might, however, be crucial during the first stages of acquisition. Table 9 indicates an additional factor, recency of cuing, in the introduction of a new past-tense form.

In addition to massing as a factor in new past-tense forms, massing also seems to facilitate use of previously employed forms. Eve produces forms when adults use them repeatedly. Effects of massed models on increases in filial production were demonstrated in previous chapters.

From Reproduction to Productivity   Table 9 suggests further influences upon filial productions of the irregular past tense. A strong tendency toward input dependency is again evident in the intervals between input and filial production presented in Table 9. With few exceptions, the irregular past forms used by Eve follow a model or a cue after intervals of approximately a dozen utterances or less. The most frequent pattern is production of the irregular past form immediately after a model or cue. The frequencies decline steeply with greater intervals. Eve's production is a direct imitation of a maternal model in many early instances. Transitions to longer intervals or cue dependency generally follow imitative trials or rehearsals.

Factors Contributing to Retention   Table 9 demonstrates that early imitations and apparent acquisitions do not guarantee permanent retention. "Brought," "lost," or "slept" do not reappear in the samples of Table 9. ("Cried" in Table 1 was seen in Table 6 to have been lost also.) Table 8 provides the explanation: These verbs were rarely used in past-tense forms by adults in the transcripts.

The acquisition courses of verbs frequently used in input can best be demonstrated by "was," "had," and "did," which indicate developmental dynamics. Input dependency for these verbs was dominant in the early samples and not until later samples did Eve produce them after longer intervals. "Was" and "did" were employed first imitatively. "Had" appeared first and more often after cues rather than following exact models. The similarity of the past-tense form of "have" to the regular past has been discussed in analyzing Table 8, but pragmatic and interactional factors are, however, probably more important in the appearance of "had."

Formulations such as "I had my coffee," "You had your cereal," and "You had your cracker" were common in this family. "To have something to eat/drink" was a formulaic expression. These remarks also referred to items of great interest to Eve, such as birthday cakes, crackers, or her grape juice. Frequency plus motivation and easy formation of this past tense contributed to its learning. Multiple causation is encountered, which is often the case.

Input dependence is not, however, absolute. Eve produced "broke" and "forgot" independently in earlier samples. Adults employed these verbs consistently, if not frequently. Toys often don't function in the nursery because "they broke," and Eve's mother often comments on things she "forgot" to do that were relevant to Eve's needs and wishes. Pragmatic importance is again a factor. The semantics of both verbs, however, are quite complex. "Forgot" is obviously a "mental"verb and difficult to conceptualize. Similarly, "it broke," in its adult meaning, requires a mental comparison between previous appearance or functioning and the present state. This complexity might have prevented Eve from employing them regularly, but it did not prevent her imitation and her delayed use of them.

Loss and Relearning of Specific Forms Presuming that Eve had learned these forms, the possibility that they were lost shortly afterward and had to be relearned has to be considered. Although Eve employed "broke" in samples 9 and 10 rather spontaneously, she uses "broke" in sample 12 only immediately after models and cues. The only other occurrence (sample 15) also follows a model. Similarly, after employing "forgot" spontaneously in sample 10, Eve employs it again only in sample 17. In sample 17, the first three instances follow three models. Eve says twice "We forgot . . ." and once, "I forgot . . ." echoing maternal utterances. The first utterance totally resembles the model that precedes it by two utterances. "You forgot to tell Fraser" becomes "We forgot to tell Fraser."

Losses of infrequently used items are well known from second language acquisition and are to be expected in first language acquisition, although this phenomenon has not caught the attention of researchers.

Microanalyses of Learning and its Sources Pragmatic factors in the three occurrences of "bought" (Table 9) are readily plausible, but are less obvious for the three uses of "gave" in samples 17 and 18. In sample 17, Eve produces "(I want mine) my book and my own favorite book Papa gave me." Although Eve struggles with the possessive pronoun and repeats the object, the word "favorite" and the relative clause (without the relative pronoun) indicate an adult source that referred repeatedly to this precious possession of Eve's. Similarly, in sample 18, Eve's statement "It's ah *Happiness Book* Cathy gave me" indicates repetition of an adult model because Eve is far from producing subordinate clauses. Eve does not cognitively master the past reference of "gave," as shown by her other production in sample 18:

C: *Yes, I drank all my . . .*
E: *Coffee*
C: *Yep.*
E: *An' you gave it to Mama.*
M: *Uh hmm. No, he still has it.*
C: *Should I give it to Mama?*
E: *Yep.*

As the mother points out, the observer had not given her his coffee or cup. "Gave" was, therefore, incorrect. It might be employed as an unanalyzed verb borrowed from the fixed phrases. Additionally, it might have been influenced by the preceding "drank," with a past tense formed by the same vowel change as that in "give." Whatever factors caused this occurrence, it is again shown that use does not imply mastery. Instances of incorrect uses suggest that correct uses too might be based on unanalyzed formulas.

The last item of Table 9, "sat," demonstrates how much information can be hidden in four occurrences of a very simple verb. Two of the four occurrences in sample 17 derived from a nursery rhyme:

E: *"Along came a spider and (he) sat down beside her."*
E: *Little Miss Muffet sat on a tuffet."*

The observers indicated that Eve recited this rhyme four times. Obviously, this rhyme is well suited to past-tense learning: "sat," "came," and "frightened" are past tenses the observers indicated that Eve reproduced very well. Two earlier instances of "sat" are given in a context that indicates influences:

L: *What happened to you?*
E: *I falled down.*
L: *What happened to you again?*

E: *I sat down again.*
L: *And what happened to you?*
E: *I sat down again.*

Three past-tense forms precede Eve's use of "sat." The adult re-peated the question with a minor change, the addition of "again," and Eve retains the past tense but changes her answer "I falled down" to "I sat down again" by using the formula from the nursery rhyme. The syntactic structures of Eve's two utterances match closely, and "again" is added from the recency position in the model. The transcript gave no indication that the exchange was meaningful or described an actual event. Close structural and vocabulary parallels exist between "he sat down beside her" from the nursery rhyme and "I sat down again," that is, pronoun-phrasal verb-adverbial. Although the application of the rote-learned nursery rhyme cannot be proven, these parallels make it highly likely. The rhyme seems recently rehearsed because Eve re-cites it so well, the observers noted.

Particular studies of the effects of nursery rhymes on first lan-guage acquisition and specifically on acquisition of tenses are needed, because little evidence exists of this, as Moerk's (1985b) survey indi-cated. Since these stories often refer to past events, they may function as an optimal training device for learning past-tense verbs and adverbs.

DISCUSSION

Several distinct domains will be considered in evaluating the analyses: methodological, logical, and two process aspects, one concerning the child and the other, adult contributions to language learning.

Methodological Aspects

The main point of consideration concerns context effects. If the pos-sibility of context effects is admitted (and from what is known about the responsiveness of all life forms, it has to be accepted as a most gen-eral principle), then the context of the child's verbal performance must be included in all studies. If the verbal context and its proximity to filial productions is not included, then its effects cannot be discovered. This easily leads to incorrect conclusions about inner rule directedness and to dogmatic pronouncements that input effects are not present. In this case, ignorance is the basis of conviction.

Conceptual Precautions

A second problem encountered in research is more logical than methodological. The concept of past tense was certainly in the minds of linguists and psycholinguists who studied child language development. It is worth questioning if and when it entered the minds of the children who were studied. No blare of trumpets marks the past from present. Experience is continuous, and children's references to the past in early stages of learning pertain to the immediate past. A clear differentiation between past and present cannot be presumed.

In contrast, the facts that do enter the mind of the attentive child are the forms of verbal input. These forms stand in some relation to nonverbal context, which is also experienced by the child. A concept of the past slowly develops from this nonverbal experience partially stored in memory, and from adult verbal input. The existence of a concept of the past has to be demonstrated before this can be assumed as the causal variable that results in past-tense formulations in child speech.

If a monolithic concept of pastness is questioned as the cause of the occurrence of past-tense forms, and if the varying nature of situational context is accepted, then the possibility is immediately apparent that the processes and the causal factors, which result in the diverse productions, might vary also. This applies both to the past tenses of different verbs and to different instances of the past tense of the same verb. In one case, a production might be imitated and only short-term memory and minimal semantic analysis might be involved, and at another time, a production might be formed by analogy based on similarity to cues or stored exemplars.

Complexity of Factors

The analysis of production suggested sensory factors and short-term memory phenomena as the "causes" for occurrences of past-tense forms. For example, the influence of "did" that resulted in overgeneralizations could be described as analogic formation.

Long-term memory of formulas was substantiated and the formulas shown to be based on frequent and pragmatically important input models. Mistakes continued to the end of the recording period and they argue against theories that emphasize general rules and concepts of pastness. Otherwise, "performance restrictions" would have to be invented for every mistake.

Increasing independence from immediate input was observed, though not analyzed in depth. Independence was due to stored formulas, as in the case of the question "What happened?" "Remember when" introduced conversations in the past tense that may have led to spontaneous past-tense productions. Absence of obvious causal variables represents, however, a more complex problem. It remains a challenging task to account for gradual productivity without leaping to premature and unsupported speculations of presumed competencies.

Adult Contributions

Parental and, more generally, adult contributions to Eve's productions and progress have been emphasized. Modeling, confirmation, and corrections have been extensively demonstrated. Several of these techniques involve direct rehearsal of specific forms by the adult or child.

Frequency Phenomena Frequency phenomena, massing, and spacing are important parts of this rehearsal. These serve not only to transfer acquired elements from short-term into long-term memory, but also to provide the basis for recognition of regularities, which might later lead to concepts or rules.

Factual explorations of frequency phenomena can also provide a possible resolution of the argument raised by Pinker and Prince (1988), counter to the assumptions of Rumelhart and McClelland (1986). Even if Pinker and Prince were correct that no extensive shift in the frequencies from irregular to regular past-tense models occurs, the findings of this study support the model of Rumelhart, McClelland, et al. Frequency of the proform "did" increased with increased discussions of past events, and "did" generally was used close to other past-tense forms. The combined frequencies of regular past-tense forms and "did" could well account for the shift to regularized forms observed in children and in the computer model.

It might have helped Pinker and Prince's argument, but it is less helpful for conceptual clarification that they employed generally irrelevant data. It is not "the percentage of [types of] children's verbs that have regular past tense forms" (Pinker & Prince, 1988, pp. 140–141), nor "the ratio of irregular to regular tokens" (p. 142) that is relevant. It is frequency of actual productions of pertinent past-tense forms, not verbs appearing in the present or other tenses, that is relevant to the argument of Rumelhart and McClelland. If those actual frequencies are considered, as in Tables 4 and 5, a different picture emerges from the one drawn by Pinker and Prince. Adult use of the regular past-tense forms increased approximately 100% between samples 13 and 17. The use of "did" increased by 100% and 50% in samples 15 and 17–18, respectively. The close temporal contiguity between adult use and filial productions and repeated massing of models can explain much of the overgeneralization.

Context Setting Adults quite conspicuously employed techniques to mark pastness. This was achieved by the introduction of an episode with "Remember when," or by emphasized and repeated forms of "did" in questions and feedback, or by other forms. One technique was employment of adverbials: "yesterday," "at your birthday party," "last week." This use was not presented in this chapter because it would have required a separate, larger study. Such contextual factors need to be considered along with frequency data in order to understand filial processing and learning.

Equational Devices   These verbal contextual cues can serve as equational devices that cue the child that specific verbal forms are required. Those cues associated with past-tense use in adult input might elicit the same past tense in filial output. Whether the child has any awareness of the obligatory nature of the relation or the meaning of the morphological items is a matter of inference that needs careful substantiation. The many instances when the past tense was not supplied when required suggest that this awareness grows slowly. Performance cannot readily be described as rule-governed.

There are two sets of equational devices. The first establishes the equivalence of forms referring to pastness. "Did" was found to be a ubiquitous cue that signaled the past. Combinations of regular and irregular past-tense forms often were encountered in the flow of conversation referring to the same time of reference. Their equivalence can thereby be learned.

The second set of equational devices pertains to the equivalence of meaning in present and past verb forms. This equation was consistently established by maternal questions and feedback that employed "did" plus the verb stem in the context of Eve's past-tense productions.

E: *He went.*
M: *He did go.*

Earlier, the adult may have provided both elements: "When did we leave?", "We left."

An almost unending variety of such equations can be found in the interactions. The provision of both elements of the equation close together and in conversationally equivalent functions provides many opportunities for the learning of these relationships.

Literary Devices   In addition, adults initiated and the child then employed literary devices such as nursery rhymes that contributed to the learning of past-tense forms. For example, "Jack and Jill," "Little Miss Muffett," and "An Eensy Weensy Spider" contained repeated and closely spaced past-tense forms. Those forms could be learned, without a full understanding of their function, in this context. Later they might be recognized in their functional pragmatic context and used conversationally, perhaps first as imitations and later, spontaneously. Examples in daily context have been more systematically summarized by Moerk and Moerk (1979). The same principle applies to many children's stories, which are often written in the past tense.

In summary, the emphasis is again shifted from a focus upon the effects of filial competence, whatever that term might mean, to relationships between causes and effects. This focus on relationships allows exploration of processes and changes. Multiple and changing causes are encountered, and so multiple and changing processes are a necessary consequence. Such fine grained, continuous-time analyses will, in the long run, lead from a simplistic postulate of filial competence to considerations of multiple factors of performance. Performance factors change with the level of mastery of individual constructions and domains such as pastness.

Chapter 5

The Transmission and Acquisition of Future-Tense Morphemes

There is always one moment in childhood
when the door opens and lets
the future in. Graham Greene: "The Power and The Glory"

Research on the perspective of future time in children and its effects upon planning and achievement motivation was actively pursued in the 1960s and 1970s in terms of a "future-time perspective" (Einstein, 1968; Kastenbaum, 1961). These studies focused on adolescents and pursued goals different from those in this study.

Piaget's discussions (1952, 1969) on the development of the temporal concepts of past, present, and future are well known. As in Chapter 4, these conceptualizations and the discussion of Werner and Kaplan (1963) are presupposed in this chapter, but they are not detailed because they address the cognitive basis, not the acquisition of the linguistic code.

More relevant are studies that report on the first appearance in children's speech of references to the future. Although in principle they are important for a comparison with Eve's first productions, they contain little information about the actual acquisition processes that are reflected in interactions between adults and children. This author, in an extended search of the literature, has not found a single study that shares the goal of this chapter, the exploration of training and learning processes of future-tense acquisition.

CONSIDERATION OF COGNITIVE BASES OF THE FUTURE PERSPECTIVE

The assertion in preceding chapters that young children live in the here and now is in agreement with most of the literature, but is, never-

111

theless, inaccurate. At the least, the concept of here and now needs to be expanded so that this assertion fits the facts.

Like every other living organism, the infant and young child are existentially future oriented. The rooting reflex, observable immediately after birth, provides the first evidence of such future orientation. This reflex "represents" first a search for the nipple and second, for need satisfaction from sucking and food intake, which will occur in the immediate future if the infant successfully locates the nipple. The activities of reaching for objects and grasping them appear later. They are also goal directed, or future oriented.

As Piaget (1952, 1969) demonstrated in detail, children first develop understanding of means–ends relationships at approximately the same time that language begins to develop, that is, they exhibit more complex goal-directed, future-oriented insights. In actual conversations between adults and Eve, adults responded verbally to aspects of the future orientation of the child. All mothers respond behaviorally when they prepare food for their infants, or prepare their baths. Those maternal preparations lead to filial anticipation of need fulfillment, including the events that regularly occur before the fulfillment. In Husserl's (1954) terminology: "Retention" of fixed sequences experienced in the past leads to "protension" in the future.

The future orientation of young children may be divided into three major dimensions that are reflected in verbal behavior: orientation toward need fulfillment, utilization of means–ends structures, and anticipation of future events.

Orientation Toward Need Fulfillment

During early stages of language acquisition needs are expressed as one-word utterances that request the desired object, for example, "milk" or "chocolate." This can also be expressed with a verb, usually "want," or with "more," and by pointing to the desired object. Much of the older literature evaluated by Werner and Kaplan (1963) reported these phenomena. These have no direct bearing upon a child's early use of specific morphemes to express the future, yet they do indicate an orientation to the future. These early uses also have a great impact on the mother's verbal behavior. In responding to the child's expression of needs and wishes, the mother often described her plans and future activities as, for example, "I'm going to give you your milk in a minute." The child was eagerly oriented to this future event, and she heard her mother describe it with morphemes that conveyed an orientation to this future. Both motivation and verbal input seem optimal for learning. Such long-standing, frequently occurring antecedents provide the basis for correspondence of filial conceptualizations and verbal codes.

Means—Ends Aspects

Eve's goal orientation expressed by means–ends behavior is reflected in her verbal behavior. She described her plans with almost the same words that her mother used, for example, "I go get it," when she ran off to fetch something. In this case, a preliminary correspondence exists between a conceptual structure, that is, the child's stepwise plan, and the verbal code modeled by the mother and imitated by the child. The maternal models precede the filial productions by several years, because they have been presented to Eve from birth.

Anticipation of Events

Anticipations of events are based on memory and are established very early. Piaget (1952) observed this with his children before the age of 1 when the infants responded to feeding preparations with sucking behavior though no bottle was yet at hand. Such sequences of events are also described to prepare children for upcoming events (e.g., "You finish eating, then I will give you your bath") or to help them delay gratification of their urgent requests (e.g., "First we need to warm it, then we will eat it"). Therefore, cognitive structures and linguistic models have been established that describe event sequences. The equivalence of cognitive structures and linguistic models could, therefore, be established. How this is done in mother–child interactions is one of the topics of the following factual analyses. The transmission and acquisition processes in the three domains of need fulfillment, means–ends conceptualizations, and anticipation of events are explored in detail.

Before the factual analyses are presented, a word of caution is needed. The remarks about elementary biologic bases of future orientation might promote one-sided nativist interpretations that would be premature as well as incorrect. The child needs to learn the linguistic means to express a variety of future-related aspects, and internal boundaries of this domain come with these linguistic means. Historical and cross-cultural research (e.g., Toulmin & Goodfield, 1965) showed that humankind has struggled through millennia to refine conceptualizations of time, and the establishment of an objective scale for time measurement is recent. For young children, the conceptualization of the future beyond immediate intentions relies upon social markers (Christmas, your birthday, next Sunday) to establish anticipation and differentiation. Parental training and teaching has to include verbal means to express future aspects and conceptual refinements. A Piagetian constructivist approach seems required to explore these developments.

ANALYSES OF THE TRAINING AND
LEARNING OF FUTURE-TENSE MORPHEMES

Presentation of factual analyses follows the format of the description of past-tense markers. Examination of the bases and early steps precedes the analyses of the course of development. Actual dialogues provide data missing from research literature, and little emphasis is placed on theoretical controversies.

Maternal feedback to early filial references of the future, as well as spontaneous models and their impact upon filial learning, are presented and explored. Filial learning strategies in the acquisition of linguistic means to refer to the future are related to information provided by adults. Longitudinal analyses follow the course of these teaching techniques and learning strategies.

Eve's Earliest Productions of Temporal
Morphemes and Their Roots in Adult Speech

Although the analyses in this chapter begin with sample 9, a few references to the future are found in samples 7 and 8. In these earlier samples, Eve referred to intentions or uttered requests without morphemes that indicate the future. Adults responded by using the future morpheme "will," the abbreviation " 'll," or the more colloquial "gonna/going to."

The thousands of parental references to the future, which certainly preceded the sample period, provided Eve with some means to refer to the future. These earliest phenomena are summarized in Table 1 and explained below.

From Main Verb to Auxiliary   The first model in Table 1, "I can go get some more," and Eve's imitation introduce an important source for Eve's acquisition of future-tense morphemes and conceptualizations of the future. "Going," in the sense of walking to a place to get something, is a common activity in caregiving procedures. It is also a common activity of a child. These actions involve goals and are therefore future oriented, but the verb "go" has not yet lost its full meaning of locomotion. Several further examples of this use are found in Table 1, sample 8, hour 3, utterance numbers 1066 and 1068. "Where's he going?" and "Going see Jack (an') Jerry" illustrate the almost imperceptible transition from the full–verb function to the auxiliary function. Sample 9, hour 1, utterance numbers 3430 and 3431, and the sequence from sample 9, hour 1, utterance numbers 3452 – 3457, illustrate feed-

Table 1.   Early steps toward future morphemes

Sample	Hour	Utterance number	Mother	Eve
7	2	3015	I can go get some more.	
		3016		Go get some more.
8	1	29	We're not ready to turn yet.	
		30	Wait a minute.	
		31	Will we turn the page in a minute?	
		34		In a minute.
8	2	471	Pour some tea.	
		472		Going pour some tea.
		473	Going pour some tea.	
		475		Mom going to have tea.
		476		Mom going to have tea.
		477	We're going to have tea . . . Fraser and I.	
		479		Fraser going have tea.
		480		Mommy going ( ) have tea.
8	2	563		Going ( ) see Jack ( ) Jerry.
		564	No, we're not gonna see Jack an' Jerry.	
8	3	1066	Where's he going?	
		1068		Going see Jack (an') Jerry.
		1069	Going to see Jack an' Jerry, is he?	
		1070	What's he gonna do when he gets there?	
		1071	What's he gonna do when he goes to see Jack an' Jerry?	
9	1	3430		Papa go get . . . Cromer.
		3431	He's not going to get Cromer.	
		3432	He's going to go see	
9	1	3433		In a minute.
		3434		In a minute.
9	1	3452		Papa (up) change clothe.
		3454	Yes, he's going go an' change his clothes.	
		3456		Go change baby Sarah clothe.
9	1	3457	Well I'm gonna change her diaper.	
		3555		Let me . . . writing.
		3556		In a minute.
		3557		In a minute.
9	1	3717		More piece of cheese.
		3718	We're gonna have a cheese sandwich.	

(continued)

Table 1.   *(continued)*

Sample	Hour	Utterance number	Mother	Eve
		3744	We'll have supper on the new table.	
		3778		Mom eat.
		3779	Yes, I'm gonna eat my sandwich.	
		3806	I'm goin' to have an apple.	
		3811		I'm goin' have choco-late.
		3812	( ) going to have chocolate?	
		3825	Are you going to eat your cheese sand-wich?	
		3832	Are you goin' to eat this one?	
		3849	Are you goin' to eat this one right here?	
9	2	3952	I'll maybe have another one in a little while.	
		3953		Fraser have little while.
		3954	He'll have another one in a little while.	
		3959		Have one little while.
		3960	In a minute.	
		3961	I'll have one in a minute.	
		3967		Hab (one a) little while.
		3968		(I) hab (one a) little while.
9	2	3991	Papa will fix it when he comes home.	
		3992	He'll cut it for you with the scissors.	
		3993		He'll cut it.
		3994		Pop cut it.

(   ) indicate reduced intelligibility.

back cycles that involve "go" as locomotion versus the feedback with "going to/gonna" as future auxiliaries. Eve employs "go" as a future auxiliary in samples 12–16 in Table 2. Later, forms closer to adult models "going to" or "gonna" replace the simple "go," based on much adult corrective feedback and modeling.

From the mass of evidence in the transcripts, it appeared that with the formulation "go get," or "go and do something," an important basis for the semantic and morphophonological mastery of reference to the future was established for Eve. Another source is encountered in the next lines of Table 1.

A Fixed Formula   The exchange in sample 8, hour 1, utterance

Table 2. Forms of maternal feedback

Sample	Hour	Utterance number	Eve	Mother
9	1	3623	Move a stool.	
		3626		Then we'll put the stool out.
9	2	4073	Hab supper.	
		4074		Tonight we'll have supper.
10	1	426	I habe (take) another one.	
		430		We'll have to cook it first.
10	2	511	S. have make more grapejuice.	
		513		I'll have to make more.
11	1	197	Fraser go eat your lunch.	
		198		Fraser'll go eat his lunch.
11	2	53	S. take a nap.	
		54		Well, S.'s gonna have some milk.
		55		She's gonna have some milk first, then she'll have a nap.
12	1	185	I go drink some more.	
		186		No, because we're gonna have lunch in just a little while.
12	2	811	You go watch me eat my lunch.	
		812		Yes, he's gonna watch you eat your lunch.
13	1	5155	Sarah go . . . Sarah go drink out Mom breast.	
		5156		Yes, she'll drink out of Mom's breast in just a little bit.
13	3	a	Cromer will do it.	
		b		Cromer will do it?
13	3	5656	I shut my eyes an' go sleep.	
		5657		You're gonna shut your eyes an' go to sleep?
14	1	252	He . . . he'll come back.	
		253		Yes, he'll come back.
14	1	421	You wipe my tears.	
		422		Yes, I will wipe your tears.
14	2	633	What we go have?	
		634		What are you gonna have?
15	1	6041	Because we haba get another one.	
		6042		Yes, we'll get another one.

(continued)

Table 2. *(continued)*

Sample	Hour	Utterance number	Eve	Mother
15	1	6185	You go take it some year. . . . some year.	
		6186ff		Some year? Yes. Next year (when) we go to New Brunswick, we'll take it along.
15	2	6839	S., they'll be on a fortnight.	
		6840		They will?
15	2	7022		You won't wake her.
		7031	I don't wake her up.	
		7032		You won't wake her up, no.
16	1	39	( ) Papa go put my jamies on.	
		40		Well,
		41		Tonight he will put your jamies on.
		42		Not now.
16	2	1278	( ) gon' make noise and . . . and I will hear her.	
		1280		You will hear her, yes.
17	1	21	C. and B. will get better, and then I may play with them.	
		22		Yes, they'll get better, and then you may play.
17	2	52	S., a lady going home to work.	
		53		Yes, she's gonna go home and have her lunch.
18	1	198	(It not) time for your lunch.	
		199		It's almost.
		200		In a little while.
		201		In a little while, it will be time for my lunch.
18	2	780	I'm ( ) play with D.	
		781		No, you're not going to play with the Ds.
19	1	10148	So we can hear S. when he wakes up.	
		10149		We'll be able to hear S. when she wakes up.
19	1	10406	And I will see Fraser.	
		10407		You will see Fraser, won't you.

(   ) indicate reduced intelligibility.

numbers 29–34, shows that in certain contexts adults responded to Eve with "in a minute" as a delaying tactic. Minor variations such as "wait a minute," or "just a minute," or "in a little while" occurred less frequently. Eve had already learned that "in a minute" was used as a way to delay gratification in this family. This use peaked in sample 8, hours 2, 3, and 5, and in this sample, mother and child employed this phrase 11 and 21 times, respectively.

In sample 9, hour 1, utterance numbers 3433–3434, Eve produces the phrase spontaneously, in a similar context, but without interactional message content, by repeating it for herself in a singsong manner. Multiple singsong productions by Eve were quite common, as shown in sample 9, hour 1, utterance numbers 3556 and 3557. Several aspects of this formula learning are examined below.

Almost without exception, adults employed the phrase either by itself (sample 9, hour 2, utterance number 3960) or in the sentence-final position, which facilitated intake and storage. The phrase stands out in its position in the input and probably through intonation, though this could not be directly evaluated from the transcripts. The most common form "in a minute" has prosodic aspects that attract attention and facilitate storage. It is composed of two trochaic feet "in a" and "minute," that is, sequences of one stressed and one unstressed syllable. Additionally, the phrase contains internal rhymes: "in," "min," and the "[it]" of the last syllable. Rhythmic alterations between stressed and unstressed syllables, and other features such as rhymes or assonance, are almost universal in children's rhymes (Burling, 1966). An example is the well-known "Sing a song of sixpence. . . ." Such rhythmic tendencies may have a biologic basis in the prenatal experience of the maternal heartbeat and its strong and weak beat. Rhymes and assonances result in patterns that facilitate information uptake and storage.

Whatever the bases, Eve learned the pattern "in a minute" by rote with minimal semantic understanding. Certainly at this developmental level Eve grasped nothing of the numerical relationship of hours and minutes, though a vague understanding of an immediately upcoming event seemed to exist. This dawning comprehension and the melodic and prosodic pattern of the formula seemed to provide a path for development of future-time understanding and the acquisition of morphemes to express this understanding.

Sample 9, hour 2, utterance numbers 3952–3968, illustrate a variant of this teaching and learning. A minor variation, "in a little while," of the form "in a minute" is employed by an adult. Eve immediately utilizes this learning opportunity by imitating the model. There is a syntactic and prosodic structural resemblance between "in a minute" and "in a little while." Both utterances are prepositional phrases, "in a little while" has three trochaic feet with the last syllable of the last foot truncated, which is very common in poetry (cf. Mayor, 1972, p. 36 and following for examples). "In a little while" exhibits other prosodic features, such as double alliteration in the three /l/ consonants and the internal rhyme of the /i/ sounds. The observer equates the two forms by alternating between "in a little while" and "in a minute," but Eve continues to work on the former construction and gradually achieves an almost complete rendition. In sample 9, hour 2, utterance number 3968, only the preposition "in" is absent, and "one," "a," and "I" were added over three repetitions. This description of the learning process exemplifies Eve's input dependency and her active work on the input. In addition, a fixed formula, "in a minute," was combined with flexibility in Eve's alert acquisition of the new phrase "I hab one a little while."

A Common Occurrence and a Standing Phrase   A third path to mastery of the future was encountered in two episodes. In sample 8, hour 2, utterance numbers 471–480, Eve demonstrates input dependency by producing her first future auxiliary "going" immediately after a model. This is followed by productivity when Eve adds the subject and changes the main verb from "pour" to "have" ("to have tea" was a standing phrase in this family). Frequent use and immediate modeling combined as causal factors in Eve's early productive achievement.

The sequence in sample 9, hour 1, utterance numbers 3717–3849, also demonstrates multiple influences. Maternal feedback that uses future auxiliaries is given to Eve's truncated utterances. Models of the future auxiliary "going to/gonna" are consistently employed and spaced over approximately 130 utterances. (Massing within a brief interval was observed in the preceding example.) Eve's use of the environmental framework is impressive. She progresses from "More piece a cheese" and "Mom eat" to "I'm going have chocolate." This was achieved following repeated maternal models. Eve replaced the object noun in her utterance while relying on the structural frame found in "going to have tea " and in similar phrases that occur in the context of meal preparations. In such instances, which are pragmatically very important, Eve relies on immediate imitation and approximates a structure to adequately express the future. This structure proved the most direct route into future-time mastery. Maternal follow-up confirmed and rewarded Eve's achievement by imitation. Later, verb and object were substituted after brief, well-spaced intervals. These learning opportunities were linked to a pragmatically motivating situation.

Sensorimotor versus Conceptual Learning   The last example in Table 1 indicates another aspect of the training process. In sample 9, hour 2, utterance numbers 3991–3994, two maternal models of the auxiliary "will/'ll" lead to an immediate imitation of the new auxiliary. Immediately afterward Eve replaces the pronoun of the subject noun phrase with "Pop," and the auxiliary is lost, although all other elements are retained. Apparent are a form of echoic or short-term memory and the rapid fading of a sound element that was not comprehended but used in a context clearly referring to the future. Learning of the auxiliary "will/'ll" is encountered in later samples.

These examples illustrate another source for future-time expressions: "I haba cool it," "Let me cool it," "Let me eat it," "Let me get it," and "Let me writing." Maternal utterances during meal preparation or in response to wishes of the child were incorporated by Eve with their orientation to the future although she did not comprehend the additional semantic features in these models.

Semantic Complexity or Input Frequency as a Causative Factor
The above examples provide a response to Brown's (1973) question of whether input frequency or semantic and syntactic complexity is the overriding factor in the acquisition of specific linguistic constructions. This author has argued (Moerk, 1980, 1983a, 1983b, 1985b) for consideration of input frequency, and the following examples provide preliminary indications of the role of, or the lack of, semantic complexity:

"I haba cool it."
"Let me cool it."
"I haba cool it."
"Let me eat it?"
"Let me get it."
"Let me writing."

The observer reported that "let me" indicated that Eve wanted something but that it did not imply that action was taken. The examples and the observer's remark shed light on the apparent paradox that semantic complexity does not necessarily interfere with early learning. When Eve employed these semantically complex constructions, she did not appear to conceptualize them as semantically complex. She utilized an adult construction in circumstances similar to those in which she had heard them. Over many trials and with much adult feedback, she will gradually construct a semantic representation identical to that of the adult. Frequency of input is the determining factor in acquisition. Semantic complexity, defined in accordance with the rules of adult language, is irrelevant for acquisition of some phrases. If it is accepted that semantic complexity is not well defined for children's speech, then it cannot be used as an independent variable.

To briefly summarize, Eve and her mother, who were oriented toward need fulfillment, were future oriented in most activities. Eve developed some understanding of this future perspective before acquiring the linguistic tools to express it. She was alert to adult linguistic expressions uttered in future-oriented situations and she repeated, that is, rehearsed, them, and so learned them. Adults generally accepted those preliminary filial attempts and simultaneously provided improving feedback, as is seen in Table 2. Finer differentiations of the linguistic forms and their meanings will be established in the learning process.

LONGITUDINAL ASPECTS OF FUTURE-MORPHEME DEVELOPMENT

Forms of Maternal Feedback

Examples of the input indicate that maternal feedback remained consistent and also changed, a form of invariance over transformations. Of the approximately 275 instances of feedback, those demonstrating a variety of teaching phenomena were selected for Table 2. In addition to variety, much maternal feedback in Table 2 contained repetitions of the same or similar phrases. Variety was integrated with repetition, and this must be considered in evaluating the data. The following discussion highlights some major principles discernible in Table 2.

The dependable and immediate provision of feedback with one or more future morphemes to Eve's reference to a future aspect is an outstanding feature of Table 2. Multiple linguistic items referring to the future were provided for Eve, especially in the later samples. Eve understood the function of at least one item referring to the future, and providing multiple items represented an equational device: A has a similar function as b. Eve increasingly relied on verbal cues for comprehension and analysis, although the nonverbal context continued in a supporting role.

Equally evident, maternal feedback was consistently positive, although it improved on Eve's formulations. This positive force was often expressed as a direct "Yes" but was most evident in the mother's imitation of the child's formulations. The mother's repetition of the filial attempt was automatically a confirmation because the mother is the authority to her young child. The only two maternal uses of "No" pertained to pragmatic aspects, or Brown's (1973) truth value, not to verbal performance. Eve's mother preferred a less obvious form to disagree. This is the hedge "Well," found in sample 11, hour 2, utterance number 54, and in sample 16, hour 1, utterance number 40.

The incidence of corrections and improvements, which consist of morphological additions or improvements, and semantic or pragmatic information was high. Sample 15, hour 1, utterance number 6185, is a production of Eve's that contained two flaws. After the initial maternal response "Some year?", the conversation that follows is both positive and corrective. "Yes" introduces the reformulation, "next" replaces Eve's incorrect determiner, " 'll" improves on "go," and a subordinate clause clarifies the meaning. Sample 17, hour 2, utterance number 52, is a statement by Eve with three mistakes. Again, the mother begins her feedback with "Yes" and eliminates all three mistakes without conveying a negative message.

Feedback is also given to what could be an imperative in Eve's statement. Imperatives are future oriented, and maternal feedback that employs future morphemes reflects this. Accepting feedback also follows correct constructions, as in sample 17, hour 1, utterance numbers 21 and 22. A variation of Eve's formulation such as in sample 19, hour 1, utterance numbers 10148 and 10149, provides more complex means, "We'll be able to," to express the same idea. Complex formulations appear in samples 17, 18, and 19 including negations of a future event, complex verb phrases, and a tag question. Maternal adaptation to filial information processing capacities, or "raising the ante," to use Bruner's (1983) term, was analyzed by Moerk (1975, 1976a).

Fine Tuning of Maternal Feedback

Table 3 exhibits two forms of adult feedback, formal and colloquial future-tense auxiliaries. Both were responses to four types of Eve's utterances referring to the future: 1) utterances without a future morpheme are labeled simple sentence, 2) utterances that employed "go" plus a main verb, 3) utterances with "going to/gonna," and 4) utterances with the formal morpheme "will/'ll." This differentiated feedback is presented for each sample to demonstrate changes in developmental dynamics.

The four verb forms are found in the second column of Table 3. Columns 3 and 4 contain the two verb forms of maternal feedback, and the numbers represent the frequency of feedback. Eve's production of a specific morpheme without feedback is expressed as zero. Eve's lack of production of a specific morpheme is represented by a dash.

Matching Feedback to Productions   Eve's mother provided the formal future morpheme as feedback more frequently than the informal morpheme "going to/gonna." This applied especially when Eve produced a simple sentence.

When Eve employs her first future-tense morpheme "go" with a main verb in samples 9 and 10, maternal feedback is matched in 100% of the cases to Eve's morpheme and consisted of the colloquial morpheme "going to/gonna."

Eve began to use "go" plus verb for the future more regularly in

Table 3. Maternal feedback to forms of filial reference to the future

Sample	Eve's production	Feedback of "will/'ll"	Feedback of "going to/gonna"
9	Simple sentence[a]	17	3
	"Go" plus verb	0[b]	3
	"Going to/gonna"	0	1
	"Will/'ll"	—[c]	—
10	Simple sentence	6	0
	"Go" plus verb	0	2
	"Going to/gonna"	0	1
	"Will/'ll"	—	—
11	Simple sentence	7	0
	"Go" plus verb	4	0
	"Going to/gonna"	—	—
	"Will/'ll"	—	—
12	Simple sentence	7	5
	"Go" plus verb	10	13
	"Going to/gonna"	0	1
	"Will/'ll"	—	—
13	Simple sentence	13	6
	"Go" plus verb	11	2
	"Going to/gonna"	—	—
	"Will/'ll"	2	0
14	Simple sentence	11	2
	"Go" plus verb	2	3
	"Going to/gonna"	—	—
	"Will/'ll"	3	0
15	Simple sentence	12	2
	"Go" plus verb	10	6
	"Going to/gonna"	0	4
	"Will/'ll"	1	0
16	Simple sentence	10	2
	"Go" plus verb	8	6
	"Going to/gonna"	3	4
	"Will/'ll"	4	1
17	Simple sentence	10	3
	"Go" plus verb	1	5
	"Going to/gonna"	0	2
	"Will/'ll"	1	0
18	Simple sentence	12	10
	"Go" plus verb	3	2
	"Going to/gonna"	3	5
	"Will/'ll"	6	0

(continued)

Table 3.   *(continued)*

Sample	Eve's production	Feedback of "will/'ll"	Feedback of "going to/gonna"
19	Simple sentence	13	0
	"Go" plus verb	1	0
	"Going to/gonna"	3	4
	"Will/'ll"	8	0
Total	Simple sentence	118	33
	"Go" plus verb	50	42
	"Going to/gonna"	9	22
	"Will/'ll"	23	1
	$\chi^2 = 46.38$, degrees of freedom $= 3, p < .001$		

[a]Eve referred to upcoming events without employing a future morpheme.

[b]Indicates lack of feedback to production of a future morpheme.

[c]Indicates that Eve did not produce the specific morpheme.

sample 11, and it reached a peak in sample 12. With Eve's increased mastery of this construction, the mother returned to her normal preference for the formal future morpheme "will/'ll." Nevertheless, "going to/gonna" were employed more often after filial utterances with "go" plus verb than what would be expected if no tendency to match existed. (The total and χ^2 show this more clearly.)

When Eve produced "going to/gonna" frequently in samples 15–17, her mother produced 13 colloquial future-tense morphemes, compared to 3 formal morphemes, in her feedback. When Eve partially mastered this auxiliary in samples 16, 18, and 19, the mother's feedback became less systematically matched and included the formal future morpheme.

Maternal matching became most evident with Eve's use of the formal future morpheme beginning in sample 13. The mother did not match Eve's form only once, in sample 16, but otherwise she matched her feedback 100% to formal production by Eve. The ratio is 25:1, formal to informal future-morpheme feedback or matched to unmatched feedback. The χ^2 of 46.38 for total distribution shows that it deviates significantly ($p < .001$) from chance, and that there was significant feedback matching in this dyad.

Positive Nature of the Feedback   Careful maternal matching not only provided feedback that was easy for the child to process, but also transmitted a positive emotional and motivational tone. The mother conveyed a message to her child that can be expressed as, "Yes, what you said is very acceptable. I would say it in exactly the same way."

This argument suggests that imitation of one's performance by an accomplished model implies acceptance and positive evaluation. This point hardly needs to be argued and is evident from common experience. (The reader will remember the impressive array of "yes" particles that introduced the maternal utterances in Table 2.)

Frequency of Feedback   Feedback in Table 3 ranges from approximately 10–40 instances per sample for future morphemes in samples of 2–3 hours. Yet these numbers underestimate maternal feedback for future morphemes. Adults often produced future morphemes in response to Eve's phrases with "let me," "I wanna," "We hafta," and similar requests. Since requests and goals obviously pertain to the future, pertinent maternal feedback can also fulfill an important teaching function. Total input frequency, including spontaneous maternal models, was considerably higher than feedback frequency. Eve not only experienced feedback that was adapted to her own processing capacities, but she also received this feedback and equivalent models frequently enough that they functioned as rehearsals and helped her to master the information. Microanalyses would show that these reminders were massed over brief intervals, which should have made learning of the input and transfer into long-term memory even easier. Schneider and Detweiler (1987) discussed this advantage of massing. Intense input and feedback referring to the future represents an additional equational device. Eve could gain insight into the many ways to refer to the future from these equivalent formulations.

In summary, Eve received consistent feedback from her mother. This feedback had a positive emotional force and was closely matched to the child's utterances and also modeled improvements. It was informative, but the load of information processing was moderate. Because this fine tuning was accompanied by frequent feedback and situational and semantic support, all conditions were close to optimal for Eve to acquire the future morphemes.

Frequency Relationships of Input and Use

Figure 1 presents the effects of the input and feedback by showing Eve's progress in producing the future-tense morphemes and provides possible causes of this progress in the total frequency of all adult models. (Profiles in Figure 1 are based on 2 hours per sample. For the 3-hour samples, two thirds of the total was computed for comparable results.) This presentation of both maternal and filial productions suggests the influences of these communication partners on each other in the course of Eve's development. The conceptual basis for discussing these mutual influences is derived from bivariate time series analysis. In this conceptualization, variables can influence each other at the same time, or the influence can be exerted after variable time lags. Lead–lag relationships provide indications of cause–effect relationships, because

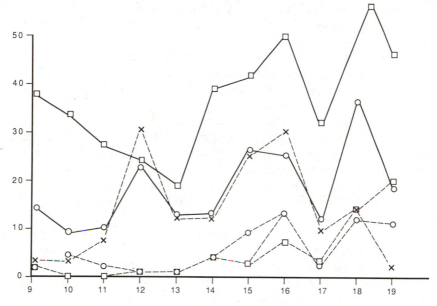

Figure 1. Overall frequency relationships. (Solid line = mother's production, dotted line = Eve's production, X = "go" plus verb, ○ = "going to/gonna", □ = "will/'ll". Vertical axis = frequency, horizontal axis = sample.)

something prior can be a cause but not an effect of something that followed. (Details of these time series considerations are presented in Chapter 7.)

Overall Trends   The correlations between age and frequencies are in the range of .70–.80. The overall correlation between total tokens of maternal and filial future use is .81, reflecting that both were correlated with Eve's age but also showing the mutual adaptation of the partners. Two exceptions to these trends are noteworthy. First, the curve for filial use of "go" plus verb is bimodal and curvilinear and reaches a first peak early in sample 12 and declines steeply after a second peak in sample 16. This makes sense because "go" plus verb is a simpler construction that made it possible for Eve to break into future-time productions and was replaced.

The second exception to increasing frequency with age is less obvious and pertains to the decline in frequency of adult productions of "will/'ll" from samples 9 to 13. The dynamics in sample 12 may provide an explanation: The steep increase in uses of the future morphemes "going to/gonna" by adults and "go" plus verb by Eve. The decrease in maternal use of "will/'ll" was due to an adjustment to Eve's progress in her use of the morphemes "go" and "gonna" to refer to future activities.

Adults provided models of the future auxiliaries "will/'ll" and "going to/gonna" with considerable baseline frequency before Eve's future expressions became productive to any degree. The frequency ranged from 40 to 50 instances per sample. Both pragmatic and informational considerations suggest that early future references by adults were employed to prepare Eve for upcoming activities or to assure her that her wishes would be fulfilled shortly.

Rapid Adult Adjustments to Filial Learning   A sudden change in adult responses was evident in sample 12 when Eve began to express future conceptualizations with "go" plus verb: Adult use of "going to/gonna" was more than doubled. This adaptation to filial usage was shown also in Table 3. Reduction of adult use of the formal future morpheme "will/'ll" in sample 13 corresponded with this attempt to match Eve's forms.

Adult use of the formal future morpheme increased beginning in sample 14 and was followed in sample 15 by a renewed increase of "going to/gonna." This emphasis on future topics resulted in Eve's second peak in the use of "go" plus verb in samples 15 and 16. This was accompanied by a corresponding increase in adult use of the future morphemes "going to/gonna" and "will/'ll." Despite the minor fluctuations in samples 17–19, adult use of the formal future morpheme was still increasing.

Regarding "going to/gonna," the adults could be returning, in the form of an oscillation, to their normal use. However, the abrupt ending of the recording does not permit an evaluation of this possibility.

In this bivariate or, more precisely, multivariate time series, the period began with an adult lead and Eve close to zero. When Eve's future morphemes became productive, adults responded both immediately and after a lag by matching Eve's morpheme and challenging her with a more formal morpheme. Discussion of Table 3 suggested that the immediate match might be due to feedback matching. The delayed challenge could have derived from the spontaneous maternal models resulting from a shift in conversation topics. This interpretation needs to be more substantiated through microanalyses.

Consistent Frequency Matching   These analyses have focused on the effects of filial change on adult responses. The cause–effect relationship was certainly bidirectional. The overall indication of adult effectiveness is seen in the gradual increase of Eve's uses of future morphemes. More impressive were the parallel shifts in curves for all future auxiliaries used by adult and child beginning in sample 14. The peaks and valleys match, so adult increases were matched by filial increases. The correlation of .81 between the sums for all samples rose for samples 14–19 to .83. This close mutual adaptation may have profound instructional implications even if based on a small number of data points.

Other analyses in this study showed that this close covariation was due to Eve's immediate imitation of new models and to adult adjustments to Eve's uses. These adaptations suggest the following dynamics: As soon as Eve was aware of a new linguistic tool (the "readiness" of many theoretical discussions, e.g., Bruner, 1983), adults could control Eve's productivity and learning of this form by using it frequently, often in episodes of massing. When Eve produced the new form, adults provided matched feedback to refine the use.

The steep increase of more than 400% in filial use of the more formal future auxiliaries "will" and "'ll" in samples 18 and 19 must be emphasized. This was preceded by an adult increase beginning in sample 14, and it was matched by a second increase and a peak in sample 18. Lead–lag relationships and concurrent cause–effect relationships are suggested by these phenomena. By sample 19, Eve's use of "going to/gonna" was not far below the maternal average, and her use of the formal auxiliary attained a level above the maternal minimum in sample 13 and was increasing steeply. Eve was on her way!

Microanalyses of Eve's Input Processing

Several major dimensions of acquisition of future-tense morphemes have been surveyed: the conceptual bases, the very first semantic and morphological roots, maternal feedback, and the longitudinal relationships between adult and filial frequency of use. Yet one aspect has been neglected that from a cognitive perspective is often considered the most important. This aspect pertains to the strategies the child uses to master input and to establish bases for productive use of linguistic items. These learning, abstracting, and storing processes are the next focus of this study.

Cognitive processes as such cannot be observed. Interactional processes observed over time have to provide the bases for hypotheses about unobservable processes. The tables following provide indications for these processes and focus upon the auxiliary "will/'ll" because a complex learning task can be observed in the acquisition of this formal future morpheme. "Will/'ll" "expresses an old concept through a new form," as stated by Werner and Kaplan (1963, p. 8), and involves creativity and flexibility.

Eve's First Productions of "Will/'ll"   Table 4 provides the earliest uses of the morphemes "will/'ll" by Eve. Eve had acquired an understanding of the immediate future and had established a morpheme for it, "go" combined with a main verb in sample 11 or 12. (This formulation continued to be used in samples 17 and 18.) If Eve had understood

Table 4. Eve's earliest productions of "will/'ll"

Sample	Hour	Utterance number	Mother	Eve
9	2	3991	Papa will fix it when he comes home.	
		3992	He'll cut it for you with the scissors.	
		3993		We'll cut it.
		3994		Pop cut it.
9	2	4159	I think I'll put an ice cube in it.	
		4160	That'll (be) much easier.	
		4161		That ice cube (easier).
		4162		That ice cube make it better.
		4163		(That) ice cube ('ll) make it better.
12	2	606		When the wind blows, cradle will rock.
		607		Down came baby, cradle will rock.
13	2	151	Pop'll do it.	
		152		Papa do it.
13	2	211		We hava fix it.
		212	We'll fix it.	
		213		We have fix the top.
13	3	271	Well, you ask Fraser if he can do it.	
		278	We'll find out by next time how it works.	
		281	But next time it'll move, I think.	
		287		Cromer will do it.
		288	Cromer will do it?	
		289		Cromer will do it.
		290	Well, I'll try it.	

(   ) indicate reduced intelligibility.

the concept of the future and its encoding by means of an auxiliary, as rule learning would imply, she should have been able to employ the auxiliary "will/'ll" in all obligatory situations. If she did not do this, it might be advisable to postulate less systematic underlying processes than rule learning to explain the observed phenomena.

Multiple Determination in Immediate Input   The data in Table 4 contrast with those expected from a rule learning perspective. The first example in Table 4, sample 9, hour 2, utterance numbers 3991–3994, contains condensed information, not only for Eve but also for the student of language acquisition. The two models of future use that produced an immediate and almost identical imitation by Eve are evident. What is less evident is the probable reason for Eve's nonidentical production in sample 9, hour 2, utterance number 3993. The reason is indicated by the phrase "we'll" in sample 13, hour 2, utterance number 212, and sample 13, hour 3, utterance number 278. This phrase was encountered frequently in the home and referred to the observers, mother and child, or father and child. Eve employed a familiar construction that was cued by the close acoustic resemblance between "he'll" and "we'll." A concise and repeated pattern "X will fix/cut/do/try it" is prevalent in Table 4. The production requires fewer processing resources because the frame is well known.

Three sources for Eve's production of "We'll cut it" have been argued: the formula "we'll," the common frame "X will do it," and the two immediately preceding models of the frame and "will/'ll." The result of all this scaffolding is that a new element, " 'll," could be incorporated into the known pattern. Nevertheless, within virtually 1 second, the auxiliary was lost when Eve rephrased the utterance in sample 4, hour 2, utterance number 3994, and progressed from mere acoustic imitation to a semantic one ("he" is replaced by the equally modeled "Papa," resulting in "Pop cut it"). Similar phenomena of rapid fading are encountered in later samples. These phenomena support the present interpretation that processes other than rule application are at work.

Syntactic Formulas Facilitate Morphological Acquisitions   Sample 9, hour 2, utterance numbers 3991–3994, contain two successive instances of a pattern in the maternal models: (subject) "will/'ll" (verb) "it," as "X will fix it," "X will cut it." Subject, object, and auxiliary are identical in this repetition, and both forms express the same content. In later examples in Table 4, we find "X'll do it," "X'll fix it," "X can do it," "X'll try it," and similar frames in Eve's utterances.

This fixed pattern is sufficient to explain Eve's spontaneous production of "Cromer will do it" in sample 13, hour 3, utterance number 287. There was no immediately preceding model for this utterance, but none was needed since this production was built on multiple supports. Shortly before this production, "He can do it" was modeled and was followed by two models with " 'll," "We'll find out," and "it'll move." Eve could rely again on the multiple supports of the known frame, the almost identical syntactic model, and two models of the future morpheme. It could be concluded that Eve's spontaneous production of "Cromer will do it" was not very spontaneous at all, considered from a sequential and microanalytic perspective that includes frames in long-term memory. This analysis does not imply that Eve never heard an identical model. It is very probable that she did, although it was not recorded in the transcripts, and that more rote remembering was involved than can be shown.

Rote Formulas Containing "Will/'ll"   Two antecedent models combined and integrated with a rote formula form the basis of the production in sample 9, hour 2, utterance numbers 4159–4163. "That'll make it better" was another common phrase in this home, helping Eve over minor aches and hurts. Eve progressed to the last utterance in this series after combining the elements "that," "ice cube," and "easier" from two preceding models. The identity of the initial elements in the model and the stored phrases "That'll be easier" and "That'll make it better" results in the retrieval of the stored formula. Eve combines her formula with the subject she previously established. Whether the future morpheme " 'll" derives from the preceding model, from the formula, or is a product of combined influences could not be determined from the data. Multiple causes for Eve's production of the utterance are certainly demonstrated.

Table 4 represents all of Eve's productions of "will/'ll" from sample 9 to sample 13. Examples were not selected to argue multiple causation. Without such multiple causation in the conversational context, Eve produced only the nursery rhyme "Rock a bye baby." Nor did the single models in sample 13, hour 2, utterance numbers 151 and 212, suffice for Eve to produce "will/'ll."

Although we have followed only the first steps in the acquisition process of this morpheme, the implications for processes that Eve employed deserve summary. Eve recalled rote formulas and fixed patterns from long-term memory, and she substituted or added items from models retained in short-term memory. The consistent retention of the main verb in Eve's imitations is also noteworthy. Integration of items from the two memory stores is common, but none of the complex analytic processes postulated in the literature that led to conclusions about rule-governed performance appear to be required to explain these early filial productions. The possibility certainly exists that at later stages other processes came into play. This is explored by following subsequent processes in the acquisition of the formal future morpheme.

Later Stages and "Level Mixture" in the Acquisition Process   Table 5 continues to follow the development of future-tense morphemes from sample 14 to sample 19, the end of the observation period. These samples cover a period of increased readiness or a zone of proximal development for the future morphemes "will/'ll," as the frequency data from Figure 1 indicated. Microanalyses of the interaction episodes summarized in Table 5 suggest how the increased mastery and changes in underlying processes from rote to abstraction of patterns develop. Eve shifted between different levels of performance in her references to the future. Piaget's concept of level mixture (cf. Feldman, 1980) expresses this and suggests an important cognitive principle. Level mixture refers to simultaneous functioning on several developmental levels. She might have noted discrepancies between the differ-

Table 5.   Input processing and effects in the acquisition of "will/'ll."

Sample	Hour	Utterance number	Mother	Eve
14	2	1	(Will you) get me the green crayon?	
		2		I'll get you a green green crayon.
14	2	20	We'll make the flower red.	
		47	Shall we make another flower?	
		50		Shall we make another flower?
		53	We'll make this one different.	
		62	We'll make the leaves green.	
		68		Shall we make it green?
14	2	635	I guess I will.	
		636		We guess I will.
		637	I guess I will.	
		640	I'll move the high chair so you can see.	
15	1	6239	He'll watch.	
		6240	He'll just watch.	
		6252		Fraser will watch.
		6253		We gonna make ( ) cubes.
		6254	Yes, we will.	
16	1	162	It will make a great big hole, if. . .	
		163		It will make a great big hole.
		164	You will, yeah.	
		165		I go make it.
		167	I'll smack your bottom if . . .	
		168		I go make a great big hole in my pants.
16	1	633	And we'll be right back.	
		634		We be right back.
		635		He going home in a fortnight.
		636		Fraser going home in a fortnight.
		637	No, I'll be back here again in a fortnight.	
		809		He go come in a week maybe.
		813	He'll come tomorrow . . .	
		814	He'll be back tomorrow.	
16	2	998		S., I I I want it off so that it'll get well.

(continued)

Table 5. *(continued)*

Sample	Hour	Utterance number	Mother	Eve
		1001	It'll get well with the Band-Aid on.	
		1015		It will get well.
		1016	Yes, it will.	
17	2	1	We'll come right back down.	
		2		We'(ll) be right back.
17	2	13		And a lady be back.
		18		A lady be back.
		20	When will she be back?	
		21		Take he nap . . . on couch, then he be back.
17	2	45	I'll come back and see you again.	
		54	But he's not gonna come back today.	
		55		He'll come.
17	3	8377	We'll read it later.	
		8378	We'll read it tonight, before you go to bed.	
		8379		Fraser will read it.
17	3	8400	We'll come right back.	
		8401		I be right back.
18	1	91	We're not ready to turn it yet.	
		92	We'll be ready in a minute.	
		93		We be ready in a minute.
18	1	562		(See it will work) this way.
		563	Well, I don't think it will.	
		582	Well, it won't work here, Eve.	
		592		It will work on here, see?
		598	I don't think it will work on there.	
18	1	608	We'll have to buy Becky a new one.	
		626		An' we will buy Becky a new one.
		628		It will be red.
18	2	960	I'll be back.	
		961		S., Fraser be back.
		964	Perhaps I will.	
		968		I will see him.
18	2	1124	Then I'll get my picture taken next time.	
		1165		So they will get dry?
		1166	They'll get dry in a little bit, uhhm.	

(continued)

Table 5.   *(continued)*

Sample	Hour	Utterance number	Mother	Eve
19	1	10050	Ok, I'll put my pencil there.	
		10068		I will put my pencil right there.
19	1	10100	( ) we'll have lunch.	
		10107		Cookie, that ('ll) make me happy.
19	1	10226	He'll share the paper with you.	
		10227		I will write right here.
19	1	10330	Maybe both of them will come.	
		10335		And they will walk.
		10336	They will walk!	
19	1	71	You'll have lunch in a little while.	
		72		My lunch will make me happy.
19	1	10538	You'll never be a man.	
		10539		Yes, I will be a man.
19	2	163	Do you think there will be enough room there?	
		164		Yeah, there'll be 'nough room there.
19	2	11057		Will . . . turn dat on?
		11059	No, it will come on by itself.	
		11061		It will turn itself.
19	2	11116	Why don't you . . .	
		11118		I will.
		11124	Are you going to do it?	
		11128		Fraser will do it.
		11129	Will Fraser do it?	
		11130	You ask F. if he'll do it for you.	
		11136		Fraser will undo it.
		11137	Fraser will do it.	

( ) indicate reduced intelligibility.

ent levels of performance and this might have been a motivating factor to progress. This "disequilibrium" derived from level mixture is the central dynamic factor in Piaget's (1977) later theorizing.

Input Dependency   Sample 14, hour 2, utterance numbers 1 and 2, suggest that multiple processes are at work in the interactions. The similarity between the adult model and the filial production is clear, yet Eve does not produce an identical imitation. The question is transformed into a declarative sentence, and the pronoun and the article of the object noun phrase are changed. The established root "I go get," discussed in Table 1, is reflected in the sample sentence although Eve substitutes the more advanced future auxiliary. A more distant reflection of this base is found in sample 16, hour 2, utterance number 998, "so that it'll get well," and in sample 18, hour 2, utterance number 1165, "So they will get dry?" More direct models for these phrases are also found in the input, and multiple determination is encountered. Changes that combine invariance with variation can be observed in the following examples from Table 5:

I	go	get	I go	make
I'	ll	get	I will	see
It will		get	It will	make

Based on a sturdy syntactic frame and with assistance from immediate models, the small changes in these phrases that indicate progress came easily.

Sample 14, hour 2, utterance numbers 20–68, involve immediate imitations, although Eve manages to make minor changes. Compare the "sophisticated" formulation of "Shall we make" with the "primitive" "We gonna make" in sample 15, hour 1, utterance number 6253, and with "I go make" in sample 16, hour 1, utterance numbers 165 and 168, a month later. This relapse to an old construction occurs despite the immediately preceding imitation "Fraser will watch" in sample 15, hour 1, utterance number 6252, and "It will make a great big hole" in sample 16, hour 1, utterance number 163. These relapses show that an increase in processing demands, whether in content or syntax, could interfere with advanced productions. These comparisons found in Table 5 again prove Eve's strong input dependency, the absence of consistent rules, and, therefore, the precarious nature of mastery of the new morpheme.

Adult Adaptation to Filial Information Processing Needs   Sample 14, hour 2, utterance numbers 635–637, indicate why a full form of a specific morpheme might precede the acquisition of the contracted form. Previous reports, such as Brown (1973), recorded with astonishment that children largely employed the full form, even though the contracted form was more frequent in input. A cause for this is suggested in Table 5. In sample 14, hour 2, utterance numbers 635 and 637; sample 15, hour 1, utterance number 6254; sample 16, hour 1, utterance number 164; and sample 16, hour 2, utterance number 1016, the full form "will" is employed by the adult in the final position of a brief sentence. The final position has an emphatic effect and attracts attention, and the recency effect facilitates short-term storage, while the brevity of the utterance promotes processing.

The full auxiliary "will" was employed by adults in 45 instances in samples 16–19, which was a period when Eve was especially alert to this new morpheme. In these samples, the ratio of full to contracted morpheme ranges between 1:5–1:2, which was higher than in preceding samples with the range between 1:7–1:13. Obviously the full form is acoustically more distinct than the contracted form. In this aspect too, adults seemed to adapt their input to fit the informational needs of the child. (These findings also indicate that the averages from long periods are not sufficiently fine grained to explain developmental changes and feedback cycles.) Regardless of the adults' didactic intentions, frequent use of the full morpheme in the final position, combined with Eve's demonstrated readiness, should positively influence Eve's grasp and retention of the form. The close imitation in sample 14, hour 2, utterance number 636, supports this interpretation. The phrase "I will," sample 14, hour 2, utterance numbers 635–637, is expanded into a longer sentence "I'll move the high chair" in sample 14, hour 2, utterance number 640, that combined teaching of a morpheme with teaching of syntax.

In sample 15, hour 1, the imitation after more than 10 utterances argues against the rapid fading encountered in previous interactional episodes. The structure and meaning of the model is retained despite Eve's substitution of the subject pronoun with a noun. The improving and emphasizing feedback of sample 15, hour 1, utterance number 6254, "Yes, we will" after the colloquial "gonna make" suggests that the mother was aware of Eve's zone of learning. Although Eve's progress is emphasized in this episode, Eve still employed "go" plus verb more often to express the future tense. Input dependency certainly was important, but habits stored in intermediate or long-term memory slowed the learning process.

Prolonged Erratic Performance   Eve's awareness and use of the future morpheme "will/'ll," at least imitatively, contrasts to sample 16, hour 1, utterance numbers 634–636 and 809. All these reflect frequent input, and sample 16, hour 1, utterance number 634, is an immediate imitation. Nevertheless, obligatory morphemes referring to the future were omitted in all. In contrast, sample 17, hour 2, utterance numbers 1 and 2, exemplify inclusion of " 'll" in an imitation, but three pages later, sample 17, hour 2, utterance numbers 13–21, again exemplify omissions, one despite an immediately preceding model. The cause of these omissions might have been that Eve overlearned the phrase "be back" at a time when she was not alert to the future morpheme "will/ 'll." The established formula acted as an obstacle to incorporation of the new morpheme already employed in other, less overlearned, contexts.

In sample 17, hour 2, utterance number 45, the model "I'll come" is followed after 10 utterances by Eve's "He'll come," which was a successful match after a considerable interval! Nevertheless, Eve employed "go" plus verb to refer to the future in the same sample.

Causes of Progress and Failure   Sample 17, hour 3, utterance numbers 8377–8379, demonstrate a double model and imitation that lead to a correct future construction. Briefly afterward, in sample 17, hour 3, utterance numbers 8400 and 8401, two substitutions in Eve's imitation that recall her well-established formula result in the loss of the future morpheme. The failure to imitate " 'll" in sample 18, hour 1, utterance number 93, reflects the rigid formula of "X be. . . ."

Phrases established early but incorrectly that become ingrained in the incorrect form seem to represent obstacles to later improvement. This phenomenon is well established as interference of a first language in the acquisition of a second language. It is also encountered in other domains of learning, especially in skill learning where incorrect procedures may become major obstacles to progress.

Otherwise, influences from long-term memory have largely positive effects. In sample 16, hour 2, utterance number 998, Eve produces "S., I I I want it off so that it'll get well." This was a perfect complex sentence, aside from minor dysfluencies in the production of the subject pronoun. The source for this production was not in the transcripts, but can be surmised. A pragmatically and emotionally important situation that involved an injury and the maternal application of a bandage resulted in the retention and adaptation of this complex phrase. Another undocumented source is reflected in sample 18, hour 1, utterance number 562, "(See it will work) this way." Adults apparently solved a nonverbal problem for Eve and accompanied the solution with the quoted words. This situation led to storage of the accompanying utterance, to spontaneous reproduction, and to the flexible adaptation in sample 18, hour 1, utterance 592. Eve moved from immediate imitation to productivity.

Evidence of Eve's Progress   Eve's achievement should not be underestimated. Both utterances were recalled from long-term storage. In both instances Eve produced a follow-up that was an altered version of the original utterance. This is evidence that the first production was not unanalyzed by Eve. Similar competence is suggested by Eve's correct imitation, after an interval of almost 20 utterances, in sample 18, hour 1, utterance numbers 608 and 626, and by the variation "It will be red" in sample 18, hour 1, utterance number 628. Yet in the next hour of the same sample, the future auxiliary is absent in imitation of the simple phrase "X be back" in sample 18, hour 2, utterance number 961. The adult "Perhaps I will" that utilized the recency position to model the full future morpheme, however, leads to "I will see him." These variable performances can be explained by memory and attention factors, but not easily by rule following!

Interspersed with spontaneous utterances such as "So they will get dry?" in sample 18, hour 2, utterance number 1165, were phrases such as "I go get" and "I go write" to refer to the future. Here also Eve was restricted by a rigid remnant of prior learning. Adult use of the forms "gonna," "going to," and "will/'ll" probably made it more difficult for Eve to achieve consistency. To the author's knowledge, rules for adult choices of future morphemes have not been established by linguists. Eve might have considered these forms as equivalent and been guided in her choices by priming or familiarity.

As Figure 1 demonstrated, Eve's use of the formal future morpheme clearly increased. Eve's productions occurred after longer intervals. Most important from a learning and cognitive perspective, Eve's performance showed increasing consistency. Although it is sometimes difficult to judge if use of the future morphemes is obligatory, there are only two constructions in sample 19 in which Eve omitted a clearly obligatory future morpheme. These involved the request: "You (please) plus verb. Eve tried to reproduce "Will you please plus verb" but failed to incorporate the unstressed initial auxiliary. The second construction contained three phrases: "When I big, I a man/I am man/I man." These lacked a future morpheme and seemed to indicate groping for the right form. In contrast, the immediate imitation in sample 19, hour 1, utterance number 10539, "Yes, I will be a man" includes the future auxiliary. In a rare instance, Eve produces "we will go drive" that was a combination of the old future construction, "go" plus verb, and the new future construction with "will."

Production Deficiency   Eve's productions in the later samples of Table 5 suggest a considerable level of mastery. Her productions of future morphemes in sample 19 could even be considered as rule governed. In sample 20, Eve conversed with her father and the observers (sample 20 was not included in the data for that reason) and did not produce a single formal future morpheme during the 2 hours of conversation. "Going to/going a" plus verb were produced several times. The obligatory future morpheme "will/'ll" was missing in "We be coming down" and "Momma be right back," and Eve's productions generally were brief and more like those in earlier samples.

The competence Eve seemed to exhibit in sample 19 appears to have been dependent on the mother's consistent scaffolding (Bruner, 1983). What Eve did with this maternal support she seemed unable to produce without it, which confirms a principle emphasized by Vygotsky (1962). From a psychological perspective, it appears that the items in long-term memory could not be independently recalled if close cues were not consistently provided. This dilemma is known from Flavell's (1970) research on "production deficiency" and is familiary to every second-language learner (Fillmore, 1976). R. Clark (1974) similarly described how toddlers "perform without competence." Such incomplete competence is, of course, a normal stage in skill learning.

The evidence presented indicates that description of Eve's productions as rule governed would be incorrect. Rote memory of surface forms cued by similar stimuli and analogic formations based on partial cues more adequately describes the phenomena.

Eve's Increased Independence from Input   Table 6 provides an integrated review of Eve's progressing independence in samples 14–19. The numbers in the column "model" refer to the interval between antecedent and production of imitations following models. Numbers in the column "cue" refer to the interval between antecedent and Eve's production with a different main verb that followed maternal use of the future.

Input Dependency versus Spontaneous Recall   Eve's productions in samples 14 and 15 follow a model or a cue in most cases and are clearly input dependent. (The one exception, "He'll come," can be explained by knowledge of conversation topics in this family.) In sample 16, "will take" (Fraser will take me up"), produced after an interval of 126 utterances from the last possible cue, seems genuinely spontaneous. (This is unique in the recorded samples and cannot be explained by matching input, but remember the discussion of Eve's "Cromer will do it.") The other utterances that appear after long intervals, "I will be very quiet" and "I will hear her," refer to the sleeping baby sister and can be considered as standing phrases. ("I/we can hear her" was found repeatedly in the transcripts.) These utterances may have functioned as patterns in which the auxiliary "can" was replaced by "will." Even if a basis is found for Eve's production, a transition to more independence is clear from the length of intervals from model or cue to production. Longer phrases such as " 'll make it better" and "It'll make a great big hole," as well as the negative future "won't," still follow immediate models. Sample 17 does not exhibit a profound change in dynamics. In sample 17, hour 1, utterance number 21, the phrase "will get" in "C. and B. will get better, and then I may play with them" is part of a complex rote consolation offered to explain the absence of playmates to Eve and to help her cope with disappointment. Otherwise, dependency on immediate input predominates.

Sample 18 is the only sample in which there is no dependency on an exact model, and productions followed cues by intervals of 10 or more utterances. This implies analogic formation and also recall of the pattern from long-term memory. Similarly in sample 19, only the negation of the future morpheme appears fully dependent on a model or cue. The phrase "will make" in "That will make me happy" (Table 5) followed twice briefly after a model, but was first produced by Eve after cues only. The utterance "I will be a man" following the adult "You'll never be a man" seems model dependent because Eve omits the future morpheme in the absence of an adult model. The general impression in sample 19 is one of increasing independence from immediately preceding environmental support. Several productions can be termed spontaneous since the intervals from cues were so long that influences were unlikely.

Productivity in Verb Phrases   Perhaps most important was the considerable increase in different phrases in which Eve employed the formal future morpheme. In sample 16 Eve added six new constructions to her repertoire. In agreement with the conclusions regarding Table 5, it can be asserted that Eve was approaching productivity even if overall environmental support was still needed. This partial independence, in combination with general dependence on the learning context maintained by the mother, has been described infrequently in the literature. Neither cognitive, rule-based interpretations nor the learning–theoretical, rote-based interpretations have attempted to account for such phenomena. Adaptations of context-retrieval models (e.g., Raaijmaker & Shiffrin, 1981) or connectionist models (e.g., Schneider & Detweiler, 1987) might account for these. Descriptive rules need to be formulated that pertain to interaction processes and information utilization, but not for internally located competence or for a linguistic theory of the child.

DISCUSSION

The starting points of Eve's conceptualizations of the future were shown in Table 1, and all could be found in frequently used input formulas, whether "in a minute," "going to/gonna" plus verb, or "go get." Although these formulas were largely unanalyzed in Eve's productions, they were usually employed in appropriate contexts, which suggested an overall understanding. The form "go get" is semantically transparent, originally referring to actual locomotion. The form also expresses intention and is similar to the colloquial future morpheme "going to/gonna," and so it contained considerable developmental potential. Adults utilized this potential and responded to Eve's demonstrated readiness by increasing their use of future morphemes, initially, the acoustically similar morpheme "going to/gonna," and then,

Table 6. Eve's increased independence from immediate models and cues

Verb/phrase	Sample 14		Sample 15		Sample 16		Sample 17		Sample 18		Sample 19	
	Model	Cue	Model	Cue	Model	Cue	Model	Cue	Model	Cue	Model	Cue
Will/'ll make					0						2,2	6[a],0,1,0
Will/'ll come		71					9					
Will/'ll ring		2										
Will/'ll get	1				13	2		+300		3,21,33		41
Shall make	3											
Shall we get		3										
I will	0											54
Will watch			11									
Will/'ll be				5		56		1		37	1	
You won't			0									
Will/'ll go get						4						
Will take						126						
Will hear						64						
Won't wear					0							
Will go						14						21,53
Will turn						5						1,29

142

	Interval (utterances)
Won't see	0
Will read	11
Will stand	79 28
Will work	9,9
Will buy	18
Will see	+100 3
Will gone	1
Will put	6
Won't hear	0,0
Will write	0,1
Will walk	4
Won't blow	+42
Will do/undo	3,5

Totals

Imitation/cued[b]	3	2	2	1	3	4	2	1	0	11	15
Spontaneous[c]	1	0	2	3		2	1	0		5	3

[a] Interval between antecedent and production measured in number of utterances.

[b] Imitation/cued corresponds to model/cue.

[c] Interval of 50 or more utterances between a model/cue and Eve's production.

143

"will." This was shown in Tables 2 and 3. Equational devices provided conceptual clarification of the functional use of these morphemes. Input provided by adults was finely attuned to Eve's needs, both as immediate feedback and in frequency of use.

Tables 4, 5, and 6 focused on specific processing aspects and demonstrated Eve's prolonged dependency upon the verbal context maintained by the mother. Models and feedback supported the child, but even with such contextual support, rapid fading of morphemes occurred. Without such contextual support, production deficiencies were common. Nevertheless, Eve's productivity, indicated by the increased intervals between adult models or cues and filial productions, was demonstrated in later samples.

From a methodological perspective, exploration of interactional processes that result in specific performances needs to be emphasized, since it has been neglected, with the exception of R. Clark (1974, 1977). Investigation of these interdependencies can provide scientific support for cause–effect relationships and clarify psychological processes. Overly global correlational analyses, analyses of variance, or the postulate of a "language acquisition device" cannot demonstrate these processes. Processes and learning involve the temporal dimension and cannot be fully understood without incorporating this dimension into research designs. This dimension includes seconds and minutes as well as weeks and months, which capture both immediate interactions and cumulative effects. The standard procedure of performing two or more cross-sections at intervals of several months represents only one, possibly the least informative, aspect of this dimension and misses most of the processes.

From a continuous-time perspective, multiple influences facilitated and were reflected in filial productions. Though multiple causes cannot be proven to have been necessary, the lack of obligatory productions without such multiple causes, and the increased complexity of productions with multiple supports, strongly suggest the necessity of such causative influences on filial progress.

Multiple causation is to be expected when language acquisition is analyzed in detail because multiple processes are involved in language. Factors must exist that support the attention to and uptake of information. One is the privileged position in maternal input of many of the morphemes. Intonational emphasis and use of a full form during the first stages were other means to facilitate filial processing of the morphemes.

Factors that pertain to frequency and massing, followed by spacing, support long-term storage. Frequency phenomena have been demonstrated for both past- and future-tense training. A special aspect of frequency, the massed presentations of models and feedback, has been shown microanalytically in the tables.

Another aspect of frequency was found in the repetition of prosodic patterns, syntactic structures, and vocabulary. Repetition simplifies not only uptake and processing but also the transfer of information from short-term to long-term memory. Despite the promising work of Weir (1962), the extensive studies of Papousek and Papousek (e.g., 1981), and some excellent reports by Fernald (e.g., 1984), too little attention has been directed to prosodic aspects. The learning of songs, poetry, and poetic language (cf. Rubin, 1988) might provide fruitful analogies for the study of first language acquisition. Phenomena found in poetry initially contribute to the uptake of linguistic information in first language learning.

Cuing and priming seemed to be effective in eliciting the reproduction of stored information. The more dense the cues, the more likely the production of an item, even if an incorrect overgeneralization.

Since the filial reproduction is rarely perfect, there must also be factors that contribute to improvement and to storage of the improved forms in long-term memory. Parental corrective feedback has been shown to fulfill this function. Since the value of corrections has been largely denied in the theoretical literature, much pertinent evidence is needed. The general principle of maternal provision of corrections has been demonstrated by Moerk (1983a, 1983b, in press), by Hirsh-Pasek, Treiman, and Schneiderman (1984), and by Demetras, Post, and Snow (1986).

Learning and retention were probably facilitated by the positive tone of the interactions established through frequent confirmations with "yes" and by maternal imitations. Early language interaction is very much a process of "vocal communion" (Malinowski, 1923), serving to cement social relationships as well as to convey information. Language use is self-rewarding.

Major theoretical implications follow from the above evidence: Phenomena of learning and forgetting are encountered that are similar to those from memory research. The cuing and priming that have been shown to be effective in experimental memory research have similar effects in the casual verbal interactions between mother and child. Filial verbal productions depend upon situational support and are influenced by multiple variables, both contextual and, later, internal. The beginning productivity that was reported could have been based on improved storage and recall from long-term memory. With frequent input, rehearsal, and extended periods of learning, such improvements in long-term memory would be expected. Evidence that simple explanations of improvement do not suffice is necessary before postulating rules to explain this process.

The demonstrated sensitivity to frequency factors is relevant to theoretical controversies of whether filial performance is rule based or based on associative networks. Demonstrated frequency effects suggest an associative network approach (Rumelhart & McClelland, 1985. A third option, cue dependency, is suggested by the data concerning the impact of conversational context. Filial performance was unreliable, and obligatory contexts often did not elicit required forms. When a discrepancy existed between verbal context and what would be expected from rule-based performance, verbal context predominated. The dominant influences on filial productions were external, not internal. Admittedly, contextual influences, for example, if–then relationships, can be regarded either as stimulus–response relations or as rule following. Classical and operant conditioning could also be so regarded, for that matter, and the heated controversy might be quite meaningless.

Flexibility is an important part of contextual dependency, since stored phrases were adapted to changing contextual and conversational demands. The process of increasing productivity is a common feature of all skill learning (cf. Moerk, 1986). The principles of schema theory (e.g., Schmidt, 1975) are applicable to filial performance: Just as elements are changed in a skilled pattern, so the auxiliary was gradually replaced in the formation of the future tense, progressing from "go" plus verb, to "going to/gonna," and finally to "will." Human beings certainly acquire skills other than language in master–apprentice relationships, which are similar to mother–child interactions.

In brief, general psychological principles and learning phenomena seem to account fully for both the reported interactions and for Eve's progress in language skills.

Chapter 6

The Training and Learning of Syntax

In spite of our increasing reliance on rules as explanations of thought and behavior,
I do not know of any clear account of what rules are and how they function.
G.A. Miller: "Four Philosophical Problems of Psycholinguistics"

This chapter, similar to others in this volume, focuses minimally on theory, although the chapter is based on the theoretical paradigm of skill training and learning. As Bates, Bretherton, Beeghly-Smith, and McNew (1982, p. 12) poignantly remarked: "In both cognitive and social areas [of developmental psycholinguistics] theory has outstripped data to a startling degree." This applies most definitely to the field of syntax acquisition. Theoretical structures that lack factual support dominate this field. Factual studies of actual acquisition processes that demonstrate how information is provided by adults and used by the child are most urgently needed. Input and feedback must guide the child because languages differ not only in vocabulary and morphology, but also in word order and other syntactic aspects. The teaching and learning processes that result in the acquisition of language-specific aspects of syntax are explored. Further research might show that the same processes also account for the acquisition of syntactic universals.

DEFINING THE DOMAIN

No single chapter could cover all syntax or explore its total development. In contrast to previous assertions (e.g., McNeil, 1970), it is now agreed that syntax acquisition is not completed by 4 years of age, but proceeds even into adulthood. Chomsky (1969) provided the first pertinent evidence for this, and Nelson (1977) summarized the pertinent findings.

To permit detailed interactional and continuous-time analyses of training and learning processes, only the early, elementary steps in syntax acquisition are explored in this chapter. Two considerations argue for this focus. First, conceptualizations of syntax acquisition are still influenced by nativist assumptions, which need to be considered in data collections and analyses. Many learning opportunities can be found in a child's interactions with adults, so that innate bases would have to be searched for in the earliest stages of acquisition. Knowledge evidenced in later stages could have been learned either through known or unknown processes. Positive evidence is needed for knowledge that precedes learning in order to posit innate knowledge. This can only be found in the very early stages of the acquisition process, if at all.

If, in contrast, the earliest and central aspects of syntax are shown to be explained on the basis of demonstrated input and observable learning procedures, then it is difficult to build a logical argument for specific innate knowledge. This is particularly applicable to later modifications and improvements of a skill acquired earlier. Since extensive language learning and training opportunities are available throughout childhood in all societies, whether literate or not, such modifications could easily be learned. The only logically permissible conclusion for these later stages would then have to be that we do not yet know how progress comes about. Factual explorations are again needed to establish this knowledge. No armchair speculations can replace them.

Second, the earliest stages of syntax acquisition are important independent of the problem raised by nativist speculations. As with all skills, basic constituents and elementary routines appear first, and later learning and improvements are affected by the earlier acquisitions. Early roots represent prerequisites for later developments and strongly influence the processes and products of these developments.

Early roots are not themselves sufficient causes for the performance of, for example, a Nobel Prize winner of literature. Decades of conversational and literary input have contributed to such an advanced level of performance. Acquisition of an advanced level of performance is not within the scope of this work but needs to be explored to understand advanced language competence.

Stimulus Dependency of Verbal Performance

It is generally accepted that the language productions of the Nobel Prize winner, when he or she sits and writes novels, are generally independent of immediately surrounding stimuli. Chomsky has stressed this independence of language from stimuli. Yet the same Nobel Prize winner riding a train and conversing with his or her partner about the passing landscape is stimulus dependent. This difference in situations and resulting linguistic products, which seems to have escaped the notice of those who argue for the stimulus independence of language productions, prompts a different conclusion about a basic principle of verbal behavior. Almost any discussion of the here and now is of necessity stimulus dependent.

Young children live primarily in the here and now. Whether the young child manages to be as stimulus independent as the person writing a novel remains a question in factual research. The quotations from nursery rhymes and discussions of past and future events in previous chapters are examples of Eve's emerging stimulus independence. Instances of stimulus dependence are more common, and three types of stimulus dependency can be differentiated.

Dependency on Nonverbal Stimuli   This is stimulus dependency Chomsky (1959) argued against in refuting Skinner (1957). Early nursery conversations prove, in contrast to Chomsky's assertion, great dependency on nonverbal stimuli. Young children talk almost exclusively about objects they see and play with, about pictures in books, and about observed or remembered events.

Dependency on Verbal Stimuli   In denying nonverbal stimulus dependency, many psycholinguists generalized to an assumption of independence from verbal stimuli. In this context, even the impact of imitations was minimized. This led to a conceptualization of the "immaculate conception," to use H. Clark's term, of language competence, or to the generativity and creativity of the child in "inventing language" (Chomsky, 1959). The motherese studies of the 1980s have shown that this generalization too was incorrect. Training variables are highly important for language acquisition (H. Clark, 1975; Cross, 1975, 1977; Hoff-Ginsburg, 1985; Moerk, 1972, 1983a; Snow 1972).

Dependency on Literary Stimuli   Dependency on literary stimuli may exist, but too little is known to draw any firm conclusions. As Moerk (1985b) has shown, however, there are considerable preliminary and informal reports of influences derived from nursery rhymes and picture books. Chapter 4 in this volume raised the possibility that past-tense learning could be supported by nursery rhymes and stories, many of which refer to the past. The recent emphasis on formulaic speech may serve as an incentive to explore this field, since the formulas of young children often derive from nursery rhymes or children's stories (cf. Moerk & Moerk, 1979). This type of stimulus dependency might also be important in syntax learning because the strong prosodic patterns in rhymes and songs can support and reinforce syntactic patterns.

Syntactic Structures in Early Learning

The syntax produced by a young child is rather simple and consists of sentence elements and a few basic structures. In these earliest syntactic constructions, obligatory elements are often missing. This chapter focuses almost exclusively on Eve's simple and largely incomplete sentences. The basic obligatory sentence constituents of subject, verb, and object are emphasized, and considerable flexibility regarding conformity with adult linguistic rules is allowed in the definition of these constituents. Whether any specific constituent structure can be imposed on a filial utterance often is left undecided. Constituent structures are linguistic means of describing data and are not necessarily an inherent feature of utterances. For example, different constituent structures could be assigned to the same utterance.

The range of semantic relations observed in filial productions is considerable even in the domain of simple sentences. Brown (1973) has described these semantic relations, which involve both full-verb and copula sentences. This chapter focuses almost exclusively on the full-verb sentence, and this restriction requires a brief justification.

Although most linguistic theories group full-verb and copula sentences under the structure subject-predicate, there are linguistic and psychological reasons to assume that they are quite different. The linguistic differentiation was argued by Pike and Pike (1977). They presented evidence that a differentiation between what could be labeled an "object and attribute frame," reflected in the copula sentence, and a "human-action frame," the full-verb sentence, is predominant in Indo-European languages as well as in unrelated languages.

From a psychological perspective, the object and attribute relation is based on a recognition of objects and their distinctive features. The full-verb sentence reflects human actions that are generally goal directed. Brentano's (1955) "act psychology" and Husserl's (1965) "act philosophy" address this aspect. Briefly, if somewhat simplistically, the copula sentence reflects the human perceptual system because it refers to objects, their features, and their class membership. The full-verb sentence reflects the human motor system because it refers, at the most basic level, to actions and, at a more abstract level, to analogies to actions. The copula sentence is basically a form of labeling: "X is red," "X is a rose." The element "X is" is often replaced by deictic verbal elements or pointing itself: "Look at the rose." "See the kitty." Thus, the root of the copula sentence in simple noticing and labeling is evident. In Latin and other languages, the copula is frequently omitted, making the labeling function even more obvious.

The situation is almost the opposite in the full-verb sentence. Verbs dominate the full-verb sentence, and subject, object, and other constituents are their arguments. The verb determines the number of object phrases required, and if the subject and actor role fully coincide.

More important, from the perspectives of psycholinguistics and learning, only in the full-verb sentence does the syntactic function of each noun element profoundly influence its semantic meaning, as Bloom (1970) argued so convincingly. When the word "Eve" functions as a subject, it represents the actor in practically all early sentences, and it assumes a meaning not included in the vocabulary item itself. The same applies also for the direct object and indirect object. Grammar adds relational meaning to the vocabulary items in a full-verb sentence, and the child has to grasp this meaning from word order or morphological markers. Acquisition of the S-V-O structure is, therefore, of considerably greater interest than acquisition of the copula sentence that largely fulfills a naming function.

For clarification, a brief consideration of the meanings of "action" and "actor" as used in this study is necessary. Most recent discussions of the role of actors and actions in early speech rely on a narrow behaviorist conception of the terms actor and action. This conception presumes that only overt action defines an actor and that every action must be observable. This may be useful from a positivist perspective, but not from a phenomenalist perspective. As every reader knows, one can actively ponder a problem while sitting completely immobile at one's desk. Neither the infant nor the naive speaker, who employ language to express their experiences, have studied positivism, but both have shared the experience that simple listening and watching are absorbing activities. In this perspective, "I see it" is therefore completely equivalent to "I get it." Both involve an agent and an act that is experienced, even if seeing is a mental act. In brief, the "experiencer" described in many analyses is the actor in the following discussions.

Method

The following analyses are restricted to Eve's earliest syntactic productions, which encompass samples 1–4 of the transcripts established by Brown. A few examples from sample 5 are provided to indicate further developments.

The analyses begin when Eve was 18 months of age and extend for the next 1½ months. Eve's mean length of utterance ranged between 1.5 and approximately 2.8 morphemes (morphemes are largely equivalent to words at this level, since Eve produced very few bound morphemes). At this level, syntactic constructions that encompass subject, verb, and object are outstanding successes because they involve at least three morphemes. As such, their roots and developments are easily traced. Most of Eve's utterances consist of one or two obligatory sentence constituents. Since one-word constructions are difficult to specify syntactically, two-word constructions, and the structural and semantic frames that they establish, are the focus of the following analyses.

A variety of methodological approaches were chosen to capture the developmental dynamics of syntax acquisition. Eve's productions and the interactional contexts in single samples are summarized to explore cross sections of the developmental process. Longitudinal analyses across samples investigate changes in input and product.

Information about training and learning dynamics was derived from continuous-time analyses of sections from single hours of observation. These demonstrate phenomena of information uptake over recurring presentations as well as gradual approximations to adult models in the child's productions.

Microanalyses of utterance sequences, based in part on computations of transitional probabilities, show the immediate relationships between maternal training techniques and filial learning strategies. Specific features of methodologies are clarified as they are introduced in the tables. Actual utterance sequences and data reduction methodologies that capture more general patterns and dynamics are employed.

THE COURSE OF EARLY SYNTAX TRAINING AND LEARNING

Several roots of the full-verb sentence can be found in Eve's interactions with her mother. These antecedents, which were initially separate and independent from each other, soon coalesced as causative factors and as paths to the full S-V-O structure. Ideally, this should be presented as it happened in the actual flow of interactions, and this is approximated in several microanalyses. To present simultaneously all the causal factors and their effects in each instance, however, would contribute more to confusion than to clarity of exposition. The following discussions focus first upon the specific factors before the combined effects are considered.

Roots of the S-V-O Structure

The complete S-V-O structure is encountered in the first sample, and its form and the gradual changes are highly informative.

A "Narrow-Scope Formula"   Eve's grasp of the structure of the full-verb sentence is built in part on a narrow-scope formula, to employ Braine's (1976) term. This formula includes the three elements of subject, verb, and object, but "it" is the only element that can serve as an object in this formula. Subjects and verbs are also restricted. Shatz (1983) reported this type of extensive simplification in processing in her daughter's phrase "I did it." All three constituents are proforms, and all three are overlearned as well as very brief. Bates's daughter also developed a formula with "it" as a general filler for the accusative, although her sentences seemed intended as subjectless imperatives (Bates et al., 1988). Subjectless imperatives are also seen in Figure 1 and reflect Eve's early full-verb sentences. Input recorded in the transcripts contained many examples of "Can you do it," "I'll do it," and even "X did it."

In the first sample of the observation period, Eve combined the fixed object element "it" with several items in the subject and verb slots, and the pertinent constructions are summarized in Figure 1.

The formulaic nature of Eve's construction is quite obvious. Recalling formulas from memory in itself conserves processing resources, and use of the proform "it" avoids the processing demands of inserting specific referents in the object slot. All the verbs in Figure 1 are one syllable and all but one are frequently encountered in Eve's household. The numbers in Figure 1 in parentheses indicate frequency of use in the input in the first sample, or 4 recorded hours. These numbers provide an indication of the average expected environment in Eve's home and demonstrate that these verbs were used frequently. Experience with the transcripts suggests that the number of uses of "find" recorded in

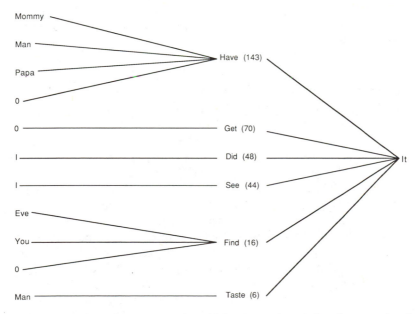

Figure 1. Eve's S-V-O constructions in sample 1. Numbers in parentheses indicate frequency of use in input.

the early samples is fewer than the number encountered in most samples. Trying to find things is a common activity and subject of discussion in this home.

The one exception to frequency of use, "Man taste it," is easily explained. The sentence appeared six times in one massed interaction episode, and Eve integrated it from two maternal models. One model referred repeatedly to the "man" (the observer), and the other consisted of "Does it taste good?" The latter model immediately preceded Eve's first "(Man) taste it." Eve's tentative formulation was immediately reinforced by a maternal repetition "I don't think the man wants to taste it." Here, the correction of truth value was clearly distinguished from the acceptance of the child's linguistic product through maternal repetition of all major elements. This led to variations of "taste it," and "Man (no) taste it?" Eve was so enchanted with repeating her new construction that her repetitions annoyed her mother. A somewhat impatient "Yes. OK. Change your record, would you please" finally stopped Eve's persistent exercise, and the phrase was not produced in later samples.

Nouns employed as subjects in these earliest S-V-O constructions obviously refer to animate beings and to actors, as the term was previously defined. The frequency factor is important here also because the actors were central to Eve's life. Detailed microanalyses would show in many cases that one or several adult models or cues preceded the filial productions in Figure 1, so that frequency and recency of input are major factors in these constructions.

The trochee in the second part of the construction deserves emphasis. All the verb-object constructions consist of one stressed and one unstressed syllable. This suprasegmental two-element pattern of the predicate might have provided a model for the emerging syntactic pattern that also involved the two major elements, verb and object.

To conclude this brief analysis, many factors, from prosodic features over a narrow semantic range to pragmatic importance and frequent modeling, facilitated storage of this first full syntactic structure in long-term memory. Immediately preceding cuing often supported retrieval, and the linguistic processing load was kept to a minimum through uniformity and familiarity.

Early Elaboration of the Formula   Table 1 presents the gradual elaboration of the full S-V-O construction from sample 1 to sample 4.

The acquisition process suggested by Table 1 is eminently plausible. The subjects, all people familiar to Eve, were engaged in a variety of activities directed toward an even larger variety of objects. Therefore, the need arose for Eve to encode these activities and their objects. This progress was achieved in two steps.

Table 1. Early elaboration of the S-V-O formula

Sample	Subject	Verb	Object
1	Mommy, Papa, you, man, Eve, I	Find, get, have, taste, see, did	It
2	I	Wipe, kick	Juice, ball
3	Lady, Mommy, you, I	Find, help, hold, read, get, write, got, shut, have, fix, drop, wipe, like	Celery, piece, door, that, cookie, coffee, paper, it, stool, pencil, soup, noodle, noodle soup
4	I, Eve, man, Mom (Mommy), lady, you	Make, change, gone, have, crack, peel, move, put, turn, want, got, sit, read, make, get, drop, write, see, climb, answer, play, wearing, banging	It, tower, pencil, paper, Eve, telephone, floor, hat, Colin, Frosty Snowman, page, spoon, nut, home, banjo, Eve-diaper, shoe, bouillon cube

In sample 2, Eve for the first time supplied two different nouns as objects of utterances:

E: *Oh grape juice.*
M: *Grape juice. Did I forget your grape juice? Well, I'll just have to get it.*
E: *( ) grape juice*
     Oh Fraser coffee.
M: *Fraser's coffee and Eve's juice, right.*
E: *Grape juice.*
M: *Oh, more grape juice*
E: *( ) wipe juice.*

Eve produced the utterance "( ) wipe juice." Shortly before this construction, Eve employed the words "grape juice" three times, once after an inaudible element that might have been a verb. The mother twice employed "grape juice" as well as the word "juice" shortly before Eve's sentence. By asking "Did I forget your grape juice?" and assuring Eve "Well, I'll just have to get it," the mother twice modeled a verb-object construction while referring to grape juice. These multiple antecedents functioned as supports for Eve's construction.

Similarly, Eve's "I kick the ball" was preceded by "Can you throw the ball?", "You catch the ball," and "(Can you) hold the ball?" An observer attempted to have Eve say "Catch the ball " and modeled this utterance three times. No immediate model of "kick the ball" was recorded, but note the acoustic, semantic, and syntactic similarity between "You catch the ball" and "I kick the ball." Two of the four elements are identical, "you" and "I" are equivalent syntactically and semantically, and "catch" and "kick" are one-syllable C-V-C verbs with velar plosives as consonants. Eve encountered multiple models for the syntactic form and multiple cues for the recall of the verb from long-term memory. Yet she also demonstrated productivity by inserting "kick," which was a verb not recently modeled.

From Formula to Flexible Frame   Little progress is evident in sample 2, but progress appeared suddenly approximately 1 month later in sample 3. Eve employed a variety of verbs and object nouns. These achievements were expanded in sample 4, and a further step in flexibility was introduced. For the first time, personal names appeared in the object slot. This might suggest a semantic restructuring because the object was not the inanimate object of action but more broadly and abstractly conceived. The schema appears to have become more abstract and syntactic and less dependent on the intention structure of agent-action-object.

Some doubts about Eve's achievement are raised by the situational context of the three sentences with personal names as objects. The utterance "(I see) Eve" immediately followed a model "I can see Eve. Hi." Obviously, this did not meet the expected felicity conditions because Eve was not standing in front of a mirror. The observer attempted to point this out by contrasting "I see Eve" and "You see Fraser," but without acknowledgment from Eve. The utterance "Mommy read Frosty Snowman" referred to a book title. The object noun was therefore a label for a book and no indication existed that Eve imagined it otherwise. Eve's "Mommy put Cromer" (an observer) and "Put Cromer" appeared in the context of discussing "Cromer shoe" and "Cromer shoe bye-bye," but it does not make sense as a verb-object construction since there was no intention to put him anywhere! ("Cromer" should probably be considered a locative adverbial since it answered the mother's question "Put where?")

These few examples were spelled out for methodological and substantive purposes. Methodologically, interpretations that focus on an utterance without considering its interactional, pragmatic, and semantic context can be very misleading. Meaningless imitations might possibly initiate progress, but they should not be confused with productive constructions. Apparently perfect S-V-O frames might consist of a vocative and a locative in the noun slots, for example, "Mommy see garden" would mean "Mommy, I see it in the garden" and not "Mommy sees the garden." Meaningless imitations and frames that contain misplaced constituents may, however, develop into correct constructions with further support and corrections. As in many instances of rote learning of surface forms, for example, the Pledge of Allegiance, mastery can proceed from surface form to semantic and syntactic analysis. Because the child deals only with surface strings in the input, this might be a common occurrence.

From the Parts to the Whole

Existence of the full S-V-O structure was demonstrated in Figure 1 and Table 1. Although the analysis indicated that this structure was derived from frequent environmental models, other causes, such as genetically programmed knowledge that facilitates learning, could easily be postulated as contributing factors. These other factors certainly could not be refuted by the evidence provided so far. The structural knowledge underlying Eve's products may appear to have arisen out of nowhere, or out of genetic knowledge, like Athena springing forth full grown from the head of Zeus.

The next sections are intended to correct this impression. It is difficult, if not impossible, to prove the nonexistence of any cause for an observed phenomenon. For a biologic event, an *elan vital* (Bergson, 1907) could be postulated, and "God's will" could serve as a causal explanation for all events. The epistemological principle of the *modus tollens* needs to be applied in order to remain within the realm of scientific methodology. If a cause is postulated to produce an effect, then the consistent absence of the specific effect argues for the absence of the cause. The following sections demonstrate Eve's structurally random combinations of words. Such random combinations should not have occurred if preexisting syntactic knowledge had guided Eve's more-word constructions. Factual evidence of probable causal factors is provided by demonstrating the maternal feedback and modeling that gradually imposed conventional structures on Eve's early combinations.

Random Constituent Selection by Eve and Maternal Structural Feedback   In the following sections, the absence of the S-V-O structure is demonstrated in Eve's utterances about human actions on objects. Eve's utterances produced reliable maternal modeling in the form of feedback, which provided a contrast between Eve's construction and the standard normally employed. This demonstrated discrepancy provided an optimal opportunity for Eve to gradually approximate the standard usage.

In Table 2, Eve obviously wanted her mother to read a book to her. A vocative (Mommy), verb (read), and object (book and book name) construction was required to convey the full message. All elements of the message were known to Eve, as seen from her utterances. But it is also clear that Eve did not recognize any syntactic constraints to produce full sentences. Eve employed a vocative-verb construction, repeated verb-object requests, a potential subject-object combination, and often expressed only one element, which was either the verb, the

Table 2. Absence of an S-V-O structure and maternal modeling

Sample	Hour	Utterance number	Eve	Mother
1	1	71	(Mommy read)	
		72–3		No, Mommy can't read.
		74		I'm busy.
		75		You read the book.
		152	Read the puzzle [repeated]	
		153	Read the puzzle	
		154	Rackety-Boom	
		262	( ) read	
		263		What?
		264	Read	
		265		Oh, you're going to read.
		266		All right.
		267		You sit on the corner and read.
		279	Mommy-book	
		280		Mommy's book?
		281–2		No, that's Eve's book.
		283	Rackety-Boom	
		284–5		Yes, that's Rackety-Boom.
		286	Rackety-Boom [repeated]	
		287–8		Yes, that's Rackety-Boom
		289	Read?	
		290–1		No, Mommy's not gonna read.
		292		Eve read book.
		293		You read the book.
		294	Rackety-Boom [repeated]	
		295	Read?	
		296–7		No, Mommy can't read.
		298		Mommy's busy.
		299		Eve read.
		300	Read choo-choo.	
		301–2		Yes, you read about the choo-choo.
		304		Mommy'll read later.
		305		I'll read to you later.
		306	Mommy [repeated]	

( ) indicate reduced intelligibility.

vocative, or the object of the full construction. These productions suggest that the various formulations were equally valid linguistic alternatives for her. The verb seems to have been of greater importance as suggested by its frequent appearance. The predominant use of the verb, however, might be explainable by purely semantic or pragmatic considerations because Eve was making requests, and requests are generally encoded by verbs in English.

The mother consistently provided learning opportunities adapted to the lack of syntactic constraints in filial productions. In Table 2, the mother provided frequent feedback with full sentences, largely S-V-O constructions, but also with copula sentences. Several closely related items of feedback were provided in response to a single utterance of Eve's. Those interactions demonstrate slot and filler principles, transformational relationships, and other linguistic aspects.

A feature of the verb "read," which applies to only a small minority of verbs, might have made Eve's progress in learning sentences with "read" more difficult. "Read" functions as both an intransitive and a transitive verb. This function was repeatedly exhibited in the feedback Eve received: "No, Mommy can't read," "You read the book," or "No, Mommy's not gonna read. Eve read book. You read the book." More intensive training might be required to clarify this exceptional feature of "read." Feedback was massed and the training and learning process extended over almost 300 utterances in 1 hour of observation alone. The opportunities for learning this pertinent linguistic request were abundant because reading picture books and being read to was a common activity in this household.

Eve had clearly not learned to correctly form pertinent sentences despite the impressive provision of information, so it is not advisable to postulate strong innate structural knowledge that facilitates such learning.

Noun-Noun Productions   The evidence in Table 3 is similar to that in Table 2, but is based on messages with a different illocutionary force and a different surface form. In the descriptive utterances in Table 3, Eve employed two nouns that referred to a readily observable person and object (demonstrating stimulus dependency), but she consistently omitted the verb from her constructions. In contrast to linguistic theories that maintain that the verb is most important in a sentence, in these examples, it appeared to be completely inessential to Eve. The perception of the objective environment seemed to guide her formulations almost exclusively. Even the extensive maternal linguistic feedback with models of correct constructions had no immediate impact on Eve. She persisted with noun-noun constructions over the approximately 200 utterances summarized in Table 3.

Eve employed in the constructions in Table 3 something similar to a "pivot and open" principle. "Fraser" filled the pivot slot in most utterances. The first two elements for the open slot were derived from models with "water" and "coffee" in the recency position. When this construction was established and repeated, Eve spontaneously added two elements in the open slot, "hat" and "pencil." After more extended training, she replaced the element in the pivot slot with "Eve," "man," and "Mommy." The gradual working up to encountered in pre-

Table 3. Constructing sentences from labels or N-N phrases

Sample	Hour	Utterance number	Mother	Eve
		109	How about a drink of water?	
		112	That's Mr. Fraser.	
		113	There, drink the water.	
		114		Fraser water?
		115–6	No, I don't think Mr. Fraser wants any water.	
		122		( ) water.
		123		Fraser water.
		124–5	Will you ask Mr. Fraser if he'd like a drink of water?	
		126		Fraser water.
		128	Mr. Fraser has coffee.	
		129	Mr. Fraser's drinking coffee.	
		130		That?
		131	What is that?	
		132	Coffee	
		133		Coffee
		134–5	Yes, he's drinking his coffee.	
		136		( ) Fraser coffee.
		137	Right.	
		138	That's Mr. Fraser's coffee.	
		160	Maybe your dolly would like a bottle.	
		162	Come see if we can find dolly's bottle.	
		164	Give dolly her bottle.	
		166		(Water) . . .
		168		(Bottle)
		169		(Water)
		170	Bottle?	
		172		(Fraser) hat
		173		Oh (Fraser) hat.
		174	What?	
		175		Oh (Fraser) hat. [repeated]
		176	I don't know what you're saying about the hat.	
		177	What about the hat?	
		178		Fraser hat.
		179	Oh, Mr. Fraser's hat.	
		180	Mr. Fraser doesn't have a hat.	
		181	He doesn't have a hat.	
		182	Would he like to have Eve's hat?	
		183	He would.	

(continued)

Table 3. *(continued)*

Sample	Hour	Utterance number	Mother	Eve
		184	Go see if he would like to have it on.	
		209		Fraser hat.
		210	Mr. Fraser doesn't have a hat, darling.	
		211	He doesn't have a hat.	
		212	Eve has a hat.	
		241		Man a pencil.
		242	What about the pencil?	
		243		Man a pencil
		244	OK man a pencil	
		245	No, that's Eve's pencil.	
		246	That's your pencil, you write with it.	
		249		( ) man
		250	The man's writing with his pencil.	
		251		Pencil
		252		Eve pencil [repeated]
		253		Man a pencil
		279		Mommy book
		280	Mommy's book?	
		281/2	No, that's Eve's book.	

(   ) indicate reduced intelligibility.

vious chapters was seen again here. Nowhere to be seen, however, was an awareness of the necessity to provide a verb in a sentence. One could even speak of Eve's "intransigence" against incorporating this element from maternal models.

No attempt is made in this chapter to completely describe all the maternal techniques of information provision. Such detailed analyses could easily provide the basis for a separate study. The points to be emphasized include immediacy of feedback and repetition, and the differentiation between truth value and grammatical information in feedback. The consistent substitutions also deserve special emphasis and have been explored by Moerk (1985a). The central importance of these for the abstraction of underlying structures from surface strings has been argued repeatedly (Kuczaj, 1983; Moerk 1983a, 1985a; Weir, 1962). The slot and filler principle for the three elements of the sentence, subject, verb, and object, was clarified for Eve by multiple substitutions. Toward the end of the interactional episode in Table 3, she employed "man," "Eve," and "Mommy" in the first position of her two-noun constructions. She had substituted the last noun consistently in earlier constructions: "water," "coffee," "hat," "pencil," and "book" filled the object slot.

Two additional maternal operating principles can be perceived in the feedback. The mother provided feedback that is as similar as possible to the child's productions. In this way, she lowered information processing demands for Eve. This feedback matching also had to reflect the probable intended meaning   that , in the case of a young child, is generally based on nonverbal situations and interactions. When the observer did not have water to drink, Eve's "Fraser water" was interpreted as "Fraser wants water." Yet in the case of Fraser drinking his coffee, Eve's "Fraser coffee" was interpreted as a Saxon genitive in a copula sentence: "That's Mr. Fraser's coffee." After "Fraser hat," the mother demonstrated both options, an expansion as a Saxon genitive and several variations of "Fraser doesn't have a hat." Semantic equivalence combined with syntactic differences, and syntactic equivalence combined with semantic differences, are demonstrated in this massed feedback. Although Eve is not ready to incorporate this information into her productions, the information was provided and some might have been understood and retained.

LEARNING PROCESSES AND PRODUCTS

Structurally Blind Input Dependency

In Tables 2 and 3, Eve's productions were guided semantically. She made requests that were conveyed predominantly by verbs, or she produced descriptive statements. Both types of productions received maternal feedback.

Table 4 provides constructions that demonstrate two distinct processing aspects: first, imitation, which was one of Eve's main approaches to learning, and second, the dominance of acoustic and prosodic factors over structural constraints in guiding her imitations. This table provides a few examples from an overwhelming diversity of instances.

In sample 1, hour 2, utterance number 149, "Write (a) paper" (a common phrase during this period) seems to reflect a verb-object structure, although the noun does not fulfill the function of the object in the model. "Change (your) record," meaning "Be quiet," in the maternal model was for Eve a meaningless imitation. "Later may" and "Later outside" are based on stressed elements in the model, and the latter is also based on primacy and the recency position. The imitation "Tapioca finger" is based on stress and recency. This resembles the noun-noun combinations in Table 3 that might have been subject-object constructions, but this example was derived from a modeled object-PPh construction.

These imitations are limited by Eve's predominant two-unit limit and not defined by any recognizable syntactic frame. To explain how

Table 4. Structurally blind input dependency

Sample	Hour	Utterance number	Mother	Eve
1	2	148	You go write on the paper.	
		149		Write (a) paper
1	2	399	Change your record, please?	
		400		Change (your) record?
1	3	134	Later maybe	
		135		Later may
1	3	632	Later we'll go outside.	
		633		Later outside
1	4	3	You have tapioca on your finger.	
		4		Tapioca finger
2	1	345	Let me put the fire on the coffee.	
		346		Fire coffee
2	4	105	That's the chair, not the table.	
		106		( ) chair table.
2	4	128	Watch your head.	
		132		Watch (a) head
3	1	22–3	Probably, yes. I think he is at home.	
		24		Probably home
3	1	98	Did you hurt yourself?	
		99		Hurt ( ) self.
3	1	117	Would you like two of those to play with?	
		118		Mommy two ( ) play with
3	1	147	You'll have to play with those.	
		148		Play those
3	1	301	Put Rangy on your lap.	
		302		Rangy lap.
3	2	1010	Well make up your mind.	
		1011		Make up mind
3	2	1082	Papa's gonna have his lunch in there.	
		1083		(Have) Papa lunch
3	2	1172	Good to eat.	
		1173		Good to eat.
3	4	949	That's the way.	
		950		That a way.
4	1	54		Sit by you.
		55	Yes, sit by you.	
		56		Man by you
4	1	97	Cromer didn't come to-day.	
		98		Cromer day.
4	1	164	You have pudding for lunch.	
		165		Pudding lunch
4	1	272–3	Be careful. Don't drop it.	
		274		Careful drop it

(   ) indicate reduced intelligibility.

163

innate syntactic knowledge could produce such constructions would be a challenge for any theorist positing preexisting syntactic information.

"Fire coffee" in sample 2, hour 1, utterance number 346, was obviously a repetition of stressed words in the model utterance. It was not meaningful in the imitation. In sample 2, hour 4, utterance number 106, "(   ) chair table" is imitated despite the model that consists of two coordinated clauses. Eve's utterance relies again upon stressed elements and possibly the word-final position in both clauses of the model.

"Watch (a) head" in sample 2, hour 4, utterance number 132, is almost certainly a semantically empty idiom since no evidence exists that Eve understood it. The principle of imitation of stressed elements observed a few utterances earlier again guides her behavior. This also points out a potential pitfall in interpretations of Eve's performance. Because parental models from which the child borrows were consistently meaningful and well structured, the blind semantic and structural imitations of the models could easily produce a false impression of filial competence. R. Clark's (1974) reference to performance without competence again comes to mind. Since most discussions of children's language acquisition do not include the immediate verbal context in the interpretation, their conclusions must greatly overestimate children's linguistic, as opposed to imitative, competence.

"Probably home" in sample 3, hour 1, utterance number 24, is a good example of two possible interpretations. From an adult perspective, the utterance could be rendered as "He is probably at home." More probably it was a rather empty imitation of the first and last words of the preceding adult utterances. Support for this hypothesis comes from sample 2, hour 4, utterance numbers 105 and 106, and from sample 4, hour 1, utterance numbers 272–274. Similar imitations are found in examples in sample 3 and sample 4.

In sample 4, hour 1, utterance numbers 272–274, the acoustic principles underlying Eve's imitation result in the utterance "Careful drop it," and the meaning is the opposite of that in the model. Factors of prosody, not meaning, are demonstrated again.

Earlier in the same hour Eve spontaneously uttered "sit by you," wanting somebody to sit beside her. The phrase was explained by her mother as a product of her models "I will sit by you." The "egocentric" (in the Piagetian sense) "you" was probably not really egocentric but was certainly semantically empty. Otherwise, Eve did not use "you" in this sample (4), with the exception of "Thank you," which did not appear to be semantically or grammatically analyzed. In Eve's utterance that immediately followed, "Man by you," she exchanges "sit" with "man" in the same three-unit formula, seemingly undisturbed by the difference in their word class membership.

These examples are not intended to deny the point, argued by Schlesinger (e.g., 1988), that children encode their intentions in early utterances. They certainly do, as the examples in previous tables indicate. Children are greatly helped in this endeavor by relying heavily on adult models, which often are also attempts to encode the child's intentions. Table 4 demonstrates the absence of syntactic constraints in filial productions, and even semantic constraints are less important than superficial acoustic and prosodic features of verbal input.

A logical truism underlies this evidence: Eve could have been guided by semantic aspects of input only if she were able to analyze it semantically. Because Eve, similar to adults learning a foreign language, was not able to semantically analyze new or complex input in normal, conversational exchanges, acoustic analysis guided her immediate responses. Acoustic features of language input are responded to first. It is a continual challenge for the mother to help her child not only to utilize these acoustic features of input, but also to use the input to lead to the gradual analysis of uncomprehended models, to the extraction of meaning from surface strings, and to the abstraction of underlying syntactic patterns.

Learning from Models and Feedback

Shaping Wishes into Predicates   Table 5, like Table 2, contains examples of Eve's requests. Here, however, Eve has adopted another way to express her request. This approach also required maternal guidance to approximate syntactic correctness. Eve relied on a constituent in the recency position in maternal models to formulate requests in early samples. Eve's mother often asked "Do you want more juice (cookies, pudding, or celery)?" Eve grasped the two stressed elements of this model and used them in her requests as "More X." This use provides evidence again that acoustic and short-term memory variables led to Eve's productions, not syntactic processing. Syntactic constraints should have led to a subject-verb imitation or a verb-object imitation, but certainly not a determiner-noun imitation. The determiner-noun imitation indicates that phenomena familiar from nonsense syllable lists were at work, not syntactic analysis.

Eve chose a learning strategy that was effective in a pragmatic sense to encode her message, and also in a linguistic sense, by selecting the main diacritical element, the object noun, which is "fortuitously" in the recency position in most simple English sentences. The linguistic result, however, did not evidence progress. The utterance was behaviorally effective by obtaining the desired "reward," but could result in learning and retention of a linguistic misconception. The two linguistic elements, indefinite numeral and noun, could be

Table 5. Short-term longitudinal training and learning processes

Sample	Hour	Utterance number	Eve	Mother
1.	**Interactional phenomena**			
1	1	1	More cookie	
		2		You . . . more cookie?
1	1	7	More cookie	
		8		You have another cookie right on the table.
1	1	9	More juice	
		10		More juice?
		11		Would you like more grape juice?
1	1	63	More . . . cookie	
		64		(You want) cookie?
		65		There's a cookie on the table.
1	1	85	More cookie [repeated]	
		86		Your cookie's there on the table.
		87		Did you eat it?
		88		Yes, you ate it.
		90		I'll give you another.
1	1	103	Milk	
		104		Milk?
		105		No, you don't want milk, honey.
		107		You've just had some juice.
1	1	143	Cookie	
		144		No more cookies, Eve.
		145		Later, we'll have a cookie.
		146		We'll have a cookie later.
1	1	316	( ) milk	
		317		You want some milk?
		318		We'll have milk for lunch.
2.	**Subsequent maternal models**			
1	2			You don't want (an) apple.
1	2			You dont want anything else to eat?
1	3			Oh, do you want a pencil too?
1	3			Oh, you want a letter on your arm?
1	3			You want more juice?
1	3			K. doesn't want a letter. No.
1	3			Do you want your diaper changed?
1	4			Because I want it shut
1	4			You want your bibby?
1	4			You don't want this.

(continued)

Table 5. *(continued)*

Sample	Hour	Utterance number	Eve	Mother
3.	**Eve employs "want X" in samples 2 and 3**			
2	1	11	More grape juice	
		12		More grape juice?
		18	More grape juice	
		19		Now be careful you don't spill it.
2	1	469		You want more soup?
		470	Yes.	
2	3	683	(Watch)	
		684		You wanna watch?
		686	Machine	
		687		You want machine? The machine?
2	4	877	More (cracker)	
		878		More cracker.
		882	(Want) watch.	
		883		You wanna watch?
2	4	920		You want a piece of celery?
		921	Yep.	
		923	Mommy celery	
		924		No. Mommy doesn't want any celery.
2	4	1016	Want lunch	
		1017		Oh you want lunch then. All right.
		1019	Want bibby	
		1020		You don't want any more sandwich?
3	1	670	(Want) 'nother one.	
		671		There isn't another one.
3	1	686	Want more grape juice.	
		687		No. No more right now.
3	2	510		You want a spoon?
		512	( ) napkin	
		513		You want a spoon in the napkin?
3	2	676		You want a cracker?
		686		Butterscotch.
		687	No	
		688		You don't want butterscotch pudding?
3	2	804	Want more . . . cheese sandwich.	
		806		More cheese sandwich?
		807		I'll give you another peanut butter . . .
		816	Papa . . . peanut butter	
		818		No. Papa doesn't want any peanut butter.
3	2	864		Do you want this peanut butter right here?
		867		Do you want your crackers?

(continued)

Table 5.   *(continued)*

Sample	Hour	Utterance number	Eve	Mother
4.	**Prolonged vacillation and gradual approximations**			
3	3	1018	Have spoon	
		1020		No, you may not have it.
3	3	1150		You want some more?
3	4	1044	No bibby	
		1045		Oh you don't want your bibby?
3	4	1050	Eve cheese	
		1051		Eve wants more cheese.
3	4	1090	Butter	
		1091		You want some butter?
3	4	1145	Mug	
		1146		You want . . . oh mug
		1147		You want it in this mug?
3	4	1181		You don't want it?
3	4	1208		Want your celery?
4	1	37	Mommy, more m . . . grape juice.	
4	1	159	(Want a) graham cracker	
4	1	457	(Want) a letter	
4	1	618	Want a page	
4	2	806	Want	
4	2	807	(Want) stool	
4	2	352	(I) want.	
		353		You want another one?
		375	(Want) 'nother one	
		376		You want another one?
		392	Mom . . . help	
		395		You want me to help?
4	2	418	('nother one)	
		419		You want another cracker.

(   ) indicate reduced intelligibility.

plotted on the cognitive elements, request and goal, and a determiner-noun construction could be learned instead of the linguistic verb-object construction. The mother's task, therefore, was to provide corrective feedback to Eve's linguistic performance while simultaneously providing positive feedback to her communicative performance.

Types of Maternal Feedback   To describe how the mother provided corrective and positive feedback, the important distinction in skill training between KR (knowledge of results) and KP (knowledge of performance) should be reintroduced. Skill learning research specifies two types of feedback. The achievement of a result (KR) is based on effectiveness of the performance. Positive results can generally be assumed in mother–child interactions, regardless of the child's linguistic level. The second type of feedback that concerns the quality of the performance (KP) provides specific information over the course of skill learning. Generally, performance continues to improve long after it has become effective (cf. e.g., Grossman, 1959). Frequent and specific linguistic feedback helps the child attain more advanced levels of performance.

Consistency and Variety in Maternal Feedback Table 5 demonstrates Eve's early attempts in formulating requests, the mother's consistent modeling and feedback, and Eve's gradual progress.

In early interactions, Eve's mother gave consistent but flexible feedback to Eve's use of the formula "More X." Consistency is found in the provision of a verb in feedback and by generally reflecting Eve's illocutionary force. Flexibility is found in the variety of verbs provided. It would have been a minor step if Eve had supplanted her rigid "More" with an equally rigid "Want." Consistent maternal substitutions in both verb and object slot increased the probability that Eve would abstract the underlying verb-object structure. She then could relate this across conversational situations and goals to other verb-object constructions, such as those in declarative sentences. Maternal feedback is also noteworthy for the relatively consistent omission of "More." Other determiners were used that supported the abstraction of the determiner-noun frame as well as the verb-object frame.

Consistent Maternal Modeling Section 2, Table 5, provides a summary of further maternal models with "want" in sample 1. Similar lists could be provided for the verbs "have" or "give." This summary gives evidence of consistency of pragmatically important input and also of the clear structure that repeated subjects and verb phrases and emphasized the open nature of the object slot. If all phrases with "have" and "give" were included, the slot and filler principle for the verb would be equally outstanding. Because the interactions involved Eve's wishes and requests, which could appear unending as with all young children, many similar models must have occurred outside the recorded situations. Nevertheless, little progress was seen in Eve's productions during this period.

Effectiveness of Training The effectiveness of maternal interventions depends on the time perspective used as the basis for judgment. Over the short term of 1 hour or even all of sample 1 and parts of sample 2, the verdict appears dismal because Eve rigidly persisted with her formula. Yet in sample 2, hour 4, Eve has absorbed the verb "want" into her vocabulary and she seemed to have made an interesting distinction. All her utterances with "want" refer to nonquantitative goals such as the actions "watch," "out," and "down," or to unitary phenomena such as "lunch" and "bibby." (For these constructions, the mother obviously did not produce models with "more.") To refer to quantitative goals, Eve still employs the construction with "more," for example, "More cracker." The distinction may have been semantic or imitative, because adults produced "more" only pertaining to quantitative goals.

A step toward further progress was apparent in sample 3, hour 1, utterance number 686, "Want more grape juice," which integrates Eve's old formula of an indefinite quantifier plus noun with the verb "want" in a linguistically correct manner. "Integrated," however, suggests spontaneity or even creativity but neglects maternal modeled constructions such as "Do you want more grape juice?" The conclusion that Eve imitated a longer sequence of a modeled utterance would be equally justified, and it might describe the psychological processes more accurately. This, however, is also progress.

Acquisition of the verb "want" posed a special difficulty. "Want" is employed in adult speech as a full verb and as an auxiliary verb. In these functions it pertains on one hand to the attainment of objects, and on the other, to the performance of actions either by the conversation partner or the speaker. At least three different messages can be conveyed through "want": "I want something," "I want to do something," and "I want you to do something." These distinctions may not be easily accessible to a listener with only minimal knowledge of the language. Conceptually, "Want pudding," meaning "I want you to give me the pudding," and "Want down," meaning "I want you to lift me down," can be considered more similar to each other than the latter would be to "Want play," meaning "I would like to play." Comparative analysis of linguistic progress must consider that such complexities could lead to prolonged confusion and slow learning.

Maternal models did not stop with Eve's early requests with "want " but were provided repeatedly with different object nouns as seen in Table 5, section 3. Further learning and rehearsal opportunities were provided for Eve.

Vacillation Between Constructions   Eve's progress was certainly not rapid. In many subsequent samples, Eve continued to produce noun-only requests, or enunciated the verb or verb equivalent so unclearly that it was not discernible from the tape. The examples from sample 3 presented in Table 5, sections 3 and 4, provide evidence of this. The phenomenon of "mumbled place holders" is especially interesting from a processing perspective. Prolonged input established a slot plus place holder, but neither the sensory pattern nor the meaning was sufficiently established to be clearly produced in motor output. This phenomenon is encountered frequently in skill learning and in learning melodies and poetry. One may know that some words are required at certain places in a song or poem, but can at best hum the melody without the lyrics. A vague whole has been learned before the constituent parts.

The old phrase "More . . ." is still encountered, noun-noun constructions show that verbs are not considered necessary, but verb-only utterances and subject-verb utterances with the object missing are encountered too. The performance could almost be labeled random from a structural perspective. In section 4, sample 3, hour 3, utterance number 1018, we find "Have spoon," which is derived from an adult infinitive construction "Do you want to have X?" The verb "have" also represented a filler for the eventual abstract verb slot. In section 3, sample 3, hour 2, utterance number 816, Eve utters "Papa . . . peanut butter." For the first time, a subject noun was included in a three-constituent request. The verb was not produced clearly, which suggests that Eve struggled to produce this more advanced construction. Note that the mother's feedback provided a model by accepting and expanding Eve's utterance but nevertheless denied the truth value!

Eve employed "Want X" more frequently in sample 4, as seen in section 4 of Table 5. In almost all instances this simple word was enunciated indistinctly, as indicated by the parentheses. Unintelligible elements that filled the slot of "want" were common in other productions, and this is slow progress indeed for such an easy and pragmatically central verb.

If this simple construction was acquired so slowly, how much maternal training and scaffolding would be required to train more complex and abstract aspects of syntax!

Intense Maternal Training

Maternal instructional efforts directed to syntax learning have to be extended and adaptable to the level of the child. Table 6 provides a glimpse of a larger domain of analyses by Moerk (1983a, 1985a) that concerned turn-taking sequences in the interactions between mothers and children. The analyses focused on the teaching techniques and learning strategies employed by the interactional partners. Table 6 presents sequences in which the mother provided concentrated linguistic information to her child in two successive maternal utterances within one conversational turn. In these utterances, the mother compared her first utterance to the preceding one by Eve or herself as well as her second utterance to her first one or to both her own and Eve's preceding utterance.

Two-utterance sequences are presented for samples 1, 3, and 5. (Equivalent data for samples 2 and 4 have not yet been established.) Both qualitative and quantitative data are provided. The qualitative as-

Table 6. Intense maternal training efforts

Sample 1		Sample 3		Sample 5	
Mother	Frequency of occurrence	Mother	Frequency of occurrence	Mother	Frequency of occurrence
2 - 25	8	25 - 25	13	2 - 80	15
1 - 6	7	25 - 28	11	80 - 2	12
6 - 99	7	28 - 25	9	29 - 25	11
80 - 6	7	25 - 23	9	29 - 29	11
6 - 27	7	80 - 2	9	51 - 51	11
80 - 2	7	80 - 25	9	2 - 27	10
29 - 29	7	27 - 27	9	80 - 29	10
25 - 27	6	25 - 29	8	25 - 28	9
29 - 27	6	24 - 29	8	25 - 25	9
29 - 28	6	80 - 29	8	2 - 25	9
80 - 51	6	29 - 29	8	51 - 29	9
6 - 28	6	28 - 28	7	25 - 23	9

Key:
1 = Simple imitation.
2 = Expansion.
6 = Incorporation of Eve's word into sentence.
23 = Breakdown sequence of own utterance.
24 = Morpheme perseveration, functors only.
25 = Replacement of major constituents.
27 = Frame variation, same meaning, different syntax.
28 = Optional transformations.
29 = Vocabulary perseveration.
51 = Linguistic mapping of situational aspects.
80 = Positive feedback, confirming force.
99 = Other, largely prosodic and nonverbal.

pect is reflected in the patterns, which can be interpreted by the table notes. Numerical patterns were chosen for presentation to make the pattern and the change more immediately obvious than lengthy verbal terms would. The quantitative aspect is given in the frequency of code patterns per sample.

The generally low frequencies for individual patterns are due to the matrix of approximately 40 maternal strategies by 40 filial techniques employed in the study. This resulted in approximately 1,600 distinct two-item sequences. Each individual sequence could be expected to appear infrequently in specific samples, and most of the 1,600 possible patterns never appeared or appeared once or twice. Compared to these random occurrences, the frequencies in Table 6 are high and significantly different from chance. Moerk (1983a) provides more extensive discussion of these statistical aspects.

Early Intensified Feedback A quick survey of the patterns shows that sample 1 is quite different from samples 3 and 5. In sample 1, code 6, "Incorporation of Eve's word into sentence," predominates in the most frequent sequences. The mother modeled how the child's one-word messages could be encoded in syntactic form. Code 2, "Expansion," and code 29, "Vocabulary perseveration," also appear frequently. The mother provided three forms of scaffolding extensively. First, she rehearsed vocabulary items (code 29), many of which had been recently introduced into Eve's active productions. Second, she supplied minor elements (code 2) that Eve largely omitted. Third, she modeled the standard of full sentences (code 6) in response to Eve's one-word expressions. She took the child's message and modeled how it would sound if fully encoded.

More complex syntactic exercises, represented by codes 23, 25, 27, and 28, were encountered more rarely in sample 1. Maternal emphasis concentrated on modeling sentences and rehearsing vocabulary items, in accordance with Eve's rudimentary level of language skills. (Her MLU was only 1.5!)

Early Advances in Syntactic Analysis and Pattern Abstraction A few weeks later in sample 3 the predominant patterns contain code 25, "Replacement of major constituents," which provides optimal opportunities for abstracting underlying syntactic patterns from surface strings. Invariances over transformations (Gibson, 1969; Jakobson, 1985; Moerk, 1989) provide the basis for pattern abstraction. Optional transformations were already modeled (code 28), and syntactic reframing (code 27), largely in exchanges between full-verb to copula sentences, also appeared. Strong patterning in maternal training also emerged. In sample 1, the most frequent pattern appeared only 8 times, but in sample 3 the highest frequency was 13. This patterning of interactional structures increased again in sample 5.

The most frequent patterns in sample 3 show that the mother related sentences to each other when she produced two utterances in one turn. In this manner, she compared similarities and differences. With code 25, similarities were maintained by syntactic structure and by most vocabulary items, and the differences exhibited by the substitution of one or two elements in specific slots. In code 27, similarities were exhibited by the retention of vocabulary items and the structure or frame was changed. Eve encountered much repetition with codes 23–29, which should have made the syntactic exercises easier to grasp.

Increased Emphasis on Minor Morphemes and Syntactic Innovation Sample 5 shows new as well as constant maternal input and feedback. Codes 25 and 23, which exhibited constituents of the sentence and solved the "segmentation problem" (Brown, 1973), were still common. New emphases are evident in the most frequent patterns, 2-80 and 80-2. Code 80 reflects a general "Yes" of agreement and confirmation, and code 2 reflects a correction when Eve omitted elements. This was an instructionally clever combination of confirmation and correction, as discussed by Moerk (1986).

Code 2 urged progress by correction, and code 51, by modeling. This code represents syntactic mapping of environmental givens, which is Quine's (1965) "radical translation." The mother showed Eve how to encode a complex environmental event or situation into a sentence, which contrasted with Eve's one-word utterances. The attainment of the sentence level of mastery is the major result of language acquisition during preschool years. This is also the center of most theoretical linguistic controversies. With this step, the mother progressed from an emphasis on repetitiveness to an emphasis on innovation. Vocabulary rehearsal, code 29, and repetitions of sentence frames in substitutions, code 25, still occurred in combination with innovation.

The selective data presented in Table 5 seem to provide persuasive answers to some old controversies. In sample 1, the mother used Eve's single words and expressed the intended meaning in a full sentence, or she modeled surface strings for known message contents. Intention structure and linguistic structure were well matched in this situation. In sample 3, Eve's mother focused on abstracting the underlying syntactic structures from the surface strings of repeated and therefore redundant sentences. This same technique partially solved the segmentation problem and the learning of kernel sentences. In sample 5, the mother encoded new messages in sentences, challenging Eve not only with syntactic analyses but also with the task of decoding the intended meaning. This maternal strategy trained matching of external and perceptual givens to linguistic structure. Codes 27 and 28 were the first steps in the training of transformational principles. In later samples, question–answer and demand–denial sequences were common. These provided opportunities to train higher levels of linguistic skills.

Certainly, the encoding of new messages, the abstraction of syntactic frames, or the handling of transformations has not yet been fully mastered, and the three types of training continued.

Verbatim Examples of Interactional and Instructional Dynamics

The interaction patterns presented in Table 6 succinctly demonstrated changes over time but suffered from severe evidence reduction. The patterns were, of course, embedded in interaction sequences and were tied to preceding and succeeding utterances. Table 7 presents verbatim examples of the interactions summarized in Table 6 to demonstrate more completely the syntactic exercises that were expressed in codes and to indicate, in part, some of the multiple links between utterances and themes.

Simple Substitutions of Elements in a Frame   Sample 1a. in Table 7 shows a simple substitution exercise matched to the early stage of Eve's language learning. Eve was learning the equivalence between her name and the pronoun "you." The immediate repetition of the same

Table 7. Intensive maternal syntax instructions in samples 1, 3, and 5

Sample 1a.	M:	That'll keep you busy.
	E:	Busy.
	M:	Busy, yes. That'll keep you busy.
		Yes. That'll keep Eve busy.
		There you write a letter.
Sample 1b.	E:	Man a pencil.
	M:	OK, man a pencil.
		No, that's Eve's pencil.
		That's your pencil.
		You write with it.
Sample 1c.	E:	Haebae?
	M:	Well you don't like it.
		You could have some if you liked it . . .
	E:	Eat it.
	E:	Mommy have it?
	M:	Yes, Mommy's gonna have it.
		[3 utterances intervened]
		I'm going to cook it.
		[3 utterances intervened]
		You wouldn't eat a wiener if I fixed it for you.
Sample 3a.	E:	Fraser cup.
	M:	Fraser's not drinking his coffee that way.
		He's not drinking his coffee with his spoon.
		Drink your juice out of the cup.
		You eat with your spoon.
		You're getting it all over you.
		You're spilling it on your dress.
		You drink it out of the cup.
		Fraser drinks his coffee that way.
		And Eve drinks her grape juice that way.
	E:	(get) grape juice cup.
	M:	You don't drink grape juice with a spoon.
		You drink it out of the cup.
Sample 3b.	M:	Eve, are you about ready to have your lunch?
	E:	( ) sugar
	M:	Would you bring the sugar here please?
		Bring Mommy the sugar.
		[5 utterances intervened]
	E:	A napkin
	M:	Will you bring the napkin please?
		Where is it?
	E:	(A) table
	M:	Would you bring me the napkin.
	E:	A napkin.
	M:	Yes. Will you bring Mommy the napkin and the spoon?
	E:	A butter
	M:	Yes, that's the butter.
		But you can't have it that way.
		You can have some for lunch.

(continued)

Table 7.   *(continued)*

Sample 3c.	E:	( ) celery
	M:	Yes, that's celery.
		Wait an' I'll fix you a piece.
	E:	( ) fix a piece
	M:	Yes, I'll fix a piece if you move out of the way.
	E:	Oh drop.
	M:	Oh what did you drop?
	E:	Celery.
	M:	Well get it.
	E:	I drop a celery.
	M:	Yes, you dropped the celery.
	M:	You put the celery right here.
	M:	An' we'll have lunch.
		I'll fix the cheese.
		You get the high chair.
		Won't you get your high chair and your bib?
Sample 5a.	E:	Eve jump . . . Mommy kitchen
	M:	You're jumping in Mommy's kitchen?
		Why don't you jump in the living room?
		You stay in the living room.
Sample 5b.	M:	You're gonna have some for lunch.
		Mommy's gonna make a goodie.
Sample 5c.	E:	There sugar Fraser.
	M:	Well, you ask Fraser if he'd like some more coffee.
	E:	Fraser more coffee.
	M:	Would he like sugar in his coffee?
	E:	Fraser more coffee.
	M:	I'll give him more coffee.
		You get your sugar bowl.
	E:	You sugar bowl.
		Fraser napkin.

(   ) indicate reduced intelligibility.

sentence frame conveying the same meaning with the same vocabulary items with the "you–Eve" replacement should have allowed Eve to process this information. "Eve" replaced "you" in a syntactic slot, so the slot and filler principle was suggested by this sequence. The follow-up sentence "There you write a letter" involved a change in syntactic frame, but was still connected with the first sentence through the pronoun "you." "You-Eve-you" constituted a brief rondo-like movement, but the conversation proceeded to a different theme.

In sample 1b., the mother shaped Eve's "man a pencil" into a full sentence, and also replaced the possessive determiner "man" with "Eve" and denied the truth value of Eve's assertion. The sentence was repeated with another substitution of the possessive determiner to simplify the processing tasks for Eve. In the first example Eve had the opportunity to learn the equivalence of a proper name and personal pronoun, and in the second example she encountered an equivalence of the Saxon genitive and the possessive pronoun.This was followed by a reframed utterance "You write with it" that was related through the "your– you" referential equivalence. Cases of reframing were common and they were expressed by code 27 in Table 6. The full informational value of reframing for the language-learning child still needs to be explored.

Multiple Substitutions in Longer Episodes Sample 1c. was more involved and cannot be fully analyzed. It was impressive how much training opportunity the mother derived from Eve's simple "Haebae." In the first step "like it," the object pronoun was clarified and corrected by avoiding the phonetic blending in Eve's utterance. The mother's next utterance established an alternating pattern: "have" (by Eve)-"like-have-like" (by the mother). Eve employed this substitution pattern with "Eat it" and "have it," followed by the maternal "have it-cook it-eat a wiener-fixed it." In a full rondo-like movement, the mother's "for you" at the end of the sample served to remind Eve of the maternal "Well you" at the beginning of the sample. The theme of eating, and the repeated references to Eve or "you," held Eve's attention. The multiple verb substitutions performed by both partners trained the slot and filler principle for the verb.

"Some" and "a wiener" were alternative fillers for the object slot that helped Eve transcend the formula that contained "it" (see Figure 1 and Table 1). Three items functioned as subjects, which demonstrates the slot and filler principle for the subject also. Contrasts in fillers and identical frames were used close together: "You have some," "you liked it," and "Mommy have it."

The transcripts indicated that the maternal correction of "Haebae" to "like it" resulted in improvement in Eve's enunciation of "it." Eve's accomplishment was confirmed with "Yes" and maternal imitation. The mother built on this accomplishment with parallels and changes:

Mommy's gonna		have	it.
I	am going	to cook	it.
You	wouldn't eat	a wiener if	
I	fixed	it	for you.

The last constituent "for you" was related to "You wouldn't eat it", and also the last clause "if I fixed it" closely resembled "if you liked it." Obviously, the two complex sentences to which these clauses belong were almost identical. If "have it" is labeled element *a* and the complex sentence as element *b*, the major pattern encountered in this sequence is *a b a a b*, interspersed with "eat it" and "cook it." Note that almost all the predicates are trochees and retain the pattern of stressed plus unstressed elements, which was presented in Figure 1 as the earliest full syntactic pattern that Eve mastered.

Balance Between Novelty and Repetition   Complexities in syntax learning were balanced by restricted conversation topics and retention of established and overlearned knowledge. Few elements were employed in the slots of Eve's sentences, and prosodic patterns often supported semantic or syntactic patterns, as Figure 1 indicated. A similar though less extreme restriction can be found in the examples of Table 7. "Mommy," "Eve," "Fraser" (the "man" in sample 1b.), and the appropriate pronouns were the main fillers for the subject slot. The semantic and categorical equivalence of these must have been relatively obvious to the young learner.

Similarly, objects in the object slot were restricted to largely real physical objects that were acted upon, played with, or eaten. Their pragmatic equivalence could be readily grasped, and their contrast to animate subject elements was maintained. Object elements were most often found in the recency position in maternal sentences. The verb pertained to obvious activities and was also frequently repeated in very similar frames. This provided multiple opportunities for analysis and learning. Finally, much of this intensive syntax training was encountered in connection with eating and drinking. This pragmatic aspect might have guaranteed Eve's attention to the verbal exchanges.

Increased Complexity Through Adverbial Phrases   Sample 3a. provides examples of increased linguistic and processing complexity that deserve attention. Four different elements plus the zero element in the imperative filled the subject slot, four verbs were used in the verb slot, and four nouns or pronouns were used in the object slot. The main innovation in this example was use of the adverbial, largely as a prepositional phrase. Various prepositions, determiners, and nouns were substituted in the course of this sequence. All the described information was presented in 22 utterances, which was a larger, if not overwhelming, information load. The many repetitions in syntax, vocabulary, and contextual support assisted Eve's analysis.

This is not to assert that Eve immediately utilized all the provided information. Vygotsky's concept of a zone of proximal development and limited filial information processing capacities suggests that much would be missed by Eve. This is not a major problem since mother and child have years of conversation ahead of them. As these examples show, the mother used learning opportunities extensively, especially to convey pragmatically important information to Eve. When the mother wanted to get her message across to Eve, she had to clarify not only the vocabulary items but also the syntactic structure. Otherwise, the child could not have understood her message. Syntactic disambiguation leads to syntax learning, which is a point often overlooked.

Maternal Building on Minimal Contributions   The episode in sample 3b., Table 7 is evidence of maternal ingenuity in building on Eve's constructions. The mother initiated the interaction with "ready to have lunch," which was well known and highly motivating. The vocative "Eve" served an alerting function and set the stage for multiple equivalences and differences. "Eve-you-your" represent equivalences, and the grammatical functions as vocative, subject, and determiner represent the differences.

After this impressive introduction, Eve's contribution in sample 3b. "(   ) sugar" was anything but impressive. This did not deter her mother. Eve's element was incorporated into a sentence, and a simplified form of the sentence was repeated in case it was too difficult for Eve to process. Lack of progress in Eve's subsequent productions "A napkin," "A table," and "A butter" intensified maternal efforts. The noun "napkin" was incorporated into a sentence that was repeated three times with minor variations and increased complexity, in the form of a double object, in the last repetition. The mother also used quite systematic alternation in auxiliaries with "Would you bring," "Will you bring," "Would you bring," and "Will you bring." This series was interrupted once with the simplified command "Bring," which clarified the message content.

Eve's "A butter" was confirmed and simultaneously corrected with "Yes, the butter." Then the reference was incorporated with well-known pronouns in two sentences. These two sentences were almost identical in structure, You-have-pronoun-adverbial, and they were also related by an optional transformation. They were obviously closely related in structure to the preceding "Will you bring." Auxiliary plus full verb were trained in various formations.

Maternal Responses to Progress   Eve's minimal linguistic contributions were stressed to emphasize maternal contributions to the interactions and to counteract the predominant assumption of filial creativity. Yet Eve obviously did show progress in her contributions to conversation, and her mother was alert to improvements.

Eve's success in producing the noun "celery," in sample 3c., was immediately rewarded with an acknowledgment and an imitation in the form of a complete copula sentence that represented a corrective model. The mother immediately proceeded to model a S-V-O sentence that incorporated a proform. When Eve provided a close imitation of this sentence, she was rewarded with another acknowledgment and imitation, with the addition of a subordinate clause.

Less accomplished productions received supporting feedback. Eve's "Oh drop" received a response that indicated "You forgot the object." When Eve supplied the object with a one-word utterance, she was prodded by a model that suggested "Form a sentence." These two hints resulted in Eve's almost correct and repeated sentence "I drop a celery." The mother responded to this achievement with the pattern of acknowledgment and imitation, or double positive feedback. This imitation, however, contained two unobtrusive corrections and was followed closely by a verb substitution. D-p-d in "dropped" became p-t in "put," with chiasmus and the repetition of the dental and labial consonants in the substitution.

The announcement of lunch at the end of sample 3c. introduced another intensive training opportunity. There are syntactic and acoustic parallels in these sentences:

| I | 'll fix | the | cheese. |
| You | get | the high chair. | |

The sentences have similar prosodic forms, and with "cheese" and "chair" we encounter assonance and a weak rhyme. In the maternal repetition, the structure was expanded through a second object. In sample 3b., the construction was "the napkin and the spoon" and in this sample, "your high chair and your bib." In addition to "high chair," "cheese" or "cheese sandwich" and "bib" or "bibby" were repeated in utterances not provided in the table. In stanza form this would be $a\ b\ b\ c\ a\ a'\ a\ c$ (a' representing the minor change to "cheese sandwich") or "cheese, high chair, high chair, bib, cheese, cheese sandwich, cheese, bibby."

These analyses suggest that rhythmic patterns were found not only within single sentences but also across sentences in interaction episodes. Further investigations are needed to provide more exhaustive evidence for those prosodic discourse patterns. Yet even without such focused studies, repetition and rehearsal of syntactic frames and elements are clearly evident in the data.

These detailed analyses do not intend to argue that a special instructional or "poetic" motivation was required for the interactions to be instructional. The repetition of content categories and the juxtaposition of frames automatically exhibited the structure. The intention of conveying a message was sufficient for the master and the intention of comprehension was sufficient for the apprentice. Playful resonance and some awareness of rhythms should not be automatically excluded from consideration, suggests Chukovsky's (1963) report on children's enjoyment of sound and word play.

Combination of Syntactic Changes   The examples in Table 7, sample 5 show that the mother utilized Eve's almost correct syntactic constructions in her substitutions. Simple frames were still trained, although more complex changes became more frequent. In sample 5a., continuity and change were combined by the maternal correction of Eve's trial and the substitution of the noun in the PPh and then the verb. In example 5b., "gonna have" and "gonna make" show continuity in the auxiliary combined with change in the main verb so that the auxiliary becomes the pivot. Multiple substitutions took place in this one step: The subject, main verb, and object were replaced, and the topic of lunch, the auxiliary "gonna," and the class equivalence "You" and "Mommy" indicate continuity.

In Table 7, sample 5c., the equivalence "Fraser" and "he" were encountered in the object and subject slot. The same referent appeared in another grammatical form and function as the indirect object "him." The noun "coffee" filled the object slot and reappeared in a prepositional phrase. Multiple elements were substituted in the subject, verb, and object slots, and the information provided was rich indeed. Again, Eve did not master all of it immediately, but the effects were seen. The word order in her first utterance was, at best, syntactically indefinite if not wrong, and her following utterances exhibited a meaningful word order copied in part from the model. Eve began to use substitutions, and the mother's "he" was replaced by "Fraser" in the subject slot. The noun-noun constructions "Fraser coffee" and "Fraser napkin," however, go back to sample 1. The old roots and overlearned formulas served as supports for Eve when maternal input became overwhelming.

As indicated by maternal support (code 80, "Positive feedback, confirming force" in Table 6), Eve was not expected to perform perfectly in very challenging tasks. Whatever she achieved was accepted and rewarded—and also improved on unobtrusively. Intense maternal syntactic instruction, exemplified here and more systematically in Moerk (1983a, 1983b, 1985a, 1985b), gave Eve many opportunities to acquire syntactic skills.

DISCUSSION

Syntactic structure, whether of the S-V-O form or the two-unit entity, the copula sentence without copula, presents structured information. Those structures are made very obvious for the infant, as 15 years of motherese studies have proven. Since these patterns are perceived, the question of how patterns are perceived must be considered first.

Pattern perception is a basic function of the nervous system in humans and many higher animals. Gibson's (1969) work on invariances over variations that exhibit patterns explains the sensory basis for visual perception. Rhythm and prosody of utterances is part of the sensory basis (cf. e.g., Crystal, 1973, 1986). Ehrenfels's (1890) work on "Gestaltsqualitaeten," arguments of the Gestalt school (Wertheimer, 1945), and common sense provide abundant evidence for the predisposition of the human nervous system to recognize and store rhythmic and melodic patterns. This predisposition is basic, because infants exhibit interactional synchrony 20 minutes after birth (e.g., Condon, 1986). This tendency is closer than anything else to a biologic basis for language training and learning.

As discussed in the conclusion of Chapter 5 of this volume, Fernald (1984), Papousek and Papousek (1981), Papousek, Papousek, and Bornstein (1985), and others have shown the intensively melodic and rhythmic features of maternal speech to infants. This chapter indicated that repeated prosodic patterns underlying syntactic structures form a model for their later abstraction in young children. Cause–effect evidence has been summarized by Snow (1977a). She reported in languages that permit flexible word order, the dominant filial word order, whether S-V-O or S-O-V, is determined by the frequency in adult language. The child's dominant order closely reflects adult, specifically maternal, dominant order.

There is, however, a profound difference between early pattern perception reported by Condon (1986) or Fernald (1984) concerning the attention infants direct to rhythmic intonation contours and the establishment of linguistic patterns. Infant attention to rhythmic intonation contours occurs shortly after birth and certainly within the first few months, but it takes at least 15 months before anything resembling syntactic patterns become established in infant productions. This slow acquisition indicates that language has few remote roots in innate tendencies.

Research on pattern learning is obviously important to language learning. In skill learning, the essence of skillful performance is the abstraction of a pattern that adjusts to changing contextual demands (Brewer & Nakamura, 1984; Holding, 1981; Schmidt, 1975). Sage (1984) formulated two central predictions of schema theory that are directly relevant to the data on language training and learning: 1) "Variable practice on a given class of movements will result in better performance on any unique variation of that same movement class." 2) "The acquisition of a diversified schema seems to be particularly relevant in learning open skills that are executed under constantly changing conditions" (p. 303). Variable practice was demonstrated in the tables of this chapter, and language skills are obviously employed under constantly changing conditions and need to be flexible.

Centuries of experience with skill training that began with the master–apprentice model in preindustrial societies, have shown that models and feedback provided by the master are the cornerstones for the perception, acquisition, and refinement of such patterns by the apprentice. Although mainstream psychology has not focused on these processes, the evidence presented in this work demonstrated the workings of the same master–apprentice relationship, the same modeling and positive correction, and the same massed and spaced rehearsals known from informal nonverbal skill training and learning.

Abstraction refers to invariant properties of stimuli that become perceptually salient when presented with other properties that do vary, and being invariant, they become stored in memory. Consequently, general patterns are much easier to learn than individual utterances because they are much more common. On one extreme, if linguists are to be taken literally, people creating an infinite variety of utterances would hear each utterance only once. On the other extreme, again following the dicta of linguists, if all utterances could be reduced to the subject-predicate structure, then children would hear the same pattern every time they heard a sentence. Based on these considerations, it is again astonishing how slow children are in picking up syntactic structure, while they discern, store, and recognize phonetic structures much earlier.

The cognitive analyses of schemas and schema acquisition in the research of Arbib and associates (e.g., Arbib, Conklin, & Hill, 1987; Hill & Arbib, 1984), in Piaget (1952), or Bartlett (1932) are applicable to syntactic structures. Bartlett argued the profound influences of schemas in memory and Piaget explored their construction and gradual differentiation and elaboration. Arbib and colleagues developed computational approaches to models underlying learning processes, specifically applied to language acquisition. These authors all argued and demonstrated the breadth and depth of influences from schemas, which can be acquired and need not be considered as innate. Piaget's (1980) debate with Chomsky on the psychogenesis of knowledge is most illuminating in this aspect.

These arguments were convincingly put forth although the authors had little evidence of how intensively adults train some patterns in their interactions with children. This intensive and effective training contributes to an understanding of how such schemas can be learned, or "re-constructed," and later abstracted through the process of reflective abstraction.

Chapter 7

The Transmission and Acquisition of Language Learning Strategies

Truly, though our element is time,
We are not suited to
the long perspectives. Philip Larkin: "Collected Poems"

PRINCIPLES OF LANGUAGE ACQUISITION

A growing consensus has emerged in the field of developmental psycholinguistics that "intuitive parental instruction" (Papousek & Papousek, 1977) and filial learning (e.g., Gleitman & Wanner, 1984) are important factors in first language acquisition. An emphasis on filial learning has prompted a focus on the cognitive and information processing devices that children may use in acquiring linguistic skills (e.g., Hoff-Ginsberg & Shatz, 1982; Snow & Goldfield, 1983). The roots and acquisition paths of these strategies, however, have gone largely unexplored. Chomsky's Language Acquisition Device (1965), with a nativist bias and strong presumptions of preexisting structures and against environmental input, has come under question. Bruner (1983) argued for a Language Acquisition Support System, which continued some nativist implications. Bruner's overall emphasis, however, accorded considerable significance to environmental factors and mother–child interactions (Bruner, 1981).

In a more radical approach, Moerk (1980b, 1989) proposed that "the LAD (Language Acquisition Device) was a lady" and that the mother performs the majority of the analytic, synthetic, abstraction, and rehearsal work for the young child (Moerk, 1985a).

Questions about this shift in emphasis to the mother suggest that the child is seen as too passive and that this argument approaches a behaviorist emphasis on environmental factors that disregards the constructive contributions of the child. Behaviorist conceptualizations are not fully satisfactory, and this work suggests a solution to this controversy. On the one hand, in some theories of first language acquisition, the child is burdened with heavy processing demands, but actual experience and research indicate that young children are not capable of highly complex learning processes. The poignant advice of Fodor, Bever, and Garret (1974) that "any model of the ideal speaker-hearer which is incompatible with whatever is known about the rest of human psychology is ipso facto disconfirmed" (p. 279) was disregarded.

On the other hand, the child's capacities are greatly underestimated in behaviorist formulations (Skinner, 1957) by assuming that very basic and universal learning processes of passive associations suffice for language acquisition. The findings of Flavell (1977) and other cognitive psychologists indirectly support this supposition. These researchers reported that preschool children do not spontaneously employ rehearsal strategies to remember arrays of items, and consequently perform quite poorly (e.g., Istomina, 1975). Since the children appeared incompetent and passive, a dilemma arose: Either the environment was involved in intensive teaching or, in the absence of such evidence, nativist conclusions were employed to explain the processes.

Multiple flaws exist in the argument that children have limited abilities. It is generally agreed that even infants are capable of information intake, pattern abstraction, and storage. Furthermore, the concept of teaching considered was too narrow, both in the behavioral and educational sense. Incidental teaching (cf. Rogoff & Lave, 1984; Warren & Kaiser, 1986) occurs continually. Moerk (e.g., 1985a) and others (e.g., Snow & Ferguson, 1977) have shown that similar informal teaching is encountered in the domain of language.

The conceptualization of filial learning was incorrect also. Children do not remain tabulae rasae who require that every bit of information be taught. Children progress in a developmental spiral and build on learned materials and skills. There is much "learning to learn" in this process. The more children advance in learning skills, the less fine tuned and direct adult teaching needs to be. At advanced levels, simple information provision is sufficient, and the child can independently analyze, abstract, and rehearse items that remain unmastered.

This chapter suggests and exemplifies the everyday mother–child interactions that model techniques for the child to manage linguistic material. Specifically, the chapter focuses on one child's acquisition of strategies to process linguistic information, or a "language acquisition device." To demonstrate these acquisitions and the mutual influences of mother and child, interactions of the dyad are followed longitudinally over almost 1 year, and incremental changes are demonstrated.

Since the study is based on one dyad and 1 year in the life of a child, it is obvious that the goal is not to test a hypothesis or to formulate nomothetic conclusions. In contrast, this study attempts to open new vistas and to suggest hypotheses for further evaluation.

Method

The entire range of Brown's transcripts, the period from 18 to 27 months in Eve's life, was used. Every second sample of the 19 was reanalyzed. In contrast to previous chapters that explored training and learning specific linguistic skills, the teaching techniques employed by the mother and the learning strategies used by the child are the focus of this chapter.

With this shift of emphasis to maternal teaching techniques and filial learning strategies, a brief clarification of conceptualizations underlying these terms is in order. Intentional instructional activities were not involved. The interactions resembled more a master–apprentice relationship, as described by Kaye (1982). The mother or master was concerned with "getting the job—of communicating—done." The child or apprentice was integral to the job of communicating, so the child needed help sufficient for the dyad to succeed. This skill transmission and acquisition involves an inseparable unity between communicative/conversational functions and teaching/learning functions. The instrumental aspect necessarily involves the informational one. For example, if a mechanic repairs many lawnmowers with the help of his apprentice, the apprentice will acquire information about lawnmowers, and if they repair cars, information is exhibited by the mechanic's work on the cars. While observing and helping, the apprentice learns how to use tools and how to take machines apart and reassemble them. The same principles apply to aspects of everyday cognition (Rogoff & Lave, 1984) and to the early acquisition of most aspects of culture.

The techniques and strategies that appeared frequently in analyzed samples and resulted in discernible trends are defined and presented. The analyses are based upon frequency data, and the conceptual basis of the analysis is found in bivariate time series approaches (e.g., Gottman, 1981). The coherence between the two series of mother and child, or their covariation, indicates either the degree of influence exerted by the communication partners on each other, or the equivalent effect of an external variable upon both. Lead–lag relationships in the trends, such as a maternal increase repeatedly preceding a filial increase, presented clear indications of the influence of the lead partner on the lag partner, which not only involved cause–effect dependencies but also concerned the direction of effects.

Continuous-Time and Quantitative Analyses of Bivariate Trends

Two approaches are employed in presentation of the data. Examples of interactions between Eve and her mother are presented from the transcripts to show that bidirectional cause–effect chains unfolded over time and to indicate the impressive rehearsals performed by both mother and child. These verbatim transcriptions also indicate how closely mother and child were attuned to each other. In subsequent sections, frequency data for specific techniques and equivalent strategies are presented for the entire observation period and the covariation in maternal and child speech is explored. The numerical and graphic presentations exhibit trends and shifts in the contributions of each conversation partner.

An Extended Training and Learning Episode

Table 1 can serve as a reminder that the probable causal influences in the course of the study are still somewhat undifferentiated. It is suggested that the mother's use of teaching techniques affected the child's

Table 1.   Introduction of the vocabulary items "crack" and "nut"

Eve	Mother
That?	
	Those are nuts.
. . . peel nut.	
	You want to peel the nut?
	Well, I'm cracking the nuts.
. . . (crack) nut.	
	No. You don't know how to crack the nuts.
(crack) nut(s) [repeated]	
	You can't crack the nuts.
	I'm cracking the nuts.
	I'm cracking the nuts.
	Would you like to have a nut? There.
There, . . . crack nut.	
	Why don't you see if the tinker toy would crack the nut.
	Go crack it with the tinker toy.
( ) crack nut.	
Eve crack nut.	
( ) crack nut.	
	Eve's cracking the nut?
( ) crack nut.	
(I) crack nut.	
	Did you, did you crack the nut?
Repeated in:	
60, 62, 64, 69, 93, 98, 101, 170, 173, 175, 188, 191, 279, 282, and approx. 450, 550, and 620.	56, 57, 61, 63, 65, 68, 70, 92, 102, 171, 172, 174, 176, 178, 180, 189, 190, 225, 240, 241, 256, 272, 273, 275, 276, 280, 283, 286, 287, and approx. 420, 440, 460, 540, 630, and 660.

(   ) indicate reduced intelligibility.

acquisition and increased use of equivalent learning strategies. (The term techniques is employed in the discussion for maternal interventions, and strategies, for filial, or Eve's, information processing attempts.) Table 1 indicates that the phenomenon of causation is complex and needs to be considered microanalytically.

Microanalytic and Qualitative Analyses The mother's introduction of the actual objects of "nuts" caused Eve's inquiry "That?", which resulted in the mother's label provision, which in turn led to the child's imitation, and so forth. Bidirectional cause–effect chains unfolded in which both causes and effects changed. The causes of immediate use consisted of a maternal nonverbal act and a label, and the cause of acquisition and retention of an item was the massed repetition by both mother and child.

Specifically, Table 1 presents the introduction of two new linguistic items by the mother, "nuts" and "cracking." Obviously, it cannot be asserted that the mother had never used these terms within earshot of the child. Eve's first two utterances, however, show that she neither knew the name nor that nuts have to be "cracked," not "peeled." The mother provided both items of information, and the second as a contrasting and camouflaged correction "You want to peel the nut? Well, I'm cracking the nuts." Eve immediately imitates the maternal model. This introduction and early rehearsal by mother and child were followed by massed modeling by the mother and soon by Eve's similarly massed rehearsals.

Interrelationships Presented Quantitatively The extended teaching and learning of these two items is indicated by the last lines of Table 1, where numbers specify repetitions of the same words. This is more clearly summarized graphically in Figure 1.

The curves for mother and child reflect occurrences of the vocabulary item "nuts." They were counted after the first occurrence to utterance number 300. After utterance number 300, approximate trends reflect the recurrence of the item. The number of these recurrences varied but was generally small. The abscissa is a logarithmic scale that expresses the flow of the conversation in utterances. The height of the curves expresses the frequency of occurrences every 10 utterances to utterance 300, and then the occurrence every 100 utterances. A pattern of massed training and spaced rehearsals is clearly evident in these curves. The pragmatic reasons for this pattern are irrelevant. Whether one frequently speaks a foreign language to get an "A" in a course or to survive in a foreign country, frequent rehearsals result in learning. The same principle applies to all skill learning.

Figure 1 also shows a close covariation between the frequency of use of the two communication partners, with the mother generally

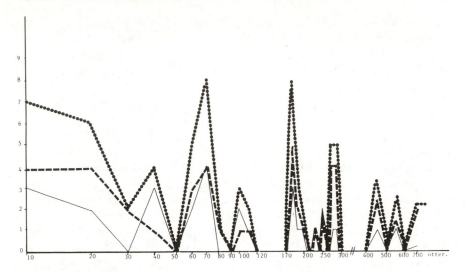

Figure 1. Massed training and spaced rehearsals of one new vocabulary item "nuts." (Broken line = mother's productions, solid line = Eve's productions, dotted line = total productions.)

having contributed more, whether in the early massed training or the later spaced rehearsals. Such close covariations were also reported by Moerk (1975). The importance of this pattern for initial learning and prolonged retention was established through experimental research in learning psychology (e.g., Estes, 1978). The early massing assured that the items were not forgotten between rehearsals, and the later spacing provided the reinstatements (Campbell & Jaynes, 1966) to ensure lasting memory.

Training and Learning Rehearsal Strategies   Figure 1, and, even more, Table 1, suggest an answer to the discongruity between Flavell's (1977) report that preschoolers do not spontaneously employ a rehearsal strategy when faced with a memory task and consequently perform rather poorly, and the demonstrated fact that preschoolers acquire many vocabulary items and much other information. The well spaced reinstatements by Eve's mother provided the rehearsal strategies that resulted in Eve's productive rehearsals. If Flavell's (1977) findings apply in the home setting, they suggest that Eve probably would not have spontaneously and independently employed such rehearsals. This suggestion is supported by evidence that the mother's absence in sample 19 resulted in a decline in the mathemagenic (knowledge producing) quality of the interactions. Yet, vocabulary items often referred to physical objects visible in the home, which might have sufficed as cues for spontaneous rehearsal of their labels. Environmental dependence may vary with the specific verbal skill: Vocabulary items can be elicited by nonverbal stimuli, but morphology and syntax are more dependent on verbal stimuli.

Long-Term Bivariate Trends in Vocabulary Training

The close covariation between mother and child in learning one vocabulary item needs to be evaluated as an exceptional case or as a frequent phenomenon. Figure 2 displays vocabulary acquisition and use from a global perspective.

Four Types of Vocabulary Training   The four categories, whose curves are depicted in Figure 2, are briefly defined. (The categories represented in this and the following figures have been more extensively described in Moerk, 1983a.) The category "Provides labels" refers to the act of naming, which expresses one content element, for example, "Cat" or "That's a dog." "Perseveration of vocabulary items" refers to rehearsal of new or rare items within a brief interval. Rehearsal of all new or rare items in each sample is reflected in the totals. "Asks for label" is self-explanatory and both the child's regular requests for infor-

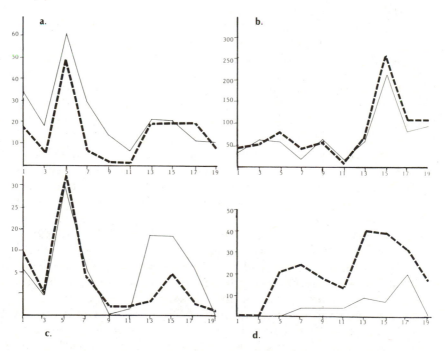

Figure 2a–d.   Techniques and strategies in training vocabulary items. **a.** Provides labels. **b.** Perseveration of vocabulary items. **c.** Asks for labels. **d.** Contrasting correction. (Broken line = mother's production, solid line = Eve's productions. Vertical axes = frequencies, horizontal axes = samples.)

mation and the mother's testing questions were included in this category. "Contrasting correction" mainly concerned vocabulary teaching and learning. For example, Eve might have said "Kitty," and the mother responded immediately, "That's a dog." The incorrect item was immediately corrected through feedback that provided the correct item. Rare corrections of morphemes and other grammatical phenomena were included in this category also, such as Eve's "Papa goed," and the mother's response "Papa went," but the overwhelming contributions to this total are vocabulary corrections.

Covariation in Trends of Mother and Child   With the exception of Figure 2d., the close relation between the curves of the child and mother is impressive in all categories, and the correlations range from .83 to .88. Figure 2d. differs for two reasons: First, the mother rarely mislabeled items, so the child did not have an opportunity to correct the mother. Second, the child at this age obviously did not know more than the mother and could not have corrected her mistakes.

Trends in Label Provision, Rehearsals, and Requests for Labels   The child had surpassed her mother in frequency of simple labeling at the beginning of the recording period, and the frequency of this for both child and mother tended to decline over the observation period. In Figure 2b., the mother led minimally in most samples, and the general trend was toward increase. Perseveration involves rehearsal, which according to Flavell's (1977) report, preschool children do not spontaneously utilize. Children ask for labels preverbally through their pointing gestures, as described by Bates, Camaioni, and Volterra (1982). Verbal requests for labels also appeared early, as Figure 2c. indicates. In early samples, Eve closely followed her mother in requesting labels, and the frequency peak occurred for both in sample 5. Not surprisingly, this is the sample in which providing labels (Figure 2a.) also peaked. In later samples, Eve surpassed her mother in the use of this strategy, though a declining trend can be seen for both partners, especially in the last two samples. Figure 2d. reveals that the mother surpassed her child considerably in the use of this advanced form. Furthermore, and in contrast to the first three categories, a clear lead–lag relationship is evident in Figure 2d.

Contrasting Correction of Vocabulary   Several aspects of Figure 2d. are theoretically and methodologically important. The mother provided corrections with considerable frequency. These corrections often involved the truth value of the child's utterances and would not have been denied by Brown and Hanlon (1970). Nevertheless, the field of developmental psycholinguistics has tended to deny (cf. MacWhinney, 1987, p. xii) or downplay the presence and instructional potential of corrections. It is an indication of maternal fine tuning that these corrections were completely absent in the earliest samples, that they rose between samples 5–11, and that the mother doubled her corrections beginning in sample 13. The corrections declined in the last two samples along with general declines in vocabulary training.

Another indication of a complex interactional relationship exists between long-term cause–effect relationships and short-term ones. The mother's long-term modeling of corrections was followed by a gradual rise in filial corrections (Figure 2d.). In sample 19, possibly foreshadowed by the slight decline in sample 17 of maternal corrections, a sharp drop in maternal corrections was accompanied by an equally sharp drop in filial corrections. Short-term cause–effect relationships seemed to predominate over long-term cause–effect relationships. Similar dynamics are discussed in the figures to follow.

General Principles from Bivariate Trends   The above interpretations need additional support. The ranking of strategies by probable difficulty may appear arbitrary, and no measures currently exist to fully support this aside from well-established evidence of the predominant sequences of language acquisition. An additional source of support for the ranking by difficulty is found in the data. The following figures, which present diverse phenomena, seem to reflect the same overriding principle: The mother modeled a language processing technique. The child gradually incorporated this form of processing into her repertoire of strategies. The mother then decreased her support, and the child surpassed her mother in frequency of use. This principle is realized in different stages in Figures 2–4. The earliest stage is found in the more difficult strategies, in Figures 2d., 3d., and most of Figure 4. With the less difficult strategies in Figure 2c., the beginning of 3c., and 4a. and 4b., stages of crossing over in frequency are observable. Eve has caught up and surpassed her mother in frequency of use of the easiest strategies in the easiest items, Figures 2a. and 2b., Figures 3a. and 3b., and large parts of Figure 3c.

The two types of evidence reinforce each other. The developmental sequence supports the postulation of developmental trends, and the general interpretative principle suggests a developmental order. Even if persuasive, these interpretations are preliminary hypotheses that need further evaluation. An evaluation is most important regarding the principle that the child acquires a learning strategy from the maternal model and becomes increasingly independent in employing the strategy in the process of language acquisition. The figures to follow provide support for this principle.

Long-Term Bivariate Trends in Simple Syntax Training

Four Types of Syntax Training   The category "Repeats own statement" refers to a meaningful utterance of several words that was repeated with little change, usually within the next five utterances. Syntactic rehearsal was necessarily involved. "Completions" are also known as vertical constructions (Scollon, 1976). Elements of one message were encoded in several separate and successive utterances, each of which ended with a falling intonation contour. "Build-up sequences" pertain to a similar but more advanced strategy where the speakers established the full message gradually. In this strategy, earlier elements were integrated with later elements in longer linguistic constructions. Figures 3a.–3c. reflect the child's rudimentary linguistic skills and her struggle to attain pragmatic and communication goals despite her limitations. The mother, in using the same stepwise constructions, simplified the task of comprehension for Eve and modeled the principle of sentence construction.

Figure 3d. may reflect more intentional, or metalinguistic endeavors. "Break-down sequences" in this figure reflect an analytic approach to utterances that successively eliminated words or entire sentence constituents. Sentence structure can be learned from this procedure without time and processing pressures because the utterance has al-

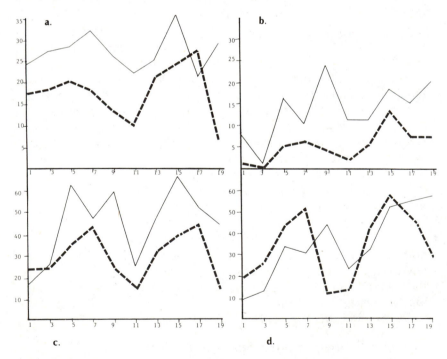

Figure 3a–d. Techniques and strategies in training simple syntactic skills. **a.** Repeats own statement. **b.** Completions. **c.** Build-up sequences. **d.** Break-down sequences. (Broken line = mother's productions, solid line = Eve's productions. Vertical axes = frequencies, horizontal axes = samples.)

ready been established. Build-up and break-down sequences were first described by Weir (1962), and the use of these terms in this work is comparable to that of Weir's.

Overall Bivariate Trends   Several trends are discernible in the relationships of the four categories. There was a clear interdependence between mother and child indicated by overall trends of the curves. The simple correlations range from .40 to .50. In addition, some indications of lead–lag relationships across samples appeared, especially in Figure 3d. If lead–lag relationships are considered for Figures 3a. and 3d., the correlations increase to .80. Interdependencies and lead–lag relationships would be more discernible with the elimination of minor "error" variations through curve fitting in the form of a cubic (or even a fourth order) parabola. There are too few data points, however, to permit this calculation. Knowledge of the transcripts and the microanalyses in Table 1 and Figure 1 indicate that the dominant pattern might be a sine wave of massing and spacing superimposed upon a linear trend of increasing mastery, which results in a progressively damped oscillation in the amplitude of the wave. Extensive analyses need to be performed to demonstrate this mathematically.

Long-Term versus Immediate Cause–Effect Dynamics   A differentiation of long-term and immediate cause–effect dynamics is suggested by a comparison of the massing and spacing phenomena to the overall learning curve. Immediate cause–effect dynamics, which occurred within single observation sessions, generally kept the frequencies of mother and child similar. Long-term dynamics, which occurred across observation sessions, involved a delay in the adjustment in the frequency of use of one partner. In Figure 3d., a sudden drop in the mother's use from sample 7 to sample 9 was followed by a similar drop in the child's frequency from sample 9 to sample 11. An equally steep increase in the mother's frequency of use from sample 11 to sample 15 was accompanied and followed by an increase in the child's use in samples 13–19. Immediate and long-term cause–effect relationships are seen to have reinforced each other. Similar phenomena can be detected in Figures 3a. and 3c. although the frequency curves changed direction, and cumulative trends were interrupted by short-term changes in interaction tendencies. Random fluctuations in the curves cannot explain the high covariations, with correlations approximately .80, if lead–lag relationships are considered. The lead–lag relationships argue against the exclusive influence of external variables, which should have affected mother and child simultaneously. In the case of lead–lag relationships, external variables might have affected the verbal behavior of one communication partner, which in turn resulted in changes in the other partner's verbal behavior after a delay. Multiple causation and complex cause–effect relationships must be assumed and will need to be traced through extensive study.

Decreases in Maternal Support   The four categories in Figure 3 suggest another interactional principle: When the child's frequency increased to approximate or surpass the mother's frequency, the mother decreased her use, often steeply. In Figure 3a., this occurred from sample 5 to sample 11 and from sample 17 to sample 19. In Figure 3b., this occurred from sample 7 to sample 11; in Figure 3c., from sample 7 to sample 11 and from sample 17 to sample 19; and in Figure 3d., from sample 7 to sample 9 and from sample 15 to sample 19. In the earlier recorded samples, Eve also decreased her use either immediately or after a lag, following a loss of maternal support. If the mother noticed that the child was not performing the linguistic procedures relatively independently, she steeply increased her frequency of use. This increase was followed by a matched increase in the child's use. In the last samples, the mother again withdrew her support, and this time Eve seemed able to maintain or increase her frequency of use above the mother's mean level.

A trend from dependency on available models to independence and strategic self-sufficiency is suggested by these curves. Whether similar principles exist in other dyads and how they are realized may be of great interest, especially because the field is now exploring information processing aspects in language transmission and acquisition.

Bimodality of Trends and Possible Causes   The pattern of longitudinal interactional fluctuations, or support followed by withdrawal followed by support, should be related to another overall pattern found in the figures. Most curves are bimodal for mother and child. The first peak was reached in sample 5 for vocabulary training and in sample 7 for syntax training. A second minor peak for vocabulary training was attained from sample 13 to sample 15. A second major peak in syntax training was reached from sample 15 to sample 17 and extended into sample 19. In easier vocabulary training, the mother "hit the mark" exactly, and Eve matched this peak performance in the same sample. The more difficult the challenge (Figure 3d.), the more the mother exceeded Eve's ability to utilize the input. The mother accordingly adjusted to Eve's decreased responses and lowered her input from sample 9 to sample 11 and then increased input, which led to the second major peak. At this time, Eve matched, or at least followed, her mother. This phenomenon corresponds to reports from the turn of the century regarding plateaus in the acquisition process (e.g., Stern & Stern, 1907). A possible plateau is reflected in Brown's (1973) MLU. From sample 9, to 10, to 11, the MLU merely increased from 2.68, to 2.86, to 2.89, respectively. In contrast, in sample 12 it jumped to 3.45, and from sample 6 to sample 8, it had increased from 2.03 to 2.58. (Brown's MLU indicates more plateaus or decreases than are reflected in the curves.)

Long-Term Bivariate Trends in Complex Syntax Training

Figure 4 represents longitudinal developments of complex syntax processing phenomena. These phenomena are labeled complex, in contrast to those in Figure 3, because they concern transformations of syntactic structures and the abstraction of underlying patterns from surface strings. Figure 3 presented the formation of sentences with additions and deletions, but with no transformations in structure or meaning.

Four Types of Complex Syntax Training   Figure 4a. focuses on "Replacement sequences" or substitutions of major content words in linguistic frames in successive utterances. For example, "The girl is playing" followed by "The boy is playing" and "The boy is running" illustrates a replacement sequence. Figure 4b. concerns a similar prin-

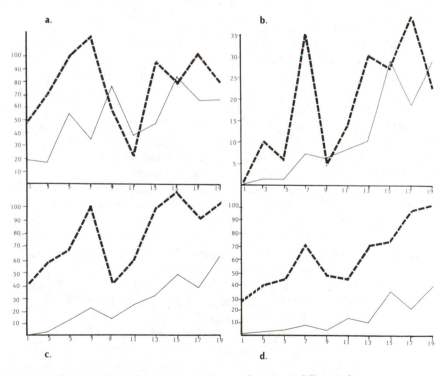

Figure 4a–d. Techniques and strategies in training complex syntactic skills. **a.** Replacement sequences (contentives). **b.** Replacement sequences (functors). **c.** Frame variation. **d.** Optional transformations. (Broken line = mother's productions, solid line = Eve's productions. Vertical axes = frequencies, horizontal axes = samples.)

ciple, replacing minor items such as auxiliaries, determiners, prepositions, or particles of separable verbs. Children focus on these "functors" later, so Figure 4b. illustrates a more advanced phenomenon than
Figure 4a. Figure 4c., "Frame variation," reflects full or partial repetitions of utterance content with extensive changes in syntactic structure. Changes from a copula sentence to a full-verb sentence were
common, such as "This is a rabbit" followed by "The rabbit is running." Frequently, the syntactic function of a single major element in
the sentence was changed. For example, "I prepare lunch for you" was
followed by "You eat your lunch." Major vocabulary items and the syntactic structure remained, which contrasts with Figure 4a., in which
vocabulary items were exchanged but the syntactic structure remained. Figure 4d. reflects "Optional transformations," as discussed
in the early writings of Chomsky (1965). Syntactic changes from declarative sentences to questions, imperatives, or negations, usually
within several successive utterances, were counted. The maximum interval for the assumption of a relationship between two utterances was
30–40 utterances.

Trends of Mother and Child　As in Figures 2 and 3, Figures 4a. and
4b. show an initial gap between maternal and filial use with clear indications that Eve began to surpass her mother in later samples. The
dynamics are different in Figures 4c. and 4d.,which represent more difficult strategies. The mother's steep increase was followed after two to
four samples by Eve's increase, although Eve was far from matching or
surpassing her mother by the end of the observation period. These figures that focus on complex syntactic techniques and strategies show
most clearly that the mother led the child in frequency of use. The large
early differences between maternal and filial frequency and Eve's minimal use of the strategies in early samples indicated the complexity of
the task for Eve. Nevertheless, the mother actively modeled these techniques, increased the use in response to Eve's use, retained a rather
consistent lead, and continued to model them intensively even at the
end of the recorded period. Indications of a plateau or decline appear
only in Figures 4a. and 4b. when Eve began to produce a considerable
number of these strategies. These lead–lag relationships were interspersed with simultaneous changes in both partners, which suggests
immediate cause–effect relationships.

Similarity in Overall Profiles　The most impressive phenomenon,
considering the differences in mastery of mother and child, is the similarity between the curves of both partners. This similarity was not
merely a function of the overall increase in frequency due to the child's
increased mastery. Almost all peaks and valleys in the mother's modeling were reflected, either with or without a delay, in the child's fre-

quency. The delayed declines are of special interest. Delayed increases are an almost expected function of learning, but minor declines in maternal frequency resulting in declines in filial frequency after an interval of two samples would not be expected. The process-based dynamics of these adaptations still need to be explored. Correlations ranging from .57 to .81 indicate the closeness of these relationships, which certainly is closer than normally expected in the social sciences, with presumably overdetermined processes.

These trends and those from previous figures strongly suggest that Eve learned to use strategies for abstracting and transforming simple and complex syntactic structures from her mother. These metalinguistic strategies are not necessarily implied in acts of verbal communication, perhaps with the exception of a minimum threshold level, which is evident because the total amount of communication did not change in any systematic manner over the course of the samples, while the use of techniques and strategies did change. The great changes that both mother and child exhibited in the use of these techniques and strategies suggest a clear effect of training and learning. As Figures 2, 3, and 4 showed, the mother progressed from teaching simple to complex skills. The child exhibited a process of learning to learn or learning to master metalinguistic strategies that was dependent on maternal modeling of the same techniques.

In Figure 4a., "Replacement sequences" or pattern abstraction, Eve twice surpassed her mother in frequency of use and was close to the maternal level by the end of the recorded period. In the abstraction of minor features of syntactic patterns reflected in Figure 4b., Eve began to surpass her mother in the last three samples. Eve was clearly below her mother in the task of syntactic transformations (Figures 4c. and 4d.) by sample 19. This is to be expected because structural transformations appear to be among the most difficult of cognitive tasks.

Cohesion in Bivariate Trends Expressed Statistically

It may have been difficult for the reader to estimate the closeness of the relationships between the curves for mother and child, particularly if overall resonance was combined with lead–lag relationships, as was often the case. Relationships between covarying profiles that were presented graphically are substantiated numerically in Table 2.

Comparing Profiles   Three aspects could be the focus of a comparison of profiles: the shape of the profiles, the level, and the emphasis, or scatter or deviation. Shape of the profiles is the main interest in a consideration of the adaptation of mother and child to each other's verbal behavior. The correlation coefficient can be used for these comparisons regardless of its weakness for comparisons of level and emphasis

Table 2. Covariation of profiles in Figures 2–4 expressed in correlation coefficients

Figure	a.	b.	c.	d.
2	r = .83	r = .98	r = .85	r = .66
				r = .82[a]
3	r = .08	r = .58	r = .57	r = .42
	r = .63[a]			r = .80[a]
4	r = .17	r = .57	r = .81	r = .79
	r = .61[a]	r = .79[a]		

[a]Coefficients computed with differential consideration of developmental dynamics and changes.

of profiles (see Cronbach & Gleser [1953] for extended discussion). Product-moment correlation coefficients are therefore presented in Table 2.

Multiple Influences on Trends and Covariations A brief theoretical discussion of system-intrinsic causal factors reflected in the profiles is needed to evaluate these correlation coefficients. External influences, virtually unlimited in their variety, are not considered but are reflected as error variance, or unmeasured influences that affect the profiles. Immediate influences of the partners on each other are the central consideration. Additionally, a cumulative influence of learning and developmental processes on the child's level of mastery was presumed. The child's level, in turn, was expected to affect the mother's input and feedback.

Finally, both the effects of maternal and filial influences could have appeared immediately or after a lag of one or more samples, and they could have appeared gradually or rather abruptly. If one partner changed interaction patterns suddenly, the other partner may have needed some time to adjust and change her own patterns. The less obvious the change, the longer the lag might be. These lead–lag cause–effect relationships occurred repeatedly. The child increased use of a strategy over several samples and the mother noticed the child's progress and decreased her modeling. Such trends could lower the covariation coefficient if these lead–lag relationships are not considered. (Any training–mastery dependency is, of course, lagged in that training has to precede mastery.) Lags between possible causes and effects have to be considered to capture such covariations.

Impressively Close Covariations Considering these complexities, the correlation coefficients reflecting similarities of the profiles might be expected to be relatively low. Table 2 shows that the straightforward correlations that do not account for lags and other complexities ranged generally from .50 to .90 with a peak of .98 for rehearsal of vocabulary items. This high correlation was due in part to pragmatic variables. A conversation about a specific topic, such as "nuts" in Table 1, led to the repetition of vocabulary items. In adult conversation, however, the vocabulary item would be replaced by pronouns and synonyms, which shows that even in this constrained conversation, pragmatic factors were reinforced by stylistic and mathemagenic factors.

Complexities of Lead–Lag Relationships   The straightforward correlations indicate beyond doubt that covariations in maternal techniques and filial strategies are not random. Even a superficial inspection of Table 2 suggests that Eve's performance in Figure 2d. lagged four samples behind the mother's performance. The exception was the sudden final drop in maternal use of the strategy that led to an immediate drop in Eve's use of contrasting corrections. If these dynamics are considered, the correlation coefficient jumps from .66, which was respectable in itself, to .82. This number suggests that approximately 65% of Eve's variance can be accounted for by maternal models generally after a lag of several samples.

The contrast is stronger using different ways of computing correlations for Figure 3a. Despite the visibly close covariation from sample 1 to sample 15, the ordinary correlation coefficient is .08, the lowest of all profile comparisons. A closer inspection of Figure 3 reveals that something special happened in sample 19 regarding maternal models. The models declined steeply in three aspects and leveled in the fourth. Comparison with Figure 4 suggests a shift to more complex forms of syntax teaching was taking place in the last samples. The new instructional emphasis in sample 19 might have been due to the mother's absence and Eve's interactions with her father and the observers. This partial change in conversation partners certainly makes interpretation of the trend more complicated. For a clearer picture of the overall trend, this sample should be excluded from the computation of correlations in Figure 3. With this exclusion and a smoothing of Eve's curve in sample 17 to eliminate the random fluctuations in the last three samples, the correlation of the maternal and filial profiles jumps to .63, which approaches the other correlations.

Figure 3d. suggests visually that Eve lagged behind her mother by two samples. The unadjusted correlation coefficient is .42, but is .80 when adjusted for this lag. The correlation coefficient adjusted further by computing only to sample 15 reaches .85. The contrast between the unadjusted and adjusted correlation coefficient is an impressive demonstration for the lag between mother and child. The contrast also indicates the importance of a flexible use of descriptive statistical tools depending on the developmental dynamics indicated by the larger pattern of results across figures.

A lead–lag relationship was already indicated in Figure 4a. by visual inspection, and it is strongly supported by the two measures of association obtained with and without consideration of the lag. The correlation is .17 without considering the lag and jumps to .61 with the lag. A smoothing of the profiles that contain smaller random fluctuations would result in higher correlations. Figure 4b. is somewhat more complicated. In early samples, maternal changes were accompanied by filial changes. The steep maternal increase that began in sample 11 and accelerated in sample 13 was reflected by Eve only after a lag in sample 15. If the delay in filial response is considered, the correlation jumps from a respectable .57 to a high .79. Again, the correlation would improve with smoothing of the curves of the last two samples. The correlations in Figures 4c. and 4d., with values of .81 and .79, could not easily be higher with a smoothing of the curves. In the most complex strategies, Eve seemed still immediately dependent on maternal support, even if her use of the strategies remained low. The contrast between 4a.–4b. and 4c.–4d. is analogous to delayed and constructive imitation compared to immediate imitation as argued in studies on imitation (e.g., Snow, 1983).

Regular versus Partial Correlations   It is obvious that the correlations and profiles discussed all reflect a trend related to Eve's increase in age, even if the trend is not monotonic. Some statisticians might argue that partial correlations only should be computed, with age partialed out. The answer to this is that age is a rough indicator of learning experience and therefore of competence. Age reflects maternal input, filial utilization of this linguistic input, and maternal feedback to this filial performance. The statistical removal of age would also remove the most meaningful factors that influenced the behavior of the interaction partners. Only the fluctuations around the larger trend would remain that are of secondary interest to this developmental perspective. Multiple time series are required to statistically separate developmental trends from other factors. Such analyses require larger sets of data points and will be presented in future studies.

DISCUSSION

The perspective of this chapter differs from that of preceding chapters and from the general perspective of first language acquisition literature. Eve's acquisition of strategies for handling linguistic material was explored, but not her acquisition of specific linguistic knowledge. The relation of this approach to other domains of research and theory is considered in this discussion as well as implications of this new emphasis for methods and conceptualizations to study language acquisition processes.

Four strategies for managing vocabulary and eight strategies for managing syntax have been presented developmentally. Vocabulary learning and retention depends considerably on rehearsal, as Table 1 and Figures 1 and 2 demonstrated. Vocabulary correction was encountered in Figure 2d. and in Table 1 with the differentiation of "peeling" bananas from "cracking" nuts.

Syntax strategies emphasized one basic invariance and three types of variation. The invariance was establishment of the basic S-V-O pattern for the affirmative sentence (Figure 3a.). Flexible applications of this schema became important before the pattern was fully established. Flexibility was seen in the number of constituents included in a sentence (Figures 3b., 3c., and 3d.), or in the specific constituents inserted in a frame (Figures 4a. and 4b.). These are strategies that pertain to phrase-structure training. Flexibility in transforming one configuration of a sentence into another (Figures 4c. and 4d.) resulted from strategies modeled by the mother concerning changes in syntactic structure.

The continuity of the instructional interactions deserves emphasis. When Eve mastered a specific skill or strategy, adults continued to provide further models to change, build, and analyze utterances, as the data presented prove. Extensive verbal interactions continued as the mother repeated known procedures and introduced new ones. The data in each figure from sample 1 to sample 19 indicate this repetition. The data in and across subsets of Figures 2, 3, and 4 showed the introduction of new strategies for handling linguistic material.

A consistent developmental function was found in the figures. The mother greatly led the child in use of a strategy; when the child began to employ the modeled strategy, the mother partially withdrew her support. If the withdrawal was too abrupt, it overtaxed the child's independent performance ability. In such cases, the frequency of the child's use declined steeply, often after a brief lag, until the mother renewed her support. This support led to a renewed increase in the child's use and rehearsal of the strategy until it could be maintained when the mother again reduced her support. These findings, so clearly demonstrated quantitatively, accord fully with Rogoff and Gardner (1984), who reported:

> The mother was often observed subtly testing the child's understanding by reducing the level of scaffolding and thereby allowing the child to participate to a great extent. But if the child indicated lack of readiness or failed, the mother quickly re-erected the scaffolding which she had momentarily removed. . . . Errors in scaffolding lead to recalibration and to adjustments of the rate at which responsibility is transferred to the child. (p. 110)

Rogoff and Gardner's report and the findings presented in this study both explain the exquisite fine tuning of maternal scaffolding that Bruner (1983) emphasized and that this writer has demonstrated in this volume and in publications that followed Moerk (1975). This chapter has shown that fine tuning applies not only to declarative knowledge or the actual linguistic items the child learned, but also to procedural knowledge.

Success in fine tuning led to a decrease in maternal modeling of mastered procedures and to an introduction of new types of procedural knowledge. This task sequencing was reported by Greenfield and Lave (1982). New strategies are trained until the child can maintain them independently. These phenomena reflect the developmental spiral or stage-wise progress emphasized by keen observers of child development. This finding does not neglect the importance of social support, but leaves much leeway for the child's productivity and constructive assimilation of socially provided information. As Piaget argued, a constructionist approach has much potential in explaining first language acquisition (Piaget, 1980).

Relation to Other Domains and Theoretical Approaches

This chapter has been concerned with the large domain of learning to learn. Four major subsets of this domain have been investigated. The first, learning set formation, derived from Harlow's (1949, 1959) research on the formation of learning sets by monkeys in discrimination studies. The concept of "positive transfer" in behaviorist psychology is relevant to this subset. The second subset, educational parallels, has been dominant in research on cognitive strategies and their training (e.g., Pressley & Levin, 1983; Segal, Chipman, & Glaser, 1985). The strategy training of this research focused on older children. The third subset, everyday learning, derived from cross-cultural psychological research, pertains to the acquisition of cultural skills as part of "everyday cognition" (Rogoff & Lave, 1984), in the course of "activities in everyday life" (Greenfield, 1984), and as a result of "adult guidance of cognitive development" (Rogoff & Gardner, 1984). Vygotsky's (1978) conceptualizations are reflected in this research. Research on skill training and acquisition (e.g., Holding, 1981; Sage, 1984), applied to the study of the acquisition of language skills by Moerk (1986), is pertinent to everyday cognition. Fourth, analogies from computer modeling involve the concepts of procedural knowledge (e.g., Anderson, 1983; Simon, 1979) and "adaptive production systems" (Waterman, 1970) related to procedures that facilitate problem solving and learning.

A few of the important aspects, some important differences, and a few conceptual and factual analogies from these domains to the findings in this chapter are elaborated.

Learning Set Formation Eve's generally increasing trends indicated that learning sets were formed. The content that Eve learned was more complex than that explored by Harlow (1949). Harlow's "interproblem learning" or learning set formation occurred largely in discrimination tasks and pertained, therefore, more to the domain of perception.

Harlow demonstrated that learning sets were formed readily in subhuman and subprimate species. In addition, learning sets were established creatively by Harlow's monkeys; that is, they were based on spontaneous abstractions from specific learning problems. Consequently, it should not be surprising that 2-year-old Eve, who received intensive support from her mother, could establish more complex learning sets. Eve's relative ease and spontaneity in acquiring learning strategies is made more plausible by these subprimate findings.

Educational Parallels A major goal of education is to train cognitive strategies to facilitate independent learning and to enhance spontaneous problem solving. This is most obvious in the training of mnemonic strategies that permit storage of a large amount of material (see the survey of Paris, Newman, & Jacobs, 1985).

Contrasts between the findings in this chapter and the main thrust of educational training deserve attention. As mentioned, most of the educational studies concern elementary school–age or older children. Generalization of specific procedures to a 2-year-old is therefore questionable. Furthermore, educational strategy training is planned and intentional. As revealed by the analyses in this chapter, this was usually not the case with Eve's mother. When children in educational studies employed the strategies, they were generally faced with a clearly defined task, for example, to remember a number of items from a brief learning period. The demands of the task defined a narrow means–end relationship. This is usually not the case in everyday verbal mother–child interactions and in language development. In these respects, Warren and Kaiser's (1986) excellent discussion of incidental teaching and Reber's research program on implicit learning (Reber, 1967, 1976) are more pertinent.

Considering these differences, caution needs to be employed in relating procedures and findings of these two domains. Yet the overall principle that mastery of learning strategies is conducive to later learning has been fully supported in literature concerning education (e.g., Segal et al., 1985). It has also been shown that strategies can be trained through social guidance. In education, as in first language acquisition, successful social guidance can turn passive learners into active processors of information. With guidance, trainees can use strategies of rehearsal, analysis, synthesis, and abstraction to master and incorporate the abundant information that is provided in educational settings and daily life.

Correspondence to Everyday Learning   Closer to the situation of Eve and her mother are studies exploring the acquisition of cognitive skills in everyday mother–child interactions. Based on the conceptualizations of Vygotsky (1978), these studies emphasized social guidance without presuming deliberate instruction. Several studies specified that mothers were unaware of the function of their guidance and asserted that the children were "learning by themselves" (Greenfield & Lave, 1982) despite the adults' responsiveness to the children's needs for scaffolding or independence. The adults maintain a consistently manageable level of difficulty for the learner, so that the child can learn by him- or herself.

These everyday learning studies profoundly changed conceptions of the roles of learner and instructor. Although the child imitates and uses adult models and scaffolding, the child is not merely a passive learner. Declarative knowledge is acquired through immediate behavior in a somewhat passive manner. Learning strategies, however, are abstracted, which make the child independent and creative. These studies demonstrated a combination of passivity and creativity that confounded the researchers who considered these features as mutually exclusive. In this respect, everyday learning of cultural skills is closer to the learning set formation of Harlow's monkeys than to intentional educational strategy teaching. Everyday learning is also a subset of the broader domain of skill learning, with the progression from dependency on environmental support to independent utilization of mastered skills. Much of skill learning is "automatic," proceeding without fully conscious awareness (cf. Polanyi, 1958). Everyday skills might seem to grow by themselves if the interactional dynamics that support their development are not carefully explored.

Specifications in Computer Modeling   Research in computer modeling provides a complement to these studies. Procedural and declarative aspects can be carefully distinguished and learning mechanisms described in a fully operational way. The nature and relationships of learning mechanisms can be explored when these have been differentiated for specific developmental stages. Flavell (1970) has shown that this differentiation is very important by his discussion of "strategy production deficiencies." This argues that strategies may exist but are not employed for specific tasks, which is a deficiency that may prevent the acquisition of declarative knowledge.

Anderson (1983), in differentiating declarative and procedural aspects, argued for stages in cognitive skill acquisition, with each skill proceeding from declarative knowledge to procedural knowledge. This seems generally the case in adult problem solving, that is, in the development of expertise. Rumelhart and Norman (1981), however, focused on the complexity of the relationship and argued that "all the data can be viewed as either data or process" (p. 243), as either declarative or procedural knowledge. Interpretation depends on the task. Their proposal, "that all knowledge is properly considered as KNOWL-EDGE HOW but that the system can sometimes interrogate this knowledge to produce KNOWLEDGE THAT" (p. 243), is especially important for the data presented in this chapter.

These considerations apply to Eve's performance. As the data showed, Eve engaged in procedures of repetitions, abstractions, or transformations (Figures 2–4). Yet it would be difficult to specify in what sense she had declarative knowledge. It appears that procedural knowledge may be acquired before declarative knowledge when learning takes place through imitation of models. "Knowledge how" to use strategies seems to come before "knowledge that" in Eve's development.

The reported findings suggest that the linguistic skills were the declarative knowledge, and the learning strategies, the procedural knowledge. Yet, linguistic skills are procedures employed to convey messages. In the communicative situation, the messages conveyed are the declarative knowledge and the linguistic skills are the procedures employed. As Langley and Simon (1981) expounded, layers of procedural knowledge are involved in learning by doing. Weak general methods (such as Eve's repetitions) are used to perform a task (maintaining a vocal interaction). Solutions to these tasks (listening to, producing, and storing maternal sound patterns) provide information to the learning mechanism for creating new productions (the strategies) that enable the learner to build more powerful solution procedures (the verbal skills).

Decades of research will be required to disentangle, conceptually and factually, these interwoven phenomena in actual life and learning situations. The developmental relations between declarative knowledge and procedural knowledge are of great importance, particularly because complex procedural knowledge may not be achieved automatically by all learners. Differentiation of types of declarative knowledge, such as the knowledge of simple facts versus the knowledge of rules, might also prove helpful in the clarification of these relationships.

Theoretical Implications

On one level, the data have implications for all aspects and theories of first language acquisition. A new theory could be built on this approach, but this is not attempted here. The present findings do, however, have the potential to resolve a basic controversy in the field of language acquisition. Much emphasis has been placed on children's linguistic creativity and the insufficiency of specific input and teaching to account for language acquisition. One answer, presented in Chapters 2–6 of this volume, in other studies of this writer (e.g., Moerk, 1972, 1976, 1983a, 1985a, 1985b), and in studies of other researchers (Bruner, 1983; Snow & Ferguson, 1977) is that input is much richer and more fine tuned to filial learning and communication needs than was ever imagined. The second and perhaps more profound answer is found in the results of this chapter that agree with previous emphases that children are creative. Children create information by operating (in the Piagetian sense) on linguistic material. This information is neither innate nor does it derive directly from input alone. It is derived from simple abstraction and reflective abstraction, in the Piagetian sense. Children learn the procedures, or required strategies, to be creative by observing their mothers and other adults perform similar operations. For example, when a child has been shown the basic principle of throwing a stone and has been provided with a large assortment of them, he or she can train and perfect his or her throwing independently and create variations of the learned behavior. Continued scaffolding is necessary only to prepare for high levels of skill.

Chukovsky's (1963) and Garvey's (1977) reports on children's linguistic play demonstrated how spontaneously and joyfully preschoolers experiment with linguistic material. Weir (1962) has also demonstrated this for a younger child. Supporting the dependence on scaffolding, Weir and others noted that the complexity of independent language play declined steeply in the absence of adult support. Such a decline was seen also in the figures in this chapter.

Besides this general implication, two consequences derived from the findings are emphasized, the first a substantive implication and the second, methodological.

A Substantive Implication   Anderson's (1983) ACT* theory stipulates that interaction with environmental stimuli over long periods is required to produce effective performance. More generally, Langley and Simon (1981) emphasized "the vast amount of learning necessary for acquiring [even] recognition skills" (p. 369), and stressed that "expert systems rest solidly on a large data base," and that "expert performance requires large amounts of knowledge" (p. 363). This principle would seem to apply for anyone to be an expert in a language, whether a first or second language. The amount of information available and frequency of provision and use would seem to be of utmost importance.

This has been clearly recognized in second language training but has been disregarded and even denied in first language acquisition. Based on these considerations, input frequency, rehearsals, and variations in input and feedback that allow the learner to abstract invariances and relate them to observed variations should be carefully considered. These phenomena, repeatedly demonstrated by this writer (e.g., Moerk, 1980a, 1980b, 1983a, 1983b, 1985a, 1985b), are still neglected in theories of learnability. The rich affordances of the linguistic environment need to be considered in their interactions with the evolving learning strategies of children.

A Methodological Implication Vygotsky (1978) stressed that "the transformation of an interpersonal process into an intrapersonal one is the result of a long series of developmental events" (p. 57). Anderson's (1983) ACT* system required interaction with environmental stimuli over long periods. Without studying constancy and change in the stimuli or input, or exploring the evolving competency in declarative and procedural knowledge, no real understanding of the acquisition process is possible. Explorations of processes, however, require truly longitudinal methodology.

The phenomena discernible in the bivariate time series earlier in this chapter indicate the methodological pitfalls if continuous-time longitudinal data are not employed. Positive covariation as well as negative covariation, or even a complete lack of covariation could be found, depending on the intervals chosen. Measurements made at the same times did not give a true picture of the covariations and the changing cause–effect dynamics because of the lead–lag relationships. Logically, they could not since competence appears after input and after repeated training opportunities. The interval between the first instances of input and the appearance of competence depends on the difficulty of the learning task, the competency of the learner, and the support of the environmental scaffolding. To quote Langley and Simon's (1981) concise formulation: "A benign environment [the instructor] can provide precisely the information that will facilitate the acquisition of the next increment of skill. . . . An adaptive production system will learn rapidly or slowly, depending on the order in which problems are presented" (p. 375). In psychological terminology, this means that optimal task sequencing, fine tuning with changing parameters across time, and the amount and consistency of information provision are important. They vary as a function of the developmental progress of the learner.

Because individual dyads are the interacting systems of interest in this study, idiosyncratic approaches must be employed since commonly used statistical methods reflect aggregates only. This does not preclude statistical analyses if much longitudinal data are collected.

Bivariate time series analyses, trend analyses, and profile comparisons can be used in macroanalyses. Transitional probabilities, joint probabilities, and lagged probabilities are promising approaches for microanalyses. The complexity of the task requires that investigators transcend "the law of the instrument" (Kaplan, 1964, p. 28), and do not remain restricted in their approaches to well-known research methods that are minimally suited to the investigation.

The complex interactional aspects discussed can be ascertained only through approximations to true longitudinal or continuous-time analyses that consider immediate interdependencies and delayed effects. Paris et al. (1985) emphasized a similar need for longitudinal studies. Bates, Bretherton, and Snyder (1988) provided an innovative approximation in considering longer developmental courses and employing complex sophisticated analyses. The data in this volume are one more contribution to this goal, even if further conceptual refinements and more extensive statistical analyses remain to be performed.

Chapter 8

Theoretical and Methodological Approaches in Research on Language Transmission and Acquisition

*The structure of inquiry must be compatible
with the structure of its object.
To the degree to which it is not,
the real nature of the object will be distorted
or its existence will be
overlooked entirely. Feldman and Toulmin: "Logic and the Theory of Mind"*

After the extensive and detailed factual reports in this work, the challenge remains to place the findings in a broader perspective and to explore possible implications for the field of first language acquisition specifically, and for conceptualizations of naturalist learning more generally. A broad theoretical conceptualization has been outlined by the writer (Moerk, 1977a) and refined as a skill learning model (Moerk, 1986). These sources indicate a broader context for the following discussion concerning the preceding chapters in this volume.

CONCEPTUAL SYSTEMS AND CONCEPTUAL TOOLS

It is presumed that language is a central part of culture. Aspects of culture are taught by adults in a community and learned by each new generation of children. In order to understand the training and learning processes and the psychological nature of the resulting product as opposed to a mere formal description, a fine grained factual or truly diachronic account of the course of the training and learning is needed.

These tasks and challenges are formidable as the progress, or the lack of it, in the field labeled culture learning, acculturation, or enculturation shows. With rare exceptions, such as Bandura's (1986) psychological outline, these fields have neither attempted nor achieved accounts of processes or immediate cause–effect relationships. No inclusive diachronic reports of culture transmission exist, and only cross sections of performances at different developmental levels are presented. This is understandable because the field of culture is so broad that a complete description of its acquisition may appear impossible. Language as only one constituent of culture may be more accessible to diachronic, developmental study.

An Empirical, Neo-positivist Approach

Because factual descriptions of the training and learning processes must be data based, it should not be surprising that the factual analyses in this volume had a behaviorist tone, though a label of empiricist or logical empiricist, or even ethologic might be more fitting. Skilled performances and goal-directed acts are forms of instrumental behavior, as they are studied in ethology. These acts are responses to an environmental signal, which has been—somewhat unfortunately— labeled as a stimulus in behaviorist approaches because of their historical roots in Pavlovian research. In much of actual goal-directed behavior, the initiating event is a complex pattern of stimuli that gives much information about the needed response. For example, there are different implications for the grazing gazelle if a pattern of stimuli represents a lion or a co-species member emerging out of the high grass of the plains. The feedback the lion provides, whether the animal initiates a chase or ignores the gazelle, will in turn influence the gazelle's behavior. All these elements of the feedback loop are highly meaningful signals and not simple stimuli. The focus is on empirical evidence and the careful description of chains of events, and this is the goal of methodological behaviorism. Therefore, correspondences are encountered in descriptions of these two domains, beyond the shadings introduced by different theoretical orientations.

Correspondences apply particularly to long-term aspects of the learning process. It is significant that they exist between the learning curves of Eppinghaus, who explored rather high level linguistic material (i.e., the learning of Greek poetry), the learning and acquisition functions of Thorndike (1913) and Hull (1952), skill learning research, and the present findings in language training and learning. General patterns, longitudinal trends, and almost identical learning principles are encountered in a wide range of reports.

The Skill Learning Model

A guiding model for process analyses and diachronic descriptions is found in the research on skill acquisition. Cognitive skill acquisition (Anderson, 1981) is a central part of skill learning because all skills are cognitively guided.

The skill learning model has shaped much of the factual analysis in this volume. The emphasis is on processes evolving over time. Skill learning relies on feedback processes or the accomplishment of a training or learning task through a three-step process. The trainer initiates a feedback cycle by inviting the response of the student and then supplies feedback to the response. The course of first language acquisition seems to follow this process with either the mother or child initiating an interaction and the mother improving on it. The mother provides an opportunity for the child to learn by comparing his or her imperfect performance with the mother's accomplished feedback. In the third step of this feedback cycle, the child incorporates improvements into his or her subsequent utterance. The skill training and learning model, by specifying input, response, and feedback processes, emphasizes the basic task of any science, which is the naturalist description of elementary events in time. This is the basis for understanding the processes and the products of learning.

Conceptualizing Cognitive Structures

Although a behaviorist- or positivist-oriented approach in its empirical focus is useful and required, it is not necessarily implied that it is sufficient. In the domain of cognitive and linguistic phenomena, structures and structural changes are of great interest. Whereas radical behaviorists have systematically bracketed all research on cognition, Piaget's structuralist approach is directly focused on this domain (though Piaget bracketed the topic of social influence). Piaget employed the term schema for such structures, and a similar concept is reflected in the structures of Miller, Galanter, and Pribam (1960). An equivalent meaning is encountered in schema theory in the field of skill learning (e.g., Schmidt, 1975; Shapiro & Schmidt, 1982) and in Arbib's cognitive research program (Arbib, Conklin, & Hill, 1987). Piaget's principles of assimilation, accommodation, and the reestablishment of a new equilibrium after disturbances describe structural learning from input and feedback. Piaget has provided valuable tools to capture the dynamic nature of these schemas as they affect learning. Miller et al. (1960) expressed these principles in their TOTE cycles.

Changes in cognitive level and performance level are central to the conceptualization of a complex and extended learning process. In a typical behaviorist approach, learning is based on simple frequency of repetitions of input in an unchanged organism, but these restrictions can be transcended with Piaget's approach. In accordance with the equilibration principle, restructuring leads to a higher level of cognition. Cognitive structures or schemas govern the perception, filtering, and analysis of new input and integration with existing structures. With cognitive progress, a "different organism" encounters the new input. This different organism interprets the new input differently, and a fine tuned social environment provides different and more complex input with the progress of the learner. Such parallel changes in the learner and the input are frequently encountered in language acquisition, as has been demonstrated in this volume. These changes obviously need to be incorporated in the conceptualization of the learning process. Identical principles are found in Gibson's (1977, 1982) affordances and in the cybernetic conceptualization of incremental feedback cycles, which are both important concepts for language acquisition research.

Integration of Behaviorist and Cognitive Approaches

A clear integration of cognitive and empiricist approaches is seen in Chapter 7 of this volume. Acquisition of learning strategies involves cognitive aspects, or procedural knowledge. Three levels or stages of learning were distinguished in Chapter 7: vocabulary learning, learning of the basic sentence frame, and learning of complex syntactic constructions and transformations. The stages would be obvious if they were integrated, as curves, into one table. Such an integration would indicate that curves pertaining to complex constructions or higher stages remained close to zero during the early samples while other curves reached high frequency of use. With progress, early strategies decline in frequency, in the same manner as performance on the level of primitive cognitive stages becomes less frequent with development, and more complex strategies arise. This reflects Piaget's (1955) principle of "vertical decalage." The increasing trends of most curves reflect the "horizontal decalage" of Inhelder, Sinclair, and Bovet (1974).

These levels of learning and processes can be represented in a stimulus–response or interaction format. Structured input leads to the acquisition and reproduction of strategies of learning.

Similarly, Chapter 6 has been concerned with the acquisition of internal patterns or schemas through analysis of input and output. Study of the acquisition of structures necessitates taking the best from behavioral learning and structural theory and enriching these with insights from two other scientific fields.

Structure of the Stimulus

The integration of behaviorist and cognitive tools leaves the domain of environmental information relatively undefined. Neither Piaget nor the behaviorists focused on the specific structure of the stimulus. Piaget used the undifferentiated concept "aliment" to denote this environmental information and behaviorists used the term stimulus. An imposed label can stifle intellectual curiosity and hinder the differentiation of the many aspects subsumed under such a vague term.

Obviously, the concept of stimulus derived from Pavlovian conditioning or from the primitive reflex arch is woefully inadequate in language acquisition. Language input is highly structured and is a pattern or gestalt, which must be a central aspect in any exploration of acquisition. The careful analyses of linguistic science, especially those of the structuralists, provide tools and a subset of information that can be employed to specify linguistic input. Prosodic and interactional structure exists in verbal mother–child interactions as well as syntactic and morphologic structure. Prosodic and stylistic analyses can provide insight into prosodic and interactional structures, and discourse analysis and interaction analysis can explore syntax and morphologic structure.

Static Conceptions of Environmental Structure

The structuralist conceptualization has also functioned as an obstacle to the exploration of first language acquisition, due to the static definition of structural linguistics chosen in response to trends in linguistics in the 19th century.

Linguistics of that period was concerned with relations and changes across time, as seen especially in the study of historical relations between the Indo-European languages. Saussure (1959) argued against dynamic 19th century linguistics in favor of synchronic structural approaches. These static and purely distributional approaches reached a level of refinement in the work of Zellig Harris. It was, however, a level that needed to be surpassed. Harris's "conversion relation" and "transformations between sentences" (1951) were the first steps in doing this and were elaborated in Chomsky's (1965) transformational grammar. With terms such as competence and performance, and base structure and transformations, the system appeared to aim at psychological dynamics and explanations of linguistic productions. Yet the system never transcended factual descriptions of relations between linguistic products. Neither Chomsky nor his colleagues utilized a dynamic psychological approach based on learning to explain language acquisition. They turned their conceptualizations into an obstacle by declaring that transformational rules are so complex that they cannot be learned. In this manner, the approach became static by relying on innate knowledge and universals, which by definition are unchangeable.

Utilizing this static system, developmental psycholinguistics too relapsed into a pre-Newtonian, pre-Darwinian disregard of the dynamics of change in time. In the extreme, it led to the postulation of innate and unchanging knowledge even by psychologists. Language learning was declared impossible without this preexisting knowledge. In less extreme cases, occurrences of specific items, but not their informational function in context, were counted as input. The phenomena that really afforded information for the young child were missed, and correlations with criteria of language acquisition were low and insignificant.

Dynamic Conceptions of Environmental Information

A way out of the dilemma between static structuralist descriptions of input and transformational defeatism does, however, exist and is best represented in Gibson's (1977, 1982) explorations of visual perception and his concept of affordances. Gibson based his approach upon Cassirer's (1944) concept of invariance over a group of transformations, and he argued that information about the environment is conveyed by higher order patterns of stimulation. These patterns are discovered on the basis of uniformity of change over time. Invariances are enhanced by variations and all information must be considered relationally.

More important from a developmental perspective, Gibson argued that affordances were relative to the perceiver. Information was not necessarily informative if the receiver could not utilize it. This emphasis is identical in principle to Vygotsky's (1978) zone of proximal development and to the emphasis in this work that the child's developmental level must be considered when evaluating the potential effects of input. With general emphasis on relational information and specific emphasis on the relation between input and receiver, Gibson laid the foundation for a third important principle, that of mutual adjustment between the information provider and user in feedback cycles. This mutual adjustment operates between mother and child in first language acquisition.

The principle that information is relational is very slightly reflected in developmental psycholinguistics. Brown's (Brown & Bellugi, 1964) expansions are relational, as are the "extensions" of Cross (1977) and the "repair sequences" of Garvey (1977). Snow (1977a) emphasized more globally the importance of "discourse parameters" and Shatz

(1982) stressed "cross-utterance information." Most systematically, Moerk (1983a, 1983b, 1985a, 1985b) constructed an analytic system on these relational categories and demonstrated the richness of linguistic information when considered in this relational and dynamic manner.

While most investigators would agree that affordances are relative to the perceiver, the implications of this have not been fully realized. For example, it has been argued that language learners are not influenced by corrections. The relation of the specific correction to the language level of the child was, however, not considered. The same problem has applied to input studies in general that did not consider linguistic constructions in relation to the child's language level. It is logical that the uptake by the child, not the input per se, results in learning. Although consistent input might gradually lead to uptake, methodological problems remain in the exploration of this changing uptake. Feedback cycles appear to be a most promising tool to explore these problems.

A Cybernetic Approach to Conversation and Learning

The regulatory cycles between readiness and affordances emphasized by Gibson were first explored in cybernetics (Wiener, 1948) and have been further developed in systems theory (e.g., Bertalanffy, 1968). The basic underlying ideas are well known and need no discussion. The TOTE cycles (Miller et al., 1960) are obviously built on the same principles. Simon (1979) employed these ideas in his exploration of problem solving and the extraction of information by comparing original performance and feedback. Feedback cycles are relevant to any conversation. If a partner misunderstands an utterance (provides negative feedback), the utterance is usually repeated and clarified. Though fine tuning is still controversial in some quarters, there is abundant evidence of motherese that represents general tuning to the child's changing level. Brown's expansions involve feedback cycles by supplying elements omitted by the child and relating two utterances across partners. We know from Slobin's (1968) analyses that children utilize these expansions to enrich their subsequent utterances.

Input, fine tuning, and other maternal adjustments have been denied, so potentially valuable systems theory conceptualizations have not been fully utilized. The wealth of affordances or information contained in these adjustments has barely been considered.

Integration of Conceptual Tools

A diagrammatic presentation may clarify these conceptual tools in their approximate order of relevance. Table 1 summarizes how tools can be integrated to explain first language acquisition.

Table 1. Conceptual tools for the study of language transmission and acquisition

Conceptualization of information (input)	Conceptualization of interaction	Conceptualization of structure
Linguistic descriptions	Behaviorist approaches	Cumulative record
Gibson's affordances	Systems theory	Skill learning
Learning psychology schedules of presentation	Skill learning research	Cognitive stage theories
Piaget's disequilibrium	Discourse analysis	Computer modeling

Concepts from research on perceptual learning need to be integrated with prosodic differentiations of structures to understand the wealth of input information available to the child. The objectivity and precision of behaviorist approaches might best capture the input–output relations, or the transfer function. More relevant and finely developed is the research on skill learning that also focuses on the transfer function between input and output. This approach emphasizes longitudinal phenomena and the feedback processes that were largely neglected in behaviorist approaches. Principles and approaches from systems theory applied in skill learning may further an understanding of the fine tuning between the changing organism, input, and the handling of input.

The conceptual tools of cognitive psychology are needed to model the internalized structures and the levels or stages (Fischer, 1980) that result from interaction with environmental information. Changing cognitive and linguistic levels, in turn, change the affordances of the child's language environment. A changed child responding to new affordances engages in new processing and arrives at new equilibria. A revision of Skinner's cumulative record, with support from multivariate time series analyses, can follow the process of the development of cognitive structures over longer time periods. Changing structures can be inferred from changing interactions by exploring discourse relations. All available conceptual and methodological tools are necessary to adequately describe these iterative interactions between a complex organism and a highly structured environment. Methodological tools are of great importance, because concepts that cannot be related to empirical phenomena remain mere speculations.

METHODOLOGICAL TOOLS FOR CONTINUOUS-TIME ANALYSES OF INTERACTIONAL TRAINING AND LEARNING

This section surveys the tools available for the process-based analyses that consider the temporal flow of training and learning. The argument is directed against the temporally undifferentiated approach of Chomsky and his colleagues who explain adult linguistic competence on the basis of input received during the first years of life, disregarding all the millions of gradated learning trials that follow. This study also attempted to transcend the correlational approaches of psychologists, because correlations are, in principle, atemporal and unsuited to phenomena of development and cumulative temporal change. Time and processes occurring across time are obviously central to learning and development, and their omission, whether conceptually or methodologically, severely detracts from the explanatory power of the results. Table 2 presents major aspects of the methodological tools that are discussed in detail in the sections to follow.

Table 2 resembles Table 1, with short-term interactions and long-term training differentiated along one dimension. Two columns in Table 2 that summarize methods reflect the major dichotomy of interest: (immediate) interaction versus long-term training and learning. Methodological tools exist for each domain: sequential analyses for immediate interaction and time and event series analyses for long-term influences. The underlying principle of both approaches is the same though the specific goals and computations differ. Both aim to relate an event at time $t + 1, t + 2,$ or $t + 3$ to an event at time t zero, the present, or at time $t - 1, t - 2,$ or $t - 3,$ the past. Time series analyses focus on the same event as it unfolds in time whereas sequential analyses capture the sequential dependency of a considerable variety of different events.

Sequential Approaches

Sequential analyses can capture the stream of behavior of an individual and provide evidence of the structure of behavior or establish in-

Table 2. Methodological tools for the study of language transmission and acquisition

Information (input)	Interaction	Long-term training and learning
Focus upon antecedents (necessity)	Bidirectional event-based analysis of contingency	Bivariate/multivariate time series analyses
Focus upon responses (sufficiency)	Traditional sequential analyses, Markov chains	Bivariate/multivariate time series analyses
Antecedents and responses with variable time window width (interval)	Lagged sequential analyses with moving moment	Lead–lag relationships, transfer function in frequency domain
Cumulative/multiple causation	Cumulative record, profile comparison with varying and changing lags	Calculus of development: first derivative = speed, second derivative = acceleration, integral = degree of mastery

teractional sequences. In the field of language acquisition, the main focus is on behaviors across persons, mainly the mother and child, to explore interactions that lead to language acquisition.

Detailed discussion of methodological approaches were provided by Gottman and Bakeman (1979), Hannan and Tuma (1979), and others. Moerk (1983a, 1983b, 1985a, 1985b) applied these methods to analyses of verbal interactions in language transmission and acquisition.

Sequential analyses are based upon transitional probabilities, or the probabilities of events N, R, or Q occurring after events E, F, or M. A square matrix of transitional probabilities for all behaviors of one person or for transitions from the behavior of one interaction partner to the other summarizes the immediate contingencies. For the case of all behaviors of one person, the diagonal contains the probabilities of each behavior following itself, because in verbal behavior all utterances can, in principle, be repeated. In the case of transitions between members of a dyad, the diagonal contains the transitional probabilities between the same types of utterances produced by the partners of the dyad. Transitional probabilities can be established between immediately antecedent and subsequent behavior, an approach that results in first order Markov chains. They can also be established for higher order dependencies, for example, the probability of event C occurring after both events A and B. Dependency between two items also can be established after longer intervals or lags. Whether a child incorporated a maternal correction after a lag, if not immediately, can be explored this way.

Higher order transitional probability approaches are appropriate to quantitatively explore and specify feedback cycles. A filial mistake results in a maternal correction with a certain probability, which studies (Moerk, in press; Snow & Goldfield, 1983) have shown to be very high, which induces the child to incorporate the corrective information. The same principle applies to the three-step sequence of model-imitation-confirmation or correction. Moerk (1972, 1975, 1976a, 1985b, 1990) described cycles that encompass several turns of interaction partners.

Necessary or Conducive Antecedents   The greatest challenge to scientists is to find the causes of an event, or the answer to the question "Why?" This applies to the causes of language acquisition. Psycholinguistic research did not establish the immediate antecedents of specific filial linguistic productions, yet researchers nevertheless desired to answer the question. As a result, speculations of unconscious rules or innate knowledge took the place of factual analyses of cause–effect relationships.

Researchers may be partly excused for this recourse to speculation, since—astonishingly—no well established statistical methods of sequential analysis exist for this question. The general approach of sequential analysis begins with a cause and looks for its consequences, or effects. This methodological orientation toward consequences probably derives from the experimental stimulus–response orientation where the cause is known. This orientation is of little help in a situation where the response is known (the filial production), and the causes need to be established.

The only method developed in this search for antecedents was presented by Watson and Hayes (1981) involving a bidirectional analysis of contingency. The theoretical question and the methodological approach are, however, simple if based on computerized counting. The theoretical question is whether X is contingent on Y, or the probability that Y precedes X. Methodologically, frequency counts of all the antecedents of X and the computation of conditional or transitional probabilities only are required. A fairly simple computer program can produce both.

If all antecedents are established and all transitional probabilities computed, a multiplicity of potential causes can be discerned and considered as each affects the probability of the particular effect. As findings in preceding chapters have shown, filial productions can result from a variety of cues. For example, a maternal model or a cue of "did" led to the child's production of a past-tense construction. A variety of antecedents, and specifically those that change with increasing filial mastery, can be captured with this method.

Higher order transitional probabilities express the degrees of dependence between multiple combined causes and subsequent acts. Causes can be found in the preceding behavior of the speaker, the interaction partner, and both. Whether first order or higher order transitional probabilities are employed, these approaches raise the causal problem from a level of mere speculation or the search for a single cause to a careful analysis of a rich database and the demonstration of multiple dependencies. The same method applied longitudinally can also provide fine grained information about changes in developmental dynamics, as reflected through changes in transitional probabilities.

Responses to Input Proceeding to the second cell in the first column of Table 2, the response of the partner to an utterance, the procedures are well-established. This is the behaviorist stimulus–response situation, and the typical question answered by sequential analysis: What is the transitional probability that Y leads to X? If this probability is higher than expected by chance, then the hypothesis of contingency or dependency is justified.

It is obvious that this approach applies equally to both directions of effects: the mother's on the child, and the child's on the mother. Questions relating to maternal feedback or the controversy about corrections can be answered objectively with this approach. Similarly, topics such as the changing nature of filial imitation or the cue dependency of productions can be studied with this methodology in a factual and objective manner.

Both of the above methods can be greatly elaborated. Instead of the effects of a single antecedent, a combination of antecedents can be defined as the possible cause. A specific behavior might appear if several antecedents occur together, but not if only one occurs. Similarly, multiple effects of one causal intervention could be studied. Those effects might appear together or in an either/or relationship: Antecedent Y produces either X or Z with a high probability but rarely or never both. A variable time interval needs to be introduced between related variables. This leads to the third cell in the left column of Table 2.

A System with Memory   This discussion of sequential contingency has been undifferentiated regarding the dimension of time. Previous approaches presumed immediately consecutive dependency. This presumption stipulates a system without memory, although it is highly incongruous to presume absence of memory in a language-learning child. In this approach, environmental influences were denied if they did not appear immediately after the intervention. As soon as memory is accepted as part of the language-learning system—and, of course, it cannot be denied—the simplification of presuming a fixed time interval between contingent acts, and of presuming immediate dependency exclusively, is lost. A variable time interval must be accepted as a central feature for sequential study of the interaction process.

The metaphor of the radar screen with its searching beam incorporated in Figure 1 expresses many features of the situation and the analytical task. The horizontal coordinate represents the time dimension and the vertical coordinate, a similarity dimension. Although in principle neither dimension has an absolute outer limit, outer limits are assumed for practical reasons. The point of origin of the radar beam is considered as time zero, or the present moment. Within the semicircle of time intervals and degrees of similarity, the "beam of attention" of the researcher, or the programmed computer, searches for antecedents at $t - 1$, $t - 2$, or $t - 3$, at the left of time zero and for consequences at $t + 1$, $t + 2$, or $t + 3$, at the right. (Simultaneous co-occurrences would appear in nonverbal behavior when turn taking has been learned by the child.)

This approach has considerable diagnostic potential. Individual differences in the contingency span with the same training could reveal differences in memory capacity and learning. Changes in the con-

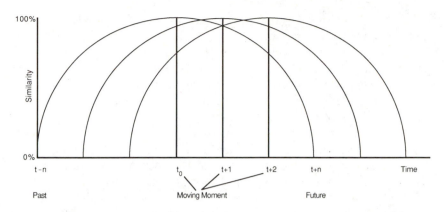

Figure 1. The temporal and similarity space of contingencies.

tingency span for the same child would express degree of learning and long-term storage. Changes in the similarity dimension would indicate progress from simple auditory imitation to pattern abstraction, which can lead to differences in elements, and to comprehension of a principle, which can be applied flexibly and lead to a variety of behaviors.

Although the approach has much potential, because it stands fixed in time, it is not true to reality. Time is obviously not fixed but continually moving. The point of origin of the search beam therefore has to move with time. The term "moving moment" might capture this: With every moment the conversation proceeds one step further, past contributions fade from memory, and present occurrences will be reflected in the future. Such an approach might appear prohibitive for manual analysis, although it has proved feasible for relatively simple goals by employing computers (see e.g., Moerk, 1983a). A relatively simple program can guide the computer to perform operations for one sweep of the beam of attention and then move on to the next item to perform the same operation. Computing transitional and joint probabilities and their deviations from chance is equally straightforward. This step differentiates real contingencies from chance co-occurrences.

A System that Changes   Relatively large numbers of events are required to ensure reasonable estimates of transitional probabilities. If some included events are relatively rare, large samples are required to obtain frequency data. Computations of probabilities of co-occurrences, however, presume a stationarity of the process and that probabilities do not change over the course of the observations that are the basis of the computations. The larger the sample, the less this stationarity can be presumed. For rapid learning, a stationary process cannot be presumed by definition.

Rapid learning is encountered with massed training followed by spaced rehearsals and testing. For example, in learning the two vocabulary items "to crack" and "nuts," Eve was at first fully dependent upon models and then soon produced the items spontaneously. Since many items might be learned in a similar manner, sequential analyses based on probability approaches are not the method of choice to study the acquisition of such specific items.

As in all careful research, exploratory data analyses (cf. Tukey, 1977) that include graphic displays can indicate changes in the dynamics during a brief learning process. The assumption of stationarity can then be immediately rejected or tests performed if the nonstationarity is less obvious. Establishment of an interactional pattern over many instances of specific acquisitions may also be informative. This pattern may take the form: *M-M-M, M-M-C-M, M-C-C-M-M-C-C-C, C-C-M*. Massed maternal modeling is followed by the child's attempt. The mother responds to this attempt with intensive modeling that leads to increasing rehearsals by the child. After intervals of unrelated conversation, the child spontaneously produces the item and receives a maternal response that confirms his or her success. This would be a very important training and learning pattern and could be objectively and quantitatively established for varying time periods. Different children and contents might reflect different patterns, providing the opportunity for differential analyses.

Nonstationary interaction sequences are also encountered with categories of interaction. For example, in the early stages of language acquisition, the child does not reliably answer when asked a question. The transitional probability from question to answer is therefore quite low. Later, most maternal questions might receive answers, and the transitional probability would rise to almost 1.00. Similarly it could be assumed that in early stages mothers provide few obvious corrections that emphasize the incorrectness of the preceding filial utterance, because most beginners' utterances contain too many mistakes or omissions to be handled by feedback with negative emotional value. Therefore, the transitional probability from filial mistake to obvious maternal correction would be low. When the child reaches a level of advanced mastery, makes few mistakes, and omits few obligatory elements, maternal feedback may be the inverse of the early stages, and most mistakes may receive a correction, which raises the transitional probability. The absolute number of corrections might still be low since by now the child makes few mistakes. This contrast between absolute number and reliability of corrections has not been fully appreciated.

Complex relationships can prove highly informative concerning interactional processes and the cognitive progress that shapes these interactional processes. Transitional probabilities can be quantitatively established for different ages. These probabilities can be compared across samples to demonstrate short-term and long-term changes.

In general, the more complex the phenomena, the more complex the information that can be abstracted. Sequential analyses are sufficiently complex and versatile to capture many forms of interaction and of training and learning over brief time intervals. For more extended processes, time series analyses appear to be optimal tools.

Dynamics of Long-Term Training

Gottman (1981) and Gregson (1983) have provided a statistical introduction to time series analyses. Cox and Lewis (1966) and Amburgey and Carroll (1984) provided equivalent presentations for event series analyses. The difference between these approaches is that time series analysis focuses on quantitative changes and the event series analysis focuses on occurrences of specific categorical events. Both methods are useful for the exploration of first language training and learning. Chapter 7 of this volume demonstrated, at least in principle, that time series conceptualizations could be applied to ascertain how the frequency of a specific strategy and technique changes over samples, months, and even 1 year. Event series methods are most useful to explore the patterns of occurrence of specific linguistic constructions or vocabulary items.

Time and event series analyses are not restricted to the study of long-term training. The only restriction for these analyses is that a sufficient number of observation points be available to permit recognition of a pattern. Middle-class children produce as many as 20,000–40,000 words per day (Wagner, 1985). One day's recording would easily suffice for a time series analysis of most linguistic aspects of filial speech performance. It appears from this author's and Brown's samples that mothers produce at least as much speech as their children. Time series for maternal input could also easily be established for a single day. If the chosen unit of recording is 1 hour per day, time series can be established over months or years to capture long-term processes. Tables in preceding chapters of this volume have represented such time series across analyzed samples, although the number of data points was too small to use the mathematical tools of time series analysis.

Time Series of Adult Input   Bivariate or multivariate time or event series, generally with some degree of lag, are appropriate to search for antecedents of specific filial developments. The figures in Chapter 7 and tables in other chapters showed that maternal input preceded filial productions by one or more samples. This is a necessary consequence of the training and learning situation where training precedes production. Some tables in Chapters 4 and 5 indicated that bivariate time series would not be sufficient to capture the complexity of the situation. In the learning of the regular past, maternal constructions with the -ed morpheme and use of the proform "did" appeared to be causal factors. Additionally, the use of the irregular past, which can help clarify the concept of the immediate past, might also have contributed to mastery of the regular past. For the learning of the future, the mother employed the two forms "will" and "going to/gonna," and the child employed "go" + verb, "going to/gonna," and, finally, "will." The time series analysis needs to consider five variables to explore the training and learning of the future morpheme.

Time Series of Filial Productions   Analyses appropriate to the study of antecedents are also appropriate to the study of responses to antecedents. Whether we explore causes or consequences of the relationships between bivariate and multivariate time series does not affect their mathematical form and computation. Cause–effect relationships exist not only within the same contents, but transfer or generalization must also be expected. With much structural similarity within a language, it almost necessarily follows that, for example, the analysis of the structure of the object-noun phrase would generalize to the analysis of the prepositional phrase. The understanding of the slot and filler principle for the object might be transferred to the verb, other constituents, or even elements of constituents. Careful methodological, mathematical, and conceptual analyses are required to explore such complicated antecedent–consequence relationships. Time and event series analyses, with their multiple approaches to establishing relationships between two or more series, are excellent instruments for this task.

Changing Lead–Lag Relationships   The problem of lead–lag relationships arises in bivariate and multivariate time series analyses. Whether one of the conversation partners takes a leading role and who is more of a respondent can be an important question. Whether these lead–lag relationships remain constant, change, or reverse are questions of developmental dynamics. In most of the factual analyses in this work, the mother led by one or more samples. Eve's frequent use of "go + verb" to express the future, however, might have been an incentive for the mother to talk more about future events. In this case, Eve would have taken the lead, and the mother would have responded after a lag.

A further complication to the conceptualization and analysis of bivariate time series is filial readiness and the possibility of a threshold function. In the analyses, the mother repeatedly attempted a new construction for which Eve was not ready. No pertinent response was made, and the mother dropped the attempt. Single, widely spaced models might never reach a necessary threshold nor produce responses until a massed training episode drew the child's attention to the item and established its use. It is also possible that unsuccessful training attempts might only appear unsuccessful because spontaneous filial productions are generally the only means available to establish an effect. Obviously, maternal training could affect filial comprehension without immediately leading to production.

Extensive and careful factual studies supported by the theoretical insights provided by learning psychology and skill learning can produce an understanding of these complex relationships. This discussion attempted to mention some challenges and to indicate generally the variety of methodologies to meet these challenges.

Time as a Dependent Variable   In these discussions, time has been considered as an independent variable, and events or frequency considered as dependent variables. In many situations it is useful to consider time as a dependent variable.

Instead of plotting frequencies against time and age or cumulative input, it is possible to plot intervals between the environmental model or cue and the dependent variable of filial production as a function of cumulative input frequency or age. As Moerk and Vilaseca (1987) have shown, this results in quite regular developmental curves and probably reflects storage of the elements in long-term memory, which permits independent retrieval. A combination of the two sets of curves might provide valuable indications of levels of learning and could operationalize this concept. For example, if an increasing variety of verbs is used in the past tense, and if these productions occur independently of preceding models or cues, then a factually specified hypothesis of rule-based, or at least, analogical performance would be indicated. This could be differentiated from rote learning by comparing speed of learning, length of delay following a model, or number of required rehearsals. The conclusions would not be based on subjective or ideological speculations but upon factually grounded interpretations.

The change from massing to spacing in the training and learning process proceeds in intermediate time intervals. The form of the inverted J-curve that results from massing followed by spacing demonstrates intensity of initial training, speed of learning, and, combined with transitional probabilities, effectiveness of learning. Widely spaced rehearsals with high probabilities of production when conversationally necessary would show this effectiveness in later periods.

A similar use of time as a dependent variable would focus on the length of massed training episodes for specific items or categories of items. Here, time would indicate the learning speed recognized by the mother and applied in her training. Differences between and within normal children and children with mental retardation would probably be found and could function as indicators of individual or dyadic differences.

Other approaches with time functioning as a dependent variable, such as the length of time before the occurrence of generalization or rate of progress from rote to analogical performances might prove very useful. Approaches that capture processes over time would all contribute to a continuous-time analysis of the training and learning process.

Some of these approaches were applied and exemplified in the factual analyses in this work. Many tables followed Eve's progress from immediate dependency on models and cues to gradual independence, regarding both the temporal interval and Eve's creativity or analogical use of a new pattern. If overall trends in these tables are sketched out, after smoothing to balance random variations and specific training dynamics, the curves seen in Figure 2 result.

Curve *a* is a typical sigmoid growth curve with a slow initial ad-

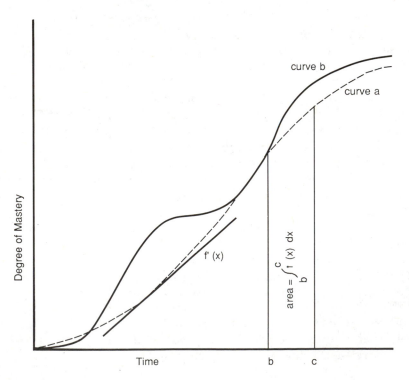

Figure 2.   A calculus of development.

vance, rapid increase during the middle stages, and a plateau following a peak in learning speed. This is the simplest phenomenon of developmental continuity, probably based on a single learning principle.
Curve b, in principle a sequential combination of several sigmoid
growth curves, is harder to demonstrate with available databases. If it
is real, as learning curves in this work suggest, it would indicate important developmental discontinuities. The first sigmoid curve could be
based on rote learning. After a certain number of acquisitions, a new
procedure of acquisition is gradually mastered, such as learning based
on schemas. A transition between learning principles could lead to the
brief plateau. Learning could accelerate with increased mastery of the
new procedure and reach another transition period. At this point, another procedure, such as rule-based performance, could come into
play and result in rapid learning.

This sketch goes beyond available evidence and borrows analogical concepts from the Inhelder et al. (1974) exploration of horizontal and
vertical decalages in Piaget's system. The specific learning procedures
of rote, analogy, and rule have been borrowed from MacWhinney's
(1978) report. Changes in the speed of learning, which are obvious and
have been reported for approximately 100 years, can be considered as
important dependent variables. These can be mathematically specified
with differential and integral calculus.

As can be seen from the previous chapters, a continuous-time approach can be applied to the learning of bound morphemes, to the formation of a verb phrase with auxiliaries, such as when Eve learned to
construct the future tense with an increasing number of verbs, and
even to mastery of the full S-V-O sentence frame.

"A Calculus of Development"   Time and event series analyses are
well suited to capture the cumulative effects of input. Maternal modeling can be recorded long before the child responds overtly. Later, the
child's lagged response, also recorded, can be related to maternal input. Chapter 7 of this volume provided conceptual examples of such an
approach. Insights can be gained from the mathematical functions derived from curves and subsections of them.

For the curve that reflects the child's acquisition, the first derivative, $f'(x)$, expresses the speed of progress or learning. The second
derivative, $f''(x)$, captures changes in this speed. Such changes could
provide valuable indications for changes in learning principles. Rote
learning should be the slowest, analogical learning would be more effective, and an established rule should be immediately applicable to all
members of a set. (This formulation begs the question of how a child
would recognize all the members of a set.) The question of whether

development proceeds in stages or with progressive acceleration would have to be explored factually for different learning contents and possibly for different learning situations.

The integral of the mathematical function would express total mastery, something resembling the competence that has never been operationalized. In a similar manner, the increase in mastery between time t and time $t + x$ could be expressed mathematically, a finding that might be relevant to educational settings because it captures the amount of material learned in a week, a month, or a semester. More possibilities could be discerned if the methodology were broadly applied. There is great potential for a conceptualization based on a calculus of development and on use of available mathematical tools.

The same principles must also be applied to curves of the input. Speed of teaching and speed of learning can then be compared and the instructor alerted to discrepancies. Amount of input per time unit could be compared across instructors or mothers, an approach that might show fascinating differences between social classes. In bivariate time series approaches, input can be related to acquisition. Speed, acceleration, or deceleration in either of the time series can be established and the two series compared regarding closeness of match, lead–lag relationships, or discrepancies. Multivariate time series can relate multiple causes and multiple effects in their temporal courses. These remarks are merely preliminary suggestions of the productiveness of continuous-time, or real developmental, approaches to the study of language training and learning.

Only if the methods of analysis match the nature of the phenomena under study can increased insights be expected. Development is a complex phenomenon, and minute processes as well as long-term trends and cumulative cause–effect relationships need to be considered. A combination of sequential techniques and time series approaches, combined with methods that employ time as a dependent variable, represent a tool set with considerable potential.

CONCLUDING REMARKS

A Return to Empirical Studies

Through an emphasis on culture learning, skill learning, and a general sociogenetic approach, language transmission and acquisition research has been brought back to an empirical level. Early bases for empirical studies were established by Brown and his associates (e.g., Brown, 1958; Brown & Bellugi, 1964). These endeavors were followed by the development of consistent research programs (Bloom, 1973;

Moerk, 1972; Snow, 1972). The extensive work by Bates and associates (Bates, Bretherton, & Snyder, 1988), Bruner and associates (Bruner, 1983), the valuable studies by Cross (1975, 1977), as well as other important approaches confirmed the basic sociogenetic perspective. Stella-Prorok (1983) has provided an excellent survey of these endeavors.

The nativist speculations and attempts of learnability theorists to prove that language learning was impossible without innate knowledge constituted a considerable setback to the field. Many aspects of environmental scaffolding were simply denied. The factual studies in this work, with this author's recent work on corrections (Moerk, in press), reflect a return to empirical evidence. When integrated with the experimental demonstrations of cause–effect relationships (cf. Nelson, 1989; Whitehurst, 1982), they can contribute to the sociogenetic approach and to the explanation of the actual processes of language transmission and acquisition.

This factual evidence suggests that something similar to "kiss feeding," described in the anthropological literature, is found in the nursery. The middle-class mother "premasticates" language for her child by simplifying it, analyzing it into smaller units (cf. Moerk, 1985a), and performing preparatory work that enables the child to "digest" information and assimilate it more easily into his or her system. (Adults do something similar for adult speakers who have mastered only the rudiments of a language. An accomplished speaker has to make the language assimilable for a novice to make communication possible.)

A Broader Perspective

The preceding remarks imply that language acquisition needs to be put into a broader perspective, that of the "sociogenetic perspective of language and culture acquisition" (Bain, 1983, p. xix). If language and language acquisition are seen as part of culture and culture acquisition, children's acquisition of language appears less miraculous and is open to normal research procedures on naturalist learning. Factually empty speculations concerning innate knowledge become implausible, because there is universal agreement that cultures, and the subsets of cultural skills, are learned through transmission from generation to generation.

It would, of course, be advantageous if the field of culture learning could provide methodological and factual guidance for the study of language transmission and acquisition. This is not yet the case, with some exceptions, notably the volume edited by Rogoff and Lave (1984). Skill training and learning, however, has provided methodological and conceptual models. Fischer and associates (e.g., Fischer, 1980; Fischer & Corrigan, 1981) developed conceptualizations of skill acquisition and applied some to language acquisition. Moerk (1986) provided a more extensive survey of parallels and correspondences in skill learning and language learning. Nevertheless, the potential of research on skill training and learning, whether sports skills, industrial skills, or performance skills in the arts, has hardly been discovered or utilized.

Neisser (1976) argued that perceptual learning is the basis of skill learning, and Ribes (1983) emphasized the connection of perceptual learning to language acquisition. A similar discussion is found in Whitehurst and DeBaryshe (1989) as "observational learning." In the analyses in this work, Gibson's system was presented as a possible model to conceptualize the linguistic information available to children. Gibson's concept of affordances focuses on conditions that enable the uptake of such information. Further work remains to be done in this field to establish how linguistic information, integrated with contextual information, appears to children at different levels of cognitive and linguistic competence. Obviously, a 1-year-old knows nothing about subject, predicate, nouns, verbs, or other word categories. These are gradually abstracted from vocal and contextual configurations that form a meaningful background for a child's interaction with adults and other children.

The Dimension of Time

The model of skill learning also serves to emphasize the temporal dimension, which should not have been overlooked in this field, which is a subset of developmental psychology. All skills are acquired over time, and complex skills undergo transformations before an individual's maximum is reached. There is, therefore, a minimal link—and no direct link—between early training and final accomplished performance. Processes and functional interdependencies must be established between immediately successive phenomena, not over months or longer.

It appears that two approaches were confounded in the studies that employed intervals of 6 months or more between presumed causes and effects. They seem to have adopted methodology from older studies, such as Gesell's (1954), of developmental milestones. In those studies, length of the interval does not systematically distort the evidence. Long intervals only result in less fine grained descriptions of successive levels of increasing mastery. These studies, however, provide little indication of cause–effect relationships and developmental processes. If the same methodology is employed in the search for processes, the long intervals eliminate all chance of resolving the question of causality or of demonstrating processes. Elements of a single learning process are not separated by intervals of up to 6 months but occur within short time periods that need to be subjected to microanalyses.

A Brief Critical Evaluation

Critics may argue that the reach of these discussions and proposals exceeds the grasp demonstrated in the factual analyses, and they are correct. The complex diachronic approaches had to be first conceptualized and demonstrated through examples. The mathematical and quantitative elaboration is, however, within our grasp and can be achieved either on the basis of the data assembled by this author, or from large databases collected by CHILDES at Carnegie Mellon University.

It can also be argued that findings from one dyad cannot be generalized to any population. This argument is partially correct also yet may be too restrictive, depending on the generalization. Admittedly, even the most careful study of one human being does not provide general parameters about the weight, metabolism rate, or level of intelligence of the species. Other generalizations, however, can be drawn with great confidence. A good knowledge of the anatomy of one normal person can be generalized to all normal persons.

Both aspects pertain to the findings concerning language transmission and acquisition established for Eve and her mother. The specific parameters may be unique to this dyad, or apply only to middle-class dyads, but the process aspects probably reflect universal principles. Just as no human being could develop physically without the major structural and functional features of the species, so children could not acquire language skills without the majority of the interaction structures that have been demonstrated. It will be the task of future research to establish the range of parameter variations for normal language acquisition and to match disturbances in language acquisition with disturbances in the structure, the functions, and the parameters of mother–child interactions.

References

Amburgey, T.L., & Carroll, G.R. (1984). Time-series models for event counts. *Social Science Research 13*, 38–54.

Anderson, J.R. (Ed.). (1981). *Cognitive skills and their acquisition.* Hillsdale, NJ: Lawrence Erlbaum Associates.

Anderson, J.R. (1982). Acquisition of skill. *Psychological Review, 89,* 369–406.

Anderson, J.R. (1983). *The architecture of cognition.* Cambridge, MA: Harvard University Press.

Arbib, M.A., Conklin, E.J., & Hill, J. (1987). *From schema theory to language.* New York: Oxford University Press.

Bain, B. (Ed.). (1983). *The sociogenesis of language and culture.* New York: Plenum.

Bandura, A. (1973). *Aggression: A social learning analysis.* Englewood Cliffs, NJ: Prentice Hall.

Bandura, A. (1986). *Social foundations of thought and action: A social cognitive theory.* Englewood Cliffs, NJ: Prentice Hall.

Bartlett, F.C. (1932). *Remembering.* Cambridge: Cambridge University Press.

Bates, E., Bretherton, I., Beeghly-Smith, M., & McNew, S. (1982). Social bases of language development: A reassessment. In H.W. Reese & L.P. Lipsitt (Eds.), *Advances in child development and behavior* (Vol. 16, pp. 8–75). New York: Academic Press.

Bates, E., Bretherton, I., & Snyder, L. (1988). *From first words to grammar: Individual differences and dissociable mechanisms.* New York: Cambridge University Press.

Bates, E., Camaioni, L., & Volterra, V. (1982). The acquisition of performatives prior to speech. *Merrill-Palmer Quarterly, 21,* 205–226.

Beckett, S. (1965). *Three Novels.* New York: Grove Press.

Beebe, B., Alson, D., Jaffe, J., Feldstein, S., & Crown, C. (1988). Vocal congruence in mother–infant play. *Journal of Psycholinguistic Research, 17,* 245–259.

Bell, S. (1903). The significance of activity in child life. *Independent, 55,* 911–914.

Bergson, H. (1907). *L'evolution creatrice* [The creative evolution]. Paris: Presses Universitaires de France.

Berko, J. (1958). The child's learning of English morphology. *Word, 14,* 150–177.

Bertalanffy, L.V. (1968). *General systems theory.* New York: George Braziller.

Bever, T.G., Fodor, J.A., & Weksel, W. (1965). Is linguistics empirical? *Psychological Review, 72,* 467–482.

Bilodeau, E.A. (Ed.). (1966). *Acquisition of skill.* New York: Academic Press.

Bloom, K. (1977). Patterning of infant vocal behavior. *Journal of Experimental Child Psychology, 23,* 367–377.

Bloom, K. (1979). Evaluation of infant vocal conditioning. *Journal of Experimental Child Psychology, 27,* 60–70.

Bloom, L.M. (1970). *Language development: Form and function in emerging grammars.* Cambridge, MA: MIT Press.

Bloom, L.M. (1973). *One word at a time.* The Hague: Mouton.

Bloom, L., Hood, P., & Lightbown, P. (1974). Imitation in language development: If, when, and why? *Cognitive Psychology, 6,* 380–420.

Bohannon, J., & Hirsh-Pasek, K. (1984). Do children say as they are told? A new perspective on motherese. In L. Feagans, C. Garvey, & R. Golinkoff (Eds.), *The origins and growth of communication* (pp. 176–195). Norwood, NJ: Ablex.

Bohannon, J., & Marquis, A.L. (1977). Children's control of adult speech. *Child Development, 48,* 1002–1008.

Bohannon, J., Stine, E.L., & Ritzenberg, D. (1982). The "fine-tuning" hypothesis of adult speech to children: Effects of experience and feedback. *Bulletin of the Psychonomic Society, 19,* 201–204.

Bolinger, D. (1976). Meaning and memory. *Forum Linguisticum, 1,* 1–14.

Braine, M.D.S. (1963). On learning the grammatical order of words. *Psychological Review, 70,* 323–348.

Braine, M.D.S. (1965). On the basis of phrase structure. *Psychological Review, 72,* 483–492.

Braine, M.D.S. (1976). Children's first word combinations. *Monographs of the Society for Research in Child Development, 41,* (1, Serial No. 164).

Brandenburg, G.C., & Brandenburg, J. (1919). Language development during the fourth year: The conversation. *Pedagogical Seminary, 26,* 27–40.

Brentano, F. (1955). *Psychologie von empirischen standpunkt.* [Psychology from an empirical point of view]. Hamburg: Felix Meiner.

Brewer, W.F., & Nakamura, G.V. (1984). The nature and function of schemas. In R.S. Wyer & T.K. Scrull (Eds.), *Handbook of social cognition* (pp. 119–160). Hillsdale, NJ: Lawrence Erlbaum Associates.

Bronfenbrenner, U. (1979). *The ecology of human development.* Cambridge, MA: Harvard University Press.

Brown, R. (1958). *Words and things.* New York: Free Press.

Brown, R. (1973). *A first language.* Cambridge, MA: Harvard University Press.

Brown, R., & Bellugi, U. (1964). Three processes in the child's acquisition of syntax. *Harvard Educational Review, 34,* 133–151.

Brown, R., Cazden, C., & Bellugi-Klima, U. (1969). The child's grammar from 1 to 3. In J.P. Hill (Ed.), *Minnesota symposia on child psychology* (Vol. 2, pp. 28–73). Minneapolis: University of Minnesota Press.

Brown, R., & Hanlon, C. (1970). Derivational complexity and order of acquisition in child speech. In J.R. Hayes (Ed.), *Cognition and the development of language* (pp. 11–53). New York: John Wiley & Sons.

Bruner, J. (1966). *Toward a theory of instruction.* Cambridge, MA: Harvard University Press.

Bruner, J. (1981). Intention and the structure of acting. In L.P. Lipsitt & C.K. Rovee-Collier (Eds.), *Advances in infancy research* (Vol. 1, pp. 41–56). Norwood, NJ: Ablex.

Bruner, J. (1983). *Child's talk: Learning to use language.* New York: Norton.

Burling, R. (1966). The metrics of children's verse: A cross-linguistic study. *American Anthropologist, 68,* 1418–1441.

Burton, R., Brown, J.S., & Fischer, G. (1984). Skiing as a model of instruction. In B. Rogoff & J. Lave (Eds.), *Everyday cognition: Its development in social context* (pp. 139–150). Cambridge, MA: Harvard University Press.

Bybee, J.L., & Slobin, D.I. (1982). Rules and schemas in the development and use of the English past tense. *Language, 58,* 265–289.

Campbell, B.A., & Jaynes, J. (1966). Reinstatement. *Psychological Review, 73,* 478–480.

Carey, S. (1978). The child as a word learner. In M. Halle, J. Brenan, & G.A. Miller (Eds.), *Linguistic theory and psychological reality* (pp. 264–293). Cambridge, MA: MIT Press.

Cassirer, E. (1944). *An essay on man.* New Haven: Yale University Press.

Cazden, C.B. (1973). The acquisition of noun and verb inflections. In C.A. Ferguson & D.I. Slobin (Eds.), *Studies of child language development* (pp. 226–240). New York: Holt, Rinehart & Winston.

Chomsky, C. (1969). *The acquisition of syntax in children from 5 to 10.* Cambridge, MA: MIT Press.

Chomsky, N. (1959). Verbal behavior by B.F. Skinner. *Language, 35,* 26–58.

Chomsky, N. (1965). *Aspects of a theory of syntax.* Cambridge, MA: MIT Press.

Chukovsky, K. (1963). *From two to five.* Berkeley: University of California Press.

Clark, E.V. (1973). Non-linguistic strategies and the acquisition of word meaning. *Cognition, 2,* 161–182.

Clark, H.H. (1973). Space, time, semantics, and the child. In T.E. Moore (Ed.), *Cognitive development and the acquisition of language* (pp. 65–110). New York: Academic Press.

Clark, R. (1974). Performing without competence. *Journal of Child Language, 1,* 1–10.

Clark, R. (1975, September). *Some even simpler ways to learn to talk.* Paper presented at the Third International Child Language Symposium, London.

Clark, R. (1977) What's the use of imitation. *Journal of Child Language, 4,* 341–358.

Condon, W.S. (1986). Communication: Rhythm and structure. In J.R. Evans & M. Clynes (Eds.), *Rhythm in psychological, linguistic and musical processes* (pp. 55–77). Springfield, IL: Charles C Thomas.

Cox, D.R., & Lewis, P.A.W. (1966). *The statistical analysis of series of events.* New York: John Wiley & Sons.

Cronbach, L.J., & Gleser, G.L. (1953). Assessing similarity between profiles. *Psychological Bulletin, 50,* 456–473.

Cross, T. (1975). Some relationships between motherese and linguistic level in accelerated children. *Papers and Reports on Child Language Development, 10,* 117–135.

Cross, T. (1977). Mothers' speech adjustments: The contribution of selected child listener variables. In C.E. Snow & C.A. Ferguson (Eds.), *Talking to children: Language input and acquisition* (pp. 151–188). Cambridge: Cambridge University Press.

Crystal, D. (1973). Non-segmental phonology in language acquisition: A review of the issues. *Lingua, 32,* 1–45.

Crystal, D. (1986). Prosodic development. In P. Fletcher & M. Garman (Eds.), *Language acquisition: Studies in first language development* (pp. 174–197). Cambridge: Cambridge University Press.

Curtiss, S. (1977). *Genie: A psycholinguistic study of a modern day "wild child."* New York: Academic Press.

Decroly, O., & Degand, J. (1913). Observations relatives au developpement de la notion du temps chez une petite fille [Observations pertaining to the development of a concept of time by a little girl]. *Archive de Psychologie, 13*, 133–161.

Delacroix, H. (1934). *Le language et la pensee* [Language and thought] (3rd. ed.). Paris: Alcan.

Demetras, M.J., Post, K.N., & Snow, C.E. (1986). Feedback to first language learners: The role of repetitions and clarification questions. *Journal of Child Language, 13*, 275–292.

Derwing, B.L., & Baker, W.J. (1986). Assessing morphological development. In P. Fletcher & M. Garman (Eds.), *Language acquisition: Studies in first language development* (pp. 326–338). New York: Cambridge University Press.

Dewey, J. (1922). *Human nature and conduct.* New York: Modern Library.

Doyle, A.C. (1950). *Adventures of Sherlock Holmes* (pp. 241–261). New York: Heritage Press.

Dray, W. (1957). *Laws and explanation in history.* Oxford: Oxford University Press.

Edelman, G.M., & Mountcastle, V. (1978). *The mindful brain.* Cambridge, MA: MIT Press.

Ehrenfels, Chr. v. (1890). Uber Gestaltsqualitaeten [About Gestalt qualities]. *Vierteljahreschrift fuer Wissenschaftliche Philosophie, 14*, 249–292.

Estes, W.K. (1978). On the organization and core concepts of learning theory and cognitive psychology. In W.K. Estes (Ed.), *Handbook of learning and cognitive processes: Vol. 6. Linguistic functions in cognitive theory* (pp. 235–292). New York: John Wiley & Sons.

Farrar, M.J. (1985). *The acquisition of grammatical morphemes from discourse: A cognitive perspective.* Unpublished doctoral dissertation, Emory University.

Feldman, C.F., & Toulmin, S. (1976). Logic and the theory of mind. In W.J. Arnold (Ed.), *Nebraska symposium on motivation 1975: Conceptual foundations of psychology* (pp. 409–476). Lincoln, NE: University of Nebraska Press.

Feldman, D.H. (1980). *Beyond universals in cognitive development.* Norwood, NJ: Ablex.

Fernald, A. (1984). The perceptual and affective salience of mothers' speech to infants. In L. Feagans, C. Garvey, & R. Golinkoff (Eds.), *The origins and growth of communication* (pp. 5–29). Norwood, NJ: Ablex.

Fernald, A. (1985). Four-month-old infants prefer to listen to motherese. *Infant Behavior and Development, 8*, 181–195.

Fillmore, L. (1976). *The second time around: Cognitive and social strategies in second language acquisition.* Unpublished doctoral dissertation, Stanford University.

Fischer, K.W. (1980). A theory of cognitive development: The control and construction of a hierarchy of skills. *Psychological Review, 87*, 477–531.

Fischer, K.W., & Corrigan, R. (1981). A skill approach to language acquisition. In R. Stark (Ed.), *Language behavior in infancy and early childhood* (pp. 245–273). Amsterdam: Elsevier/North Holland.

Fitts, P.M. (1964). Perceptual-motor skill learning. In A.W. Melton (Ed.), *Categories of human learning* (pp. 243–285). New York: Academic Press.

Flavell, J.H. (1970). Concept development. In P.H. Mussen (Ed.), *Carmichael's manual of child psychology* (Vol. 1, pp. 983–1059). New York: John Wiley & Sons.

Flavell, J.H. (1977). *Cognitive development.* Englewood Cliffs, NJ: Prentice Hall.

Fletcher, P. (1985). *A child's learning of English.* Oxford: Basil Blackwell.

Fodor, J.A., Bever, T.G., & Garret, M.F. (1974). *The psychology of language.* New York: McGraw-Hill.

Friedman, W.J. (1982). *The developmental psychology of time.* New York: Academic Press.

Gagne, R.M. (1968). Contributions of learning to human development. *Psychological Review, 75,* 177–191.

Garfinkel, H. (1967). *Studies in ethnomethodology.* Englewood Cliffs, NJ: Prentice Hall.

Garvey, C. (1977). Play with language. In B. Tizard & D. Harvey (Eds.), *Biology of play* (pp. 74–99). Philadelphia: J.B. Lippincott.

Gesell, A. (1954). The ontogenesis of infant behavior. In L. Carmichael (Ed.), *Manual of child psychology* (2nd ed., pp. 335–373). New York: John Wiley & Sons.

Gibson, J.J. (1969). *Principles of perceptual learning and development.* New York: Appleton-Century-Crofts.

Gibson, J.J. (1977). The theory of affordances. In R. Shaw & J. Bransford (Eds.), *Perceiving, acting, and knowing: Toward an ecological psychology* (pp. 67–82). Hillsdale, NJ: Lawrence Erlbaum Associates.

Gibson, J.J. (1979). *The ecological approach to visual perception.* Boston: Houghton Mifflin.

Gibson, J.J. (1982). Notes on affordances. In E. Reed & R. Jones (Eds.), *Reasons for realism: Selected essays of James J. Gibson* (pp. 401–418). Hillsdale, NJ: Lawrence Erlbaum Associates.

Gleitman, L.R., & Wanner, E. (1982). Language acquisition: The state of the art. In E. Wanner & L.R. Gleitman (Eds.), *Language acquisition: The state of the art* (pp. 3–48). Cambridge: Cambridge University Press.

Gleitman, L.R., & Wanner, E. (1984). Current issues in language learning. In M.H. Bornstein & M.E. Lamb (Eds.), *Psychology: An advanced textbook* (pp. 181–240). Hillsdale, NJ: Lawrence Erlbaum Associates.

Gottman, J.M. (1981). *Time-series analysis: A comprehensive introduction for social scientists.* Cambridge: Cambridge University Press.

Gottman, J.M., & Bakeman, R. (1979). The sequential analysis of observational data. In M.F. Lamb, S.J. Suomi, & G.R. Stephenson (Eds.), *Social interaction analysis: Methodological issues* (pp. 185–206). Madison: University of Wisconsin Press.

Gottman, J.M., & Notarius, C. (1978). Sequential analysis of observational data using Markov chains. In T.R. Kratochwill (Ed.), *Single subject research: Strategies for evaluating change* (pp. 237–285). New York: Academic Press.

Greene, G. (1946). *The power and the glory.* New York: Viking Press.

Greenfield, P.M. (1984). A theory of the teacher in the learning activities of everyday life. In B. Rogoff & J. Lave (Eds.), *Everyday cognition: Its development in social context* (pp. 117–138). Cambridge, MA: Harvard University Press.

Greenfield, P., & Lave, J. (1982). Cognitive aspects of informal education. In D.A. Wagner & H.W. Stevenson (Eds.), *Cultural perspectives on child development* (pp. 181–207). San Francisco: Freeman & Co.

Gregson, R.A.M. (1983). *Time series in psychology.* Hillsdale, NJ: Lawrence Erlbaum Associates.

Grossman, E.R.F. (1959). A theory of the acquisition of speed-skill. *Ergonomics, 2,* 153–166.

Hannan, M.T., & Tuma, N.B. (1979). Methods for temporal analysis. *American Review of Sociology, 5,* 303–328.

Harlow, H.F. (1949). The formation of learning sets. *Psychological Review, 56,* 51–65.

Harlow, H.F. (1959). The development of learning in the Rhesus monkey. *American Scientist, 47,* 459–479.

Harris, Z.S. (1951). *Methods in structural linguistics*. Chicago: University of Chicago Press.

Heritage, J. (1984). *Garfinkel and ethnomethodology*. Cambridge: Polity Press.

Hill, J.C., & Arbib, M.A. (1984). Schemas, computation, and language acquisition. *Human Development, 27*, 282–296.

Hirsh-Pasek, K., Treiman, R., & Schneiderman, M. (1984). Brown & Hanlon revisited: Mothers' sensitivity to ungrammatical forms. *Journal of Child Language, 11*, 81–88.

Hockett, C.F. (1960). The origin of speech. *Scientific American, 203*, 1–10.

Hoff-Ginsberg, E. (1985). Some contributions of mothers' speech to their children's syntactic growth. *Journal of Child Language, 12*, 367–385.

Hoff-Ginsberg, E., & Shatz, M. (1982). Linguistic input and the child's acquisition of language. *Psychological Bulletin, 92*, 3–26.

Holding, D.H. (Ed.). (1981). *Human skills*. New York: John Wiley & Sons.

Hull, C.L. (1943). *Principles of behavior.* New York: Appleton-Century-Crofts.

Hull, C.L. (1952). *A behavior system: An introduction to behavior theory concerning the individual organism*. New Haven: Yale University Press.

Husserl, E. (1954). *Erfahrung und urteil* [Experience and judgment]. Hamburg: Felix Meiner.

Husserl, E. (1965). *Phenomenology and the crisis of philosophy*. New York: Harper Torchbooks.

Inhelder, B., Sinclair, H., & Bovet, M. (1974). *Learning and the development of cognition*. Cambridge, MA: Harvard University Press.

Istomina, Z.M. (1975). The development of voluntary memory in preschool-age children. *Soviet Psychology, 13*, 5–64.

Jacoby, L.L., & Witherspoon, D. (1982). Remembering without awareness. *Canadian Journal of Psychology, 36*, 300–324.

Jakobson, R. (1973). *Main trends in the science of language*. London: George Allen & Unwin.

Jakobson, R. (1985). Poetry of grammar and grammar of poetry. In K. Pomorska & S. Rudy (Eds.), *Verbal art, verbal sign, verbal time* (pp. 37–46). Minneapolis: University of Minnesota Press.

Johnston, J.R., & Slobin, D.I. (1979). The development of locative expressions in English, Italian, Serbo-Croatian and Turkish. *Journal of Child Language, 6*, 529–545.

Kaplan, A. (1964). *The conduct of inquiry*. San Francisco: Chandler.

Kastenbaum, R. (1961). The dimension of time perspective: An experimental analysis. *Journal of General Psychology, 65*, 203–218.

Kaye, K. (1982). *The mental and social life of babies: How parents create persons*. Chicago: University of Chicago Press.

Kelso, J.A. (Ed.). (1982). *Human motor behavior.* Hillsdale, NJ: Lawrence Erlbaum Associates.

Kleinman, M. (1983). *The acquisition of motor skill*. Princeton, NJ: Princeton Book Co.

Kluckhohn, C., Murray, H.A., & Schneider, D.M. (1967). *Personality in nature, society, and culture*. New York: Alfred A. Knopf.

Kuczaj, S.A. (1983). *Crib speech and language play*. New York: Springer-Verlag.

Langley, P., & Simon, H.A. (1981). The central role of learning in cognition. In J.R. Anderson (Ed.), *Cognitive skills and their acquisition* (pp. 361–380). Hillsdale, NJ: Lawrence Erlbaum Associates.

Larkin, P. (1988). *Collected poems*. London: Marvell Press.

Lashley, K.S. (1951). The problem of serial order in behavior. In L.A. Jeffress (Ed.), *Cerebral mechanisms in behavior* (pp. 112–136). New York: John Wiley & Sons.

Leopold, W. (1949). *Speech development of a bilingual child* (Vol. III). Evanston, IL: Northwestern University Press.

Mace, W.M. (1977). J.J. Gibson's strategy of perceiving: Ask not what's inside your head, but what your head's inside of. In R. Shaw & J. Bransford (Eds.), *Perceiving, acting, and knowing: Towards an ecological psychology* (pp. 43–65). Hillsdale, NJ: Lawrence Erlbaum Associates.

MacWhinney, B. (1978). The acquisition of morphophonology. *Monographs of the Society for Research in Child Development. 43* (Whole No. 1–2, Serial No. 174).

MacWhinney, B. (1982). Basic syntactic processes. In S. Kuczaj, II. (Ed.), *Language development: Vol. 1. Syntax and semantics* (pp. 73–136). Hillsdale, NJ: Lawrence Erlbaum Associates.

MacWhinney, B. (1987). Preface. In B. MacWhinney (Ed.), *Mechanisms of language acquisition* (pp. ix–xii). Hillsdale, NJ: Lawrence Erlbaum Associates.

MacWhinney, B., & Snow, C. (1985). The child language exchange system. *Journal of Child Language, 12*, 271–295.

Malinowski, B. (1923). The problem of meaning in primitive languages. In C.K. Ogden & I.A. Richards (Eds.), *The meaning of meaning* (pp. 296–336). London: Routledge & Kegan Paul Ltd.

Maratsos, M.P., & Chalkley, M.A. (1979). The internal language of children's syntax: The ontogenesis and representation of syntactic categories. In K. Nelson (Ed.), *Children's language* (Vol. 2, pp. 127–214). New York: Gardner Press.

Mayor, J.B. (1972). *A handbook of modern English metre.* New York: Lemma.

McNeil, D. (1970). *The acquisition of language.* New York: Harper & Row.

Mead, G.H. (1934). *Mind, self, and society.* Chicago: University of Chicago Press.

Meisel, J. (1985). Les phases initiales du developpement de notions temporelles, aspectuelles et de modes d'action [The initial phases of the development of concepts of time, aspect, and modality]. *Lingua, 66*, 321–374.

Menyuk, P. (1977). *Language and maturation.* Cambridge, MA: MIT Press.

Miller, G.A. (1970). Four philosophical problems of psycholinguistics. *Philosophy of Science, 37*(2), 183–191.

Miller, G.A., Galanter, E., & Pribram, K.H. (1960). *Plans and the structure of behavior.* New York: Holt, Rinehart & Winston.

Miller, G.A., & Johnson-Laird, P.N. (1976). *Language and perception.* Cambridge, MA: Harvard University Press.

Moerk, E.L. (1972). Principles of dyadic interaction in language learning. *Merrill-Palmer Quarterly, 18*, 229–257.

Moerk, E.L. (1975). Verbal interactions between children and their mothers during the preschool years. *Developmental Psychology, 11*, 788–794.

Moerk, E.L. (1976a). Processes of language teaching and training in the interactions of mother–child dyads. *Child Development, 47*, 1064–1078.

Moerk, E.L. (1976b). Motivational variables in language acquisition. *Child Study Journal, 6* (2), 55–84.

Moerk, E.L. (1977a). *Pragmatic and semantic aspects of early language development.* Baltimore: University Park Press.

Moerk, E.L. (1977b). Processes and products of imitation: Additional evidence that imitation is progressive. *Journal of Psycholinguistic Research, 6*, 187–202.

Moerk, E.L. (1980a). Relationships between parental input frequencies and children's language acquisition: A reanalysis of Brown's data. *Journal of Psycholinguistic Research, 7,* 105–118.

Moerk, E.L. (1980b, May). *The LAD was a lady.* Paper presented at the annual meeting of the Western Psychological Association, Honolulu.

Moerk, E.L. (1983a). *The mother of Eve—as a first language teacher.* Norwood, NJ: Ablex.

Moerk, E.L. (1983b). A behavioral analysis of controversial topics in first language acquisition: Reinforcements, corrections, modeling, input frequencies, and the three-term contingency pattern. *Journal of Psycholinguistic Research, 12,* 129–155.

Moerk, E.L. (1985a). Analytic, synthetic, abstracting, and word-class defining aspects of verbal mother–child interactions. *Journal of Psycholinguistic Research, 14,* 263–287.

Moerk, E.L. (1985b). Picture-book reading by mothers and young children and its impact upon language development. *Journal of Pragmatics, 9,* 547–566.

Moerk, E.L. (1986). Environmental factors in early language acquisition. In G.J. Whitehurst (Ed.), *Annals of child development* (Vol. 3, pp. 191–235). Greenwich, CT: JAI Press.

Moerk, E.L. (1989). The LAD was a lady and the tasks were ill-defined. *Developmental Review, 9,* 21–57.

Moerk, E.L. (1990). Three-term contingency patterns in mother–child verbal interactions during first-language acquisition. *Journal of the Experimental Analysis of Behavior, 54,* 293–305.

Moerk, E.L. (in press). Positive evidence for negative evidence. *First Language.*

Moerk, E.L., & Moerk, C. (1979). Quotations, imitations, and generalizations: Factual and methodological analyses. *International Journal of Behavioral Development, 2,* 43–72.

Moerk, E.L., & Vilaseca, R. (1987). Time-binding in mother–child interactions: The morphemes for past and future. *Papers and Reports on Child Language Development, 26,* 80–87.

Neisser, U. (1976). *Cognition and reality.* San Francisco: W.H. Freeman.

Nelson, K.E. (1977). Aspects of language acquisition and use from age 2 to 20. *Journal of the American Academy of Child Psychiatry, 16,* 584–607.

Nelson, K.E. (1989). Strategies for first language teaching. In M.L. Rice & R.L. Schiefelbusch (Eds.), *The teachability of language* (pp. 263–310). Baltimore: Paul H. Brookes Publishing Co.

Newell, K.M. (1981). Skill learning. In D. Holding (Ed.), *Human skills* (pp. 203–226). New York: John Wiley & Sons.

Newport, E., Gleitman, L., & Gleitman, H. (1977). Mother, I'd rather do it myself: Some effects and noneffects of maternal speech style. In C.E. Snow & C.A. Ferguson (Eds.), *Talking to children* (pp. 109–149). Cambridge: Cambridge University Press.

Ochs, E. (1986). Introduction. In B.B. Schieffelin & E. Ochs (Eds.), *Language socialization across cultures* (pp. 1–13). Cambridge: Cambridge University Press.

Orne, J.E. (1969). *Time, experience and behavior.* New York: American Elsevier.

Papousek, H., & Papousek, M. (1977). Mothering and the cognitive headstart: Psychological considerations. In H.R. Schaffer (Ed.), *Studies in mother–infant interaction* (pp. 63–85). New York: Academic Press.

Papousek, M., & Papousek, H. (1981). Musical elements in the infant's vocalization: Their significance for communication, cognition, and creativity. In L.P.

Lipsitt (Ed.), *Advances in infancy research* (Vol. 1, pp. 164–225). Norwood, NJ: Ablex.

Papousek, M., Papousek, H., & Bornstein, M.H. (1985). The naturalistic vocal environment of young infants. In T.M. Field & N. Fox (Eds.), *Social perception in infants* (pp. 269–297). Norwood, NJ: Ablex.

Paris, S.G., Newman, S., & Jacobs, J.E. (1985). Social contexts and functions of children's remembering. In M. Pressley & C.J. Brainerd (Eds.), *Cognitive learning and memory in children: Progress in cognitive development research* (pp. 81–115). New York: Springer-Verlag.

Parisi, D., & Antinucci, F. (1970). Lexical competence. In G.B. Flores d'Arcais & W.J.M. Levelt (Eds.), *Advances in psycholinguistics* (pp. 197–210). Amsterdam: North Holland.

Peters, A. (1983). *The units of language acquisition.* Cambridge: Cambridge University Press.

Piaget, J. (1952). *The origins of intelligence in children.* New York: Norton & Co.

Piaget, J. (1955). Les stades du developpement intellectuel de l'enfant et de l'adolescent [The stages of intellectual development of the child and adolescent]. In P. Osterreich (Ed.), *Le probleme des stades en psychologie de l'enfant [The problem of stages in child psychology]* (pp. 33–113). Paris: Presses Universitaires de France.

Piaget, J. (1969). *The mechanisms of perception.* New York: Basic Books.

Piaget, J. (1977). *The development of thought: Equilibration of cognitive structures.* New York: Viking Press.

Piaget, J. (1980). The psychogenesis of knowledge and its epistemological significance. In M. Piatelli-Palmarini (Eds.), *Language and learning* (pp. 23–24). Cambridge, MA: Harvard University Press.

Pierce, C.S. (1934). *Collected papers* (Vol. 1). Cambridge, MA: Harvard University Press.

Pike, K.L., & Pike, E.G. (1977). *Grammatical analysis.* Arlington, TX: Summer Institute of Linguistics Academic Publications.

Pinker, S., & Prince, A. (1988). On language and connectionism: Analysis of a parallel distributed processing model of language acquisition. *Cognition, 28,* 73–193.

Polanyi, M. (1958). *Personal knowledge.* Chicago: University of Chicago Press.

Preez, P. du (1974). Units of information in the acquisition of language. *Language and Speech, 17,* 369–376.

Pressley, M., & Levin, J.R. (Eds.). (1983). *Cognitive strategy research: Psychological foundations.* New York: Springer-Verlag.

Quine, W. (1965). *Word and object.* Cambridge, MA: MIT Press.

Raaijmaker, J.G., & Shiffrin, R.M. (1981). Search for associative memory. *Psychological Review, 88,* 93–134.

Reber, A.S. (1967). Implicit learning of artificial grammars. *Journal of Verbal Learning and Verbal Behavior, 5,* 855–863.

Reber, A.S. (1976). Implicit learning of synthetic languages: The role of instructional set. *Journal of Experimental Psychology, 81,* 115–119.

Ribes, E. (1983). Has behavior analysis actually dealt with language? In N. Smith, P. Mountjoy, & D. Rubem (Eds.), *Reassessment in psychology: The interbehavioral alternative* (pp. 233–250). Washington, DC: University Press of America.

Rivers, W. (1964). *The psychologist and the foreign-language teacher.* Chicago: University of Chicago Press.

Rogoff, B., & Gardner, W. (1984). Adult guidance of cognitive development. In

B. Rogoff & J. Lave (Eds.), *Everyday cognition: Its development in social context* (pp. 95–116). Cambridge, MA: Harvard University Press.

Rogoff, B., Gauvain, M., & Ellis, S. (1984). Development viewed in its cultural context. In M. Bornstein & M.E. Lamb (Eds.), *Developmental psychology* (pp. 533–571). Hillsdale, NJ: Lawrence Erlbaum Associates.

Rogoff, B., & Lave, J. (Eds.). (1984). *Everyday cognition: Its development in social context.* Cambridge, MA: Harvard University Press.

Rondal, J.A. (1979). Mama est au courant: Une etude des connaissances maternelles quant aux aspects formels du langage de jeune enfant [Mommy is informed: A study of maternal knowledge about formal aspects of the language of the young child]. *Enfance, 2,* 95–105.

Rondal, J.A. (1985). *Adult–child interaction and the process of language acquisition.* New York: Praeger.

Rubin, D.C. (1988). Learning poetic language. In F.S. Kessel (Ed.), *The development of language and language researchers* (pp. 339–351). Hillsdale, NJ: Lawrence Erlbaum Associates.

Rumelhart, D.E., & McClelland, J.L. (1985). *On learning the past tense of English verbs* (ICS Report 8507). San Diego: University of California Institute for Cognitive Science.

Rumelhart, D.E., McClelland, J.L., & PDP research group (Eds.). (1986). *Parallel distributed processing* (Vols. 1 & 2). Cambridge, MA: Bradford Books.

Rumelhart, D.E., & Norman, D.A. (1981). Analogical processes in learning. In J.R. Anderson (Ed.), *Cognitive skills and their acquisition* (pp. 335–359). Hillsdale, NJ: Lawrence Erlbaum Associates.

Sachs, J. (1979). Topic selection in parent–child discourse. *Discourse Processes, 2,* 145–153.

Sachs, J. (1983). Talking about the there and then: The emergence of displaced reference in parent–child discourse. In K.E. Nelson (Ed.), *Children's language* (Vol. 4, pp. 1–28). Hillsdale, NJ: Lawrence Erlbaum Associates.

Sage, G.H. (Ed.). (1984). *Motor learning and control.* Dubuque, IA: Wm. C. Brown.

Salzinger, K. (1975). Are theories of competence necessary? In D. Aaronson & R.W. Rieber (Eds.), Developmental psycholinguistics and communication disorders. *Annals of the New York Academy of Sciences, 263,* 178–196.

Saussure, F. de (1959). *Course in general linguistics.* New York: McGraw-Hill.

Schlesinger, I.M. (1988). The origin of relational categories. In Y. Levy, I.M. Schlesinger, & M.D.S. Braine (Eds.), *Categories and processes in language acquisition* (pp. 121–178). Hillsdale, NJ: Lawrence Erlbaum Associates.

Schmidt, C.R., & Paris, S.G. (1984). The development of verbal communicative skills in children. In H.W. Reese (Ed.), *Advances in child development and behavior* (Vol. 18, pp. 1–47). New York: Academic Press.

Schmidt, R.A. (1975). A schema theory of discrete motor learning. *Psychological Review, 82,* 225–260.

Schneider, W., & Detweiler, M. (1987). A connectionist/control architecture for working memory. In G.H. Bower (Ed.), *The psychology of learning and motivation* (Vol. 21, pp. 53–119). San Diego, CA: Academic Press.

Schneider, W., & Shiffrin, R.M. (1977). Controlled and automatic human information processing: 1. Detection, search, and attention. *Psychological Review, 84,* 1–66.

Scollon, R. (1976). *Conversations with a one-year-old.* Honolulu: University Press of Hawaii.

Segal, J.W., Chipman, S.F., & Glaser, R. (1985). (Eds.). *Thinking and learning skills: Vol. 1. Relating instruction to research.* Hillsdale, NJ: Lawrence Erlbaum

Associates.

Shapiro, D.C., & Schmidt, R.A. (1982). The schema theory: Recent evidence and developmental implications. In J.A.S. Kelso & J.E. Clark (Eds.), *The development of movement and coordination* (pp. 113–150). New York: John Wiley & Sons.

Shatz, M. (1982). On mechanisms of language acquisition: Can features of the communicative environment account for development? In E. Wanner & L.R. Gleitman (Eds.), *Language acquisition: The state of the art* (pp. 102–127). Cambridge: Cambridge University Press.

Shatz, M. (1983). Communication. In J.H. Flavell & E.M. Markman (Eds.), *Handbook of child development: Vol. III. Cognitive development* (pp. 841–889). New York: John Wiley & Sons.

Simon, H.A. (1979). *Models of thought.* New Haven: Yale University Press.

Skinner, B.F. (1957). *Verbal behavior.* New York. Appleton-Century-Crofts.

Slama-Cazacu, T. (1977). Les exchanges verbaux entre les enfants et entre adults et enfants [The verbal exchanges between children and between adults and children]. In J.P. Bronckart, P. Malrieu, M. Siguan-Soler, H. Sinclair, T. Slama-Cazacu, & A. Tabouret-Keller (Eds.), *La genese de la parole* [The development of the utterance] (pp. 179–229). Paris: Presses Universitaires de France.

Slobin, D.I. (1968). Imitation and grammatical development in children. In N.S. Endler, L.R. Boutler, & H. Osser (Eds.), *Contemporary issues in developmental psychology* (pp. 437–443). New York: Holt, Rinehart & Winston.

Slobin, D.I. (Ed.). (1985). *The crosslinguistic study of language acquisition* (Vols. 1 & 2). Hillsdale, NJ: Lawrence Erlbaum Associates.

Smith, G. (1984). Plea for a process-oriented psychology. In K.M.J. Lagerspetz & P. Niemi (Eds.), *Psychology in the 1990s* (pp. 367–381). Amsterdam: Elsevier/North Holland.

Snow, C.E. (1972). Mothers' speech to children learning language. *Child Development, 43*, 549–565.

Snow, C.E. (1977a). Mothers' speech research: From input to interaction. In C.E. Snow & C.A. Ferguson (Eds.), *Talking to children: Language input and acquisition* (pp. 31–49). Cambridge: Cambridge University Press.

Snow, C.E. (1977b) The development of conversation between mothers and babies. *Journal of Child Language, 4*, 1–22.

Snow, C.E. (1981). The uses of imitation. *Journal of Child Language, 8*, 205–212.

Snow, C.E. (1983). Saying it again: The role of expanded and deferred imitations in language acquisition. In K.E. Nelson (Ed.), *Children's language* (Vol. 4, pp. 29–58). Hillsdale, NJ: Lawrence Erlbaum Associates.

Snow, C., & Ferguson, C. (Eds.). (1977). *Talking to children.* Cambridge: Cambridge University Press.

Snow, C.E., & Goldfield, B.A. (1983). Turn the page please: Situation-specific language acquisition. *Journal of Child Language, 10*, 551–569.

Soederberg, R. (1974). *Barnets spraokutveckling och dess konsekvenser* [The child's language development and its consequences]. Stockholm: Stockholm University Institute for Nordic Languages.

Stella-Prorok, E.M. (1983). Mother–child language in the natural environment. In K. Nelson (Ed.), *Children's language* (Vol. 4, pp. 187–230). Hillsdale, NJ: Lawrence Erlbaum Associates.

Stern, W., & Stern, C. (1907). *Die kindersprache: Eine psychologische und sprachtheoretische untersuchung* [Child language: A psychological and theoretical investigation]. Leipzig: Barth.

Stokes, T.F., & Baer, D.M. (1977). An implicit technology of generalization. *Journal of Applied Behavior Analysis, 10*, 349–367.

Sullivan, H.S. (1947). *Conceptions of modern psychiatry.* Washington, DC: W.A. White Foundation.

Thorndike, E.L. (1913). *Educational psychology.* New York: Columbia University Press.

Thurstone, L.L. (1919). The learning curve equation. *Psychological Monographs, 26,* 1–51.

Toulmin, S., & Goldfield, J. (1965). *The discovery of time.* Chicago: University of Chicago Press.

Tukey, J.W. (1977). *Exploratory data analysis.* Reading, MA: Addison-Wesley.

Vos, G.A. de, & Hippler, A.A. (1969). Cultural psychology: Causative studies of human behavior. In G. Lindzey & E. Aronson (Eds.), *The handbook of social psychology* (Vol. 4, pp. 323–417) Reading, MA: Addison-Wesley.

Vygotsky, L.S. (1962). *Thought and language.* Cambridge, MA: MIT Press.

Vygotsky, L.S. (1978). *Mind in society.* Cambridge, MA: Harvard University Press.

Wagner, K.R. (1985). How much do children say in a day? *Journal of Child Language, 12,* 475–487.

Wales, R. (1986). Deixis. In P. Fletcher & N. Garman (Eds.), *Language acquisition: Studies in first language development* (2nd ed., pp. 401–428). Cambridge: Cambridge University Press.

Warren, S.F., & Kaiser, A.P. (1986). Incidental language teaching: A critical review. *Journal of Speech and Hearing Disorders, 51,* 291–299.

Waterman, D. (1970). Generalization learning techniques for automating the learning of heuristics. *Artificial Intelligence, 1,* 121–170.

Watson, J.S., & Hayes, L.A. (1981, April). *A new method of infant-environment interaction analysis.* Paper presented at the Biennial Meeting of the Society for Research in Child Development, Boston.

Watson, J.S., & Ramey, C.T. (1972). Reactions to response-contingent stimulation in early infancy. *Merrill-Palmer Quarterly, 18,* 219–228.

Weir, R. (1962). *Language in the crib.* The Hague: Mouton.

Wells, G. (1985). *Language development in the pre-school years.* Cambridge: Cambridge University Press.

Werner, H. (1948). *Comparative psychology of mental development.* New York: International Universities Press.

Werner, H., & Kaplan, B. (1963). *Symbol formation.* New York: John Wiley & Sons.

Wertheimer, M. (1945). *Productive thinking.* New York: Harper.

Whitehurst, G.J. (1982). Language development. In B.B. Wolman (Ed.), *Handbook of developmental psychology* (pp. 367–386). Englewood Cliffs, NJ: Prentice Hall.

Whitehurst, G.J., & DeBaryshe, B.D. (1989). Observational learning and language acquisition: Principles of learning, systems, and tasks. In G.E. Speidel & K. Nelson (Eds.), *The many faces of imitation in language learning* (pp. 251–276). New York: Springer-Verlag.

Whitehurst, G.J., & Vasta, R. (1975). Is language acquired through imitation? *Journal of Psycholinguistic Research, 4,* 37–59.

Wiener, N. (1948). *Cybernetics: Or control and communication in the animal and the machine.* Cambridge, MA: MIT Press.

Wilson, B., & Peters, A. (1988). What are you cookin' on a hot? *Language, 64,* 249–273.

Index

Abstraction, 12–13, 183
  see also Pattern abstraction
Acquisition
  iterative and incremental, *see* Iterative and incremental acquisition
  meanings of, 11
  processes of, in context, 76–77
  see also Language acquisition; *specific types, e.g.,* Syntax acquisition
ACT* theory, 208, 209
Adaptive production systems, 204
Adjacent utterances, relationships between, 15
Adult interventions
  adaptations of, to filial information processing needs, 136–137
  effectiveness of, syntax learning and, 169–170
  intense, syntax acquisition and, 171–174
  positive effects of, 89–92
  see also specific type, e.g., Corrective feedback
Adult speech, roots of future morphemes in, 114–122
Affordances
  culture learning and, 3
  language learning and, 11
  readiness and, 217
Antecedents, in sequential analysis, 220–221
Anticipation, future orientation and, 113–114
Augmented feedback, skill learning and, 7
Automatization
  culture learning and, 5–6
  gradual, 14–15
  language learning and, 14–15
  skill learning and, 9

Behaviorism
  cognitive approach integrated with, 214–215
  language acquisition and, 185–186
Bivariate trends
  cohesion in, expressed statistically, 199–202
  language acquisition and, 187
  general principles from, 193
  long-term
    in complex syntax training, 197–199
    in simple syntax training, 193–197
    in vocabulary training, 191–193
Break-down sequences, 194–195
Build-up sequences, 194

"Calculus of development," 229–230
Cause–effect relationships
  frequency relationships of input and use and, future morphemes and, 126–127, 128–129
  multiple, past-tense morphemes and, 80–81
  syntax acquisition and, 182
    long-term versus immediate dynamics in, 195–196
CHILDES database, 1, 233
Cognitive approach, 213–214
  behaviorist approach integrated with, 214–215
Cognitive development, future perspective and, 111–114
Cognitive processes, in input processing, future morphemes and, 129–141
Cognitive skill acquisition, stages in, 207
Cognitive structures, conceptualization of, 213–214

247

Competence
cues and, present progressive
and, 36–37
prepositional phrases and, 70
Completions, 194
Complex skills, progress from simple skills to, 12–13
Complex syntax training, bivariate
trends in, 197–199
Computer modeling, specifications
in, 204, 206–207
Conceptual learning, sensorimotor
learning versus, future-tense
morphemes and, 120–121
Conceptual models and tools, 1–15,
211–218
see also Theoretical perspectives;
specific models
Confirmation, minor corrections
and, 81–83
Context
acquisition processes in, temporal
morphemes and, 76–77,
108–109
dependency on, future-tense morphemes and, 146
see also Environment
Contingency, sequential, 222–223
Continuity, present progressive and,
35
Continuous-time analyses, 16
adult interventions and, temporal
morphemes and, 90–92
of bivariate trends, 188
methodological tools for, 218–230
see also Methodology
Conversation, learning and, cybernetic approach to, 217
Copula sentence
full-verb sentence and, 198
prepositional phrase and, 48
present progressive and, 32
S-V-O structure versus, 151
Corrective feedback
confirmation with, 81–83
consistency of, past-tense morphemes and, 83–87
grammatical, past-tense morphemes and, 87
past-tense morphemes and, 80–81
prepositional phrases and, 64–69
production without mastery and,
40–42

skill learning and, 7
see also Feedback
Correlations, regular versus partial,
202
Covariations
frequency of, temporal morphemes and, 90–92, 128–129
methodology and, 209
multiple influences on, 200
in trends of mother and child, vocabulary training and, 192
Cue(s)
through "did," see "Did," as past-
tense marker
future-tense morphemes and, 145
present progressive and, 26, 27,
36–40
see also Present progressive
(PPr), acquisition of
see also Modeling
Cue dependency
creativity versus, past-tense morphemes and, 94
future-tense morphemes and, 146
prepositional phrase and, 53
present progressive and, 42–44
speed of progress and, 94–95
see also Input dependency
Culture learning, 2–6
from controlled to automatic processing in, 5–6
flexibility of cultural skills and, 5
interactional routines and, 4
iterative and incremental acquisition in, 4–5
sociogenetic perspective of,
231–232
ubiquity of information and, 3–4
Cybernetic approach to conversation
and learning, 217

Data
reduction and synthesis of, 16–17
relational, 15–16
Declarative knowledge, procedural
knowledge versus, 207
"Did," as past-tense marker, 78, 80,
82
cue value of, overgeneralization
and, 87–89
cuing through, 83, 85
see also Past-tense morphemes

Dyadic interactions, 10–11
    see also Interactional routines

Early learning, syntactic structures
        in, 150–151, 152–162
Echoing, imitation and, past-tense
        morphemes and, 80
Educational parallels, 204, 205–206
Effectiveness of training, syntax
        learning and, 169–170
Empirical, neo-positivist approach,
        212–213
Environment
    behaviorist emphasis on, language
        acquisition and, 185–186
    interaction with stimuli in, 208
    structure of, static conceptions of,
        215–216
    temporal morphemes and, 76–77,
        78, 89
    see also Context
Environmental information, dynamic
        conceptions of, 216–217
Equational devices, temporal mor-
        phemes and, 109
Errors, in present progressive, 21
Event series analyses, 225
    "calculus of development" and,
        229–230
Everyday learning, 204, 206
Expansions, in feedback, 11, 69–70

Factual analyses, generalizations
        from, 233
Feedback
    consistency of, syntax and, 169
    cycles of, 217
    fine tuning of, 217
        future-morpheme development
            and, 123–126
    forms of, future-morpheme devel-
            opment and, 122–123
    frequency of, future-morpheme
            development and, 126
    imitation and, 11
    informative, prepositional phrases
            and, 59–64
    intensified, early, 172–173
    interactional routines and
        culture learning and, 4
        language learning and, 11

    skill learning and, 7
    matching of, to productions,
        123–125
    misleading effects of, past-tense
        morphemes and, 86–87
    positive nature of, future-
        morpheme development and,
        125–126
    structural, random constituent se-
        lection and, 157–159
    syntax and, 165–171
    temporal morphemes and, 78, 80
        future-tense, 117–118, 122–126
        past-tense, 78, 80, 85–86
    types of, syntax and, 168–169
    unobtrusive, past-tense mor-
        phemes and, 85
    variety of, 169
    versatility of, past-tense mor-
        phemes and, 85–86
    see also Corrective feedback; Input
        entries
Figure–ground relationship, pre-
        positional phrases and, 72
Filial learning, 185, 186
    see also Language acquisition
Filial productions
    prepositional phrase and, 53, 69,
        71
    rapid adult adjustments to, 128
    temporal morphemes and, 75–76
        future, 128, 136–137
        irregular past, 99–103
    time series of, 226
Fine tuning
    of maternal feedback, 217
        future-morpheme development
            and, 123–126
    readiness and, 12
Formula learning, future-tense mor-
        phemes and, 116–120
Frame variation, 198
Frequency
    input and use relationships,
        126–129
    present progressive and, 24–26
    temporal morphemes and, 90–92,
        108
        future, 126–129, 144–145, 146
        irregular past, 99
    see also Input frequency
Frequency matching, consistent,
        128–129

Full-verb sentence, changing from
     copula sentence to, 198
Functors, 198
Future orientation, 112, 113–114
Future-tense morphemes, 76
     acquisition of, 111–146
          analyses of, 114–122
          anticipation of events and,
               113–114
          causes of progress and failure
               in, 138
          cognitive bases of future per-
               spective and, 111–114
          evidence of progress in, 138–139
          first productions of "will/'ll" in,
               129–132
          fixed formula in, 116–120
          frequency relationships of input
               and use in, 126–129
          increased independence from
               input in, 140–141
          input dependency and, 135–136
          input frequency and, 121
          input processing in, 129–141
          level mixture in, 132–140
          longitudinal aspects of develop-
               ment in, 122–141
          from main verb to auxiliary in,
               114–116
          maternal feedback and, 122–126
          means–ends aspects of, 113
          need fulfillment and, 112–113
          production deficiency and,
               139–140
          prolonged erratic performance
               in, 137–138
          semantic complexity and, 121
          sensorimotor versus conceptual
               learning in, 120–121
          standing phrase and, 120
     earliest productions of, roots in
          adult speech and, 114–122
     see also Temporal morphemes

Generalizations, from factual anal-
     yses, 233
Grammar, corrections of, past-tense
     morphemes and, 87

Imitation, feedback and, 11
Imitative utterances

prepositional phrase and, 49–50,
     51
     see also Prepositional phrase
          (PPh), acquisition of
present progressive and, 26–27, 30
     see also Present progressive
          (PPr), acquisition of
temporal morphemes and, 75,
     78–80
Incidental learning, 4
Incremental progress, 13–14
Information
     environmental, dynamic concep-
          tions of, 216–217
     ubiquity of
          culture learning and, 3–4
          language learning and, 9–10
          skill learning and, 6–7
Information display, prepositional
     phrases and, 71
Information processing needs, filial,
     adult adaptation to, 136–137
Input
     filial learning and, irregular past
          and, 99–103
     immediate, multiple determina-
          tion in, 130–131
     increased independence from, fu-
          ture-tense morphemes and,
          140–141
     responses to, sequential analysis
          and, 221–222
     see also Feedback
Input dependency
     future-tense morphemes and,
          135–136, 140–141
     past-tense morphemes and, 94
          irregular past, 103–104
     spontaneous recall versus, 140–141
     structurally blind, 162–165
     see also Cue dependency
Input frequency
     future-tense morphemes and, 121
     past-tense morphemes and, 98–99
     use frequency and, 126–129
Input processing, microanalyses of,
     future morphemes and,
     129–141
Interactional phenomena
     consistency of corrective feedback
          and, 83–87
     continuous-time analyses of, see

Continuous-time analyses;
  Methodology
decreases in maternal support in,
  83–87
Interactional routines
  culture learning and, 4
  language learning and, 10–11
    present progressive in, 24
  skill learning and, 7
  syntax acquisition and, 174–181
Interactional sequences, nonstationary, 224
Interactional structure, 215
Irregular past
  acquisition of, 99–106
    factors contributing to retention
      in, 103–104
    loss and relearning of specific
      forms in, 104
    maternal input and filial learn-
      ing in, 99–103
    microanalyses of, 105–106
    from reproduction to productiv-
      ity in, 103
  see also Past-tense morphemes
Iterative and incremental acquisition
  culture learning and, 4–5
  language learning and, 11–14
  skill learning and, 7–8

Knowledge
  declarative versus procedural, 207
  tacit, skill learning and, 9

Labeling, vocabulary training and,
  192
Language acquisition, 185–210
  bivariate trends in, 187–202
    see also Bivariate trends
  learning mechanisms in, 203
  method of analysis of, 187
  principles of, 185–187
  relation of, to other domains and
    theoretical approaches,
    204–207
  sociogenetic perspective of,
    231–232
  see also specific aspects, e.g., Tem-
    poral morphemes, acquisition
    of

Language Acquisition Device (LAD),
  185
Language Acquisition Support System, 185
Language learning, 185–210
  from controlled to automatic pro-
    cessing in, 14–15
  flexibility of skills and, 14
  interactional routines and, 10–11
  iterative and incremental acquisi-
    tion in, 11–14
    progress from simple to com-
      plex skills and, 12–13
    readiness principle and, 12
  theoretical perspectives and, 9–15
  see also Language acquisition; spe-
    cific aspect
Lead–lag relationships, 200
  changing, in time series analyses,
    226–227
  complexities of, 201–202
  methodology and, 209
  simple syntax training and,
    195–196
Learning
  early, syntactic structures in,
    150–151, 152–162
  everyday, 204, 206
  filial, 185, 186
    see also Filial productions; Lan-
      guage acquisition
  sociogenetic perspective and,
    231–232
Learning set formation, 204, 205
Learning strategies, 202–210
  see also Language acquisition
Level mixture, in acquisition process, future-tense morphemes
  and, 132–140
Literary devices, temporal morphemes and, 109–110
Long-term memory
  past-tense morphemes and, 81
  prepositional phrases and, 72
  see also Memory span
Long-term training, dynamics of,
  225–230

Macroanalytic domain, relational
  data and, 16
Massing, 224

Massing—*continued*
  prepositional phrase and, 49
  present progressive and, 25
  temporal morphemes and, 108
    irregular past, 103
Mastery
  defined, 20
  production without, present pro-
    gressive and, 40–42
  of temporal concepts, 75
Maternal feedback, *see* Feedback
Maternal influences, *see* Interactional
  *entries; specific topics or types of
  influence*
Maternal training, *see* Adult
  interventions
Mean length of utterance (MLU)
  past-tense morphemes and, 78
  prepositional phrase and, 50
  syntax training and, 196–197
Memory, sequential contingency
  and, 222–223
Memory span
  future-tense morphemes and,
    145–146
  past-tense morphemes and, 80,
    81, 107
  prepositional phrases and, 72
  present progressive and, 24, 43–44
  see also Recall; Retention
Methodology
  continuous-time analysis and,
    218–230
  data reduction and synthesis and,
    16–17
  empirical studies and, 230–231
  learning strategies and, 209–210
  long-term training dynamics in,
    225–230
  measurement and, 15–16
  sequential approaches in, 219–225
  syntax and, 151–152
  temporal morphemes and, 106,
    144
Microanalytic domain, relational
  data and, 15
MLU, *see* Mean length of utterance
Modeling
  consistent, syntax and, 169
  past-tense morphemes and
    exact post-modeling, 83
    see also Past-tense morphemes,
    acquisition of

prepositional phrase and, 49
  see also Prepositional phrase
    (PPh), acquisition of
present progressive and, 26–27,
  29–32
  see also Present progressive
    (PPr), acquisition of
syntax learning and, 165–171
Models, conceptual, 1–15, 211–218
  see also Theoretical perspectives;
  specific models
Morpheme(s)
  minor, syntactic innovation and,
    173–174
  prepositional, *see* Prepositional
    phrase (PPh)
  present progressive, *see* Present
    progressive (PPr)
  temporal, *see* Temporal
    morphemes
Mother–child interactions, *see* Interactional *entries; specific type*

Narrow-scope formula, S-V-O structure and, 152–154
Need fulfillment, orientation toward,
  112–113
Neo-positivist approach, empirical,
  212–213
Nonverbal stimuli, dependency on,
  149
Noun-noun productions, in syntax
  acquisition, 159–162
Novelty, repetition and, balance between, 178
Novelty problem, 8

Observational learning, 232
Optional transformations, 198
Overgeneralization, temporal morphemes and, 76, 77
  cue value of "did," 87–89
  input frequency, 98

Past-tense morphemes, acquisition
  of, 77–110
  cause–effect relationships and,
    80–81
  clarification through confirmation
    and correction in, 81–89

confirmation with minor correc-
    tions in, 81–83
consistency of corrective feedback
    and, 83–87
corrective feedback in confirming
    responses and, 83
creativity versus cue dependency
    and, 94
cue value of "did" and over-
    generalization in, 87–89
first steps in, 78–81
grammar corrections and, 87
immediate imitation in, 78–80
input dependency and, 94
input frequency effects on, 98–99
irregular past, 99–106
positive effects of adult interven-
    tions and, 89–92
prolonged confusion and partial
    learning in, 96–98
from reproduction to productivity
    in, 92–99
results of analysis of, 78–106
slow versus rapid progress in,
    94–96
theoretical considerations of,
    77–78, 89
truth value corrections and, 87
Pattern abstraction, 12–13, 199
    prepositional phrases and, 71
    syntactic analysis and, early ad-
        vances in, 173
Pattern display, prepositional phrase
    and, 56
Pattern learning, 182
Pattern perception, syntax acquisi-
    tion and, 181–182
Perceptual learning, significance of,
    232
Phrase, prepositional, see Preposi-
    tional phrase (PPh)
Positive transfer, 204
Possessive determiners, preposi-
    tional phrases and, feedback
    and, 64, 68
PPh, see Prepositional phrase
PPr, see Present progressive
Predicates, wishes shaped into,
    165–168
Prepositional phrase (PPh), 19
    acquisition of, 47–73
        intensive teaching episodes
            and, 53–58

maternal feedback effects in,
    64–69
maternal informative feedback
    and, 59–64
method of analysis of, 50–51
results of analysis of, 51–69
uptake of new and rare preposi-
    tions in, 51–53
Prepositions
    uptake of, 51–53
    see also Prepositional phrase (PPh)
Present progressive (PPr), 19
    acquisition of, 19–45
        antecedents and intervals before
            production in, 28, 33, 38–39
        cue dependency in, 42–44
        early uses and, 27–32
        fine grained analyses of process
            in, 26–27
        method of analysis of, 21–22
        overall longitudinal trends in,
            22–24
        production without mastery in,
            40–42
        range of effective cues and,
            36–40
        results of analysis of, 22–44
        variety of verbs and, 32–36
    errors in, 21
Priming
    future-tense morphemes and, 145
    present progressive and, 29, 37
    see also Cue(s); Cue dependency
Procedural knowledge, declarative
    knowledge versus, 207
Production deficiency, future-tense
    morphemes and, 139–140
Productions
    filial, see Filial productions
    noun-noun, in syntax acquisition,
        159–162
    see also Utterance(s)
Productivity
    irregular past and, 103
    past-tense morphemes and,
        92–99, 103
    in verb phrases, future-tense mor-
        phemes and, 141
Progress
    evidence of, future-tense mor-
        phemes and, 138–139
    incremental, 13–14
    maternal responses to, syntax ac-

Progress—*continued*
quisition and, 179–180
from simple to complex skills,
12–13
slow versus rapid, past-tense morphemes and, 94–96
Prosodic structure, 215
Proximal development, zone of, iterative and incremental acquisition and, 5, 12

Quantitative analysis, 15–16
of bivariate trends, 188

Readiness
affordances and, 217
iterative and incremental acquisition and, 5, 12
Recall
spontaneous, input dependency
versus, 140–141
see also Memory span; Retention
Rehearsal strategies, 186, 190–191
simple syntax training and, 194
vocabulary training and, 192
Relational data, 15–16
environmental, 216–217
Repetition, novelty and, balance between, 178
Replacement sequences, 197, 199
Reproduction, to productivity from
irregular past tense and, 103
past-tense morphemes and,
92–99, 103
Requests, for labels, 192
Retention
factors contributing to, irregular
past and, 103–104
see also Memory span; Recall
Rhythmic patterns
prepositional phrases and, 56
syntax acquisition and, 180, 182
Rote formulas, containing "will/'ll,'"
131–132
Rule-governed use, present progressive and, 41
Rule learning, 11–12, 13

Schema theory, 8
syntax acquisition and, 182, 183

Semantic complexity, future-tense
morphemes and, 121
Sensorimotor learning, conceptual
learning versus, 120–121
Sequential analyses, 219–225
antecedents in, 220–221
changing system in, 223–225
contingency in, 222–223
responses to input in, 221–222
Serial methods, 16
Short-term memory
prepositional phrases and, 72
see also Memory span
Skill(s)
flexibility of
culture learning and, 5
language learning and, 14–15
skill learning and, 8
progress from simple to complex,
12–13
Skill learning, 6–9, 213
from controlled to automatic processing in, 8
everyday learning and, 206
flexibility of skills and, 8
interactional routines and, 7
iterative and incremental acquisition in, 7–8
sociogenetic perspective of,
231–232
time dimension in, 232
ubiquity of information and, 6–7
Slot and filler principle, syntax acquisition and, 159, 161, 169
Sociogenetic perspective, 231–232
Spacing
prepositional phrase and, 49
present progressive and, 26
temporal morphemes and, 108
Spontaneous utterances
prepositional phrase and, 49–50
see also Prepositional phrase
(PPh), acquisition of
present progressive and, 26–27,
29–30
see also Present progressive
(PPr), acquisition of
Statistics
inferential, 50
see also specific topics
Stimuli
environmental, interaction with,
208

structure of, 215
Stimulus dependency, syntax and,
    148–149
Strategy production deficiencies, 206
Structure
    environmental, 215–216
    information and, 10
    stimulus, 215
    syntactic, *see* Syntactic construc-
        tions; Syntactic structure
Substitutions
    multiple, syntax acquisition and,
        177–178
    simple, syntax acquisition and,
        174–177
S-V-O sentence structure
    acquisition of, 151
        see also Syntax acquisition
    early elaboration of formula for,
        154–156
    from formula to flexible frame
        and, 156–157
    narrow-scope formula and,
        152–154
    prepositional phrase and, 57
    roots of, 152–157
Syntactic analysis, pattern abstrac-
    tion and, 173
Syntactic constructions
    complexity of, future-tense mor-
        phemes and, 121
    formulas and, 131
    groping for, past-tense mor-
        phemes and, 88–89
    vacillation between, 170–171
    vertical, 194
Syntactic frames
    elements in, simple substitutions
        of, 174–177
    variation in, 198
Syntactic structures, in early learn-
    ing, 150–151
Syntax acquisition, 147–183
    domain definition and, 147–152
    early, course of, 152–162
    effectiveness of training and,
        169–170
    intense maternal training and,
        171–174
    learning processes and products
        in, 162–181
    method of analysis of, 151–152
    models and feedback in, 165–171

from parts to whole in, 157–162
stimulus dependency and,
    148–149
structurally blind input depen-
    dency and, 162–165
S-V-O structure and, 152–157
syntactic structures in early learn-
    ing and, 150–151
verbatim examples of dynamics in,
    174–181
Syntax training
    complex
        bivariate trends in, 197–199
        types of, 197–198
    simple
        bivariate trends in, 193–197
        types of, 193–195

Tacit knowledge, skill learning and, 9
Teaching
    defined, 47
    instructional dynamics in, syntax
        acquisition and, 174–181
    intensive, prepositional phrase
        and, 53
    long-term, dynamics of, 225–230
    see also Adult interventions; *specific
        topic*
Temporal morphemes
    acquisition of, 75–110, 111–146
        adult contributions to, 108–110
        complexity of factors in, 107–108
        conceptual precautions for anal-
            ysis of, 106–107
        context of processes in, 76–77
        context setting and, 108–109
        equational devices and, 109
        frequency phenomena and, 108
        literary devices and, 109–110
        methodology of analysis of, 106
    see also Future-tense morphemes;
        Past-tense morphemes
Temporal relations, 15–16
    see also Time *entries*
Theoretical perspectives, 1–15
    broadening, 231–232
    cognitive structures and, 213–214
    conceptual systems and tools and,
        211–218
    culture learning model, 2–6
    cybernetic approach to conversa-
        tion and learning, 217

Theoretical perspectives—*continued*
  dynamic conceptions of environ-
    mental information, 216–217
  empirical, neo-positivist approach,
    212–213
  environmental structure and,
    215–216
  integrated behaviorist/cognitive
    approach, 214–215
  language teaching and learning
    and, 9–15
    see also Language learning
  learning strategies and, 207–210
  methodological implications of,
    15–17
  past-tense morphemes and,
    77–78, 89
  skill learning model, 6–9, 213
  stimulus structure and, 215
Time
  dimension of, 232–233
  see also Temporal *entries*
Time series analyses, 225
  of adult input, 225–226
  "calculus of development" and,
    229–230
  changing lead–lag relationships
    in, 226–227
  of filial productions, 226
  time as dependent variable in,
    227–229
Training, *see* Teaching
Transformations
  invariances over, 16
  optional, 198, 199
Transparency of language, automa-
    tization and, 14
Truth value, corrections of
  misleading, 87
  past-tense morphemes and, 87
  present progressive and, 42
Turn taking
  in interactional routines, 10–11
  iterative and incremental acquisi-
    tion and, 12

past-tense morphemes and, 89
syntax acquisition and, 171

Utterance(s)
  adjacent, relationships between, 15
  matching feedback to, future-
    morpheme development and,
    123–125
  mean length of, *see* Mean length
    of utterance (MLU)
  spontaneous versus imitative
    prepositional phrase and, 49–50
    present progressive and, 26–27,
    29–30
    temporal morphemes and, 75
    see also Productions

Verbal performance, stimulus de-
    pendency of, 148–149
Verbal stimuli, dependency on, 149
Verbs, variety of, present progres-
    sive and, 32–36
Vertical constructions, 194
Vocabulary, correction of, contrast-
    ing, 192–193
Vocabulary training
  long-term bivariate trends in,
    191–193
  types of, 191–192

"Will/'ll"
  first productions of, 129–132
  multiple determination in immedi-
    ate input and, 130–131
  rote formulas containing, 131–132
  syntactic formulas and, 131
  see also Future-tense morphemes
Wishes, shaping into predicates,
    165–168

Zone of proximal development, iter-
    ative and incremental acquisi-
    tion and, 5, 12